Heimo Zeilinger

Bionically Inspired Information Representation

Heimo Zeilinger

Bionically Inspired Information Representation

Realizing Neuropsychoanalytic Concepts of Information Processing Within the Computational Framework ARSi10

Südwestdeutscher Verlag für Hochschulschriften

Impressum/Imprint (nur für Deutschland/only for Germany)
Bibliografische Information der Deutschen Nationalbibliothek: Die Deutsche Nationalbibliothek verzeichnet diese Publikation in der Deutschen Nationalbibliografie; detaillierte bibliografische Daten sind im Internet über http://dnb.d-nb.de abrufbar.
Alle in diesem Buch genannten Marken und Produktnamen unterliegen warenzeichen-, marken- oder patentrechtlichem Schutz bzw. sind Warenzeichen oder eingetragene Warenzeichen der jeweiligen Inhaber. Die Wiedergabe von Marken, Produktnamen, Gebrauchsnamen, Handelsnamen, Warenbezeichnungen u.s.w. in diesem Werk berechtigt auch ohne besondere Kennzeichnung nicht zu der Annahme, dass solche Namen im Sinne der Warenzeichen- und Markenschutzgesetzgebung als frei zu betrachten wären und daher von jedermann benutzt werden dürften.

Verlag: Südwestdeutscher Verlag für Hochschulschriften GmbH & Co. KG
Dudweiler Landstr. 99, 66123 Saarbrücken, Deutschland
Telefon +49 681 37 20 271-1, Telefax +49 681 37 20 271-0
Email: info@svh-verlag.de

Approved by: Wien, TU, Diss., 2010

Herstellung in Deutschland:
Schaltungsdienst Lange o.H.G., Berlin
Books on Demand GmbH, Norderstedt
Reha GmbH, Saarbrücken
Amazon Distribution GmbH, Leipzig
ISBN: 978-3-8381-2841-2

Imprint (only for USA, GB)
Bibliographic information published by the Deutsche Nationalbibliothek: The Deutsche Nationalbibliothek lists this publication in the Deutsche Nationalbibliografie; detailed bibliographic data are available in the Internet at http://dnb.d-nb.de.
Any brand names and product names mentioned in this book are subject to trademark, brand or patent protection and are trademarks or registered trademarks of their respective holders. The use of brand names, product names, common names, trade names, product descriptions etc. even without a particular marking in this works is in no way to be construed to mean that such names may be regarded as unrestricted in respect of trademark and brand protection legislation and could thus be used by anyone.

Publisher: Südwestdeutscher Verlag für Hochschulschriften GmbH & Co. KG
Dudweiler Landstr. 99, 66123 Saarbrücken, Germany
Phone +49 681 37 20 271-1, Fax +49 681 37 20 271-0
Email: info@svh-verlag.de

Printed in the U.S.A.
Printed in the U.K. by (see last page)
ISBN: 978-3-8381-2841-2

Copyright © 2011 by the author and Südwestdeutscher Verlag für Hochschulschriften GmbH & Co. KG and licensors
All rights reserved. Saarbrücken 2011

Abstract

This work describes the bionically inspired representation of information in a control unit for embodied software agents. It focuses on the first ever realization of neuropsychoanalytic concepts for generating and processing mental data structures in computer science and compares said approach to established bionically inspired methodologies. The approach is completely new to Artificial Intelligence and should allow the design of systems following the principles of the human being's mental apparatus, thus enabling them to operate in dynamically changing environments.

An existing decision unit is supplemented with an information representation system composed of an information representation concept, a data storage, and an information management unit. By use of a top-down design approach, the resulting adaptations are introduced into a new model whose implementation in embodied software agents produces the computational framework ARSi10.

The multi-agent framework-based simulator 'Bubble World' is developed as a test-bed with predefined use cases, and the agents' abilities are evaluated through internal and external performance indicators. These show the benefits of the developed system. Internal and external sensor data are mapped to neuropsychoanalytically inspired data structures and used for the decision making process. This allows the agents to interact with their environment while keeping their system resources balanced and thus retaining their functional abilities.

Acknowledgements

The work with this dissertation has been extensive and challenging, but in the main exciting, instructive, and fun. Without encouragement and support from several persons, I would never have been able to write this work.

First of all, I thank my supervisor Prof. Dr. Dietmar Dietrich for his inspiring and encouraging way to guide me to a deeper understanding of scientific work, and his inestimable comments.

This work would not have been possible without the expert guidance of my second advisor, Prof. Etienne Barnard, Ph.D. Not only was he available for me anytime but he always commented and responded to the drafts of each chapter of my work more quickly than I could have wished.

Thanks also to all my colleagues at the Institute of Computer Technology for providing a fantastic working atmosphere and especially to the current and former members of the ARS project team who supported me with their knowledge and programming skills.

My appreciation goes to my family who motivated me to write this work and whose love and support still sustain me today.

Most of all I thank my loving and patient partner in life Iris whose faithful support in managing difficulties of this work is so appreciated. Thank you.

Table of Contents

1. Introduction 1
   1.1 Heading Towards Intelligence 1
   1.2 The Neuropsychoanalytic Approach for Engineering Applications 5
   1.3 Methodology 10
2. Related Work 15
   2.1 Embodiment, Emotions, and Common Misunderstandings in Artificial Intelligence . 15
      2.1.1 Embodiment in Autonomous Agents 15
      2.1.2 Emotions in Autonomous Agents 18
   2.2 Psychoanalysis meets Artificial Intelligence 24
   2.3 Information Representation in Autonomous Agents 30
      2.3.1 Knowledge Representation Techniques 31
      2.3.2 Memory Based Control Architectures 34
      2.3.3 Information Representation Concepts in Autonomous Agents 37
   2.4 Evaluation of the Information Representation System 45
      2.4.1 Entering Artificial Worlds 46
      2.4.2 Multi-Agent Simulation Platforms 48
      2.4.3 Agent Performance Evaluation 51
   2.5 From Sensor Signals to Neuro-symbols 53
   2.6 Outcomes 56
3. Concept and Model 59
   3.1 Psychoanalytic Terms and Technical Definitions 59
   3.2 Technical Conceptualization of Psychoanalytically Inspired Data Structures 65
      3.2.1 Atomic Data Structures 66
      3.2.2 Images, Scenarios, and Acts 71
   3.3 The Artificial Recognition System Decision Unit 75
      3.3.1 Top-down Design Approach 76
      3.3.2 Topological View of the Body 78
      3.3.3 Fourth Topological Layer 80
      3.3.4 Third Topological Layer 82

  3.3.5 Second Topological Layer 85
  3.3.6 First Topological Layer 87
 3.4 Information Representation Management 96
  3.4.1 Information Management System 96
  3.4.2 Activation and Retrieval of Stored Data Structures 100

4. Examined Solution 105
 4.1 Simulation Environment and Embodied Software Agents 105
 4.2 Realization of Primary and Secondary Data Structures 114
 4.3 ARSi10 Implementation 122

5. Simulation and Results 131
 5.1 Evaluation Toolkit 131
 5.2 Definition of Use Cases 133
  5.2.1 Use Case 1 134
  5.2.2 Use Case 2 143

6. Conclusion and Outlook 154
 6.1 Achieved Solution 154
 6.2 Future Research Hot Spots 158
 6.3 Ethical Questions and Upcoming Challenges 161

References 165

Internet References 176

A. Unified Modeling Language Notation 177

B. Additional Acknowledgment 179

Abbreviations

ACT-R	Adaptive Control of Thought-Rational
AI	Artificial Intelligence
AMOUSE	Artificial Mouse
ARS	Artificial Recognition System
ARS-PA	ARS-Psychoanalysis
ARS-PC	ARS-Perception
ARSi10	ARS implementation number 10
BWsim	Bubble World simulator
CS	Cognitive Science
DM	Drive Mesh
EPM	External perception management module
HM	Homeostatic Mesh
HPM	Homeostatic perception management
MAS	Multi-agent System
MASON	Multi-Agent Simulator Of Neighborhoods… or Networks… or something…
OWL	Web Ontology Language
PAM	Perceptive Awareness Model
PDSM	Primary data structure management
PAIAS	Neuro-Psychoanalytically Inspired Automation System
RDF	Resource Description Framework
SDSM	Secondary data structure management
SENSE	Smart Embedded Network of Sensing Entities
SmaKi	Smart Kitchen
SOAR	State, Operator Apply Result
TI	Template Image
TP	Thing Presentation
TPM	Thing Presentation Mesh
UML	Unified Modeling Language
WP	Word Presentation
XML	Extensible Markup Language

1. Introduction

Can a machine show human-like intelligence? Back in 1956, when the term Artificial Intelligence (AI) was introduced, there were notions that this aim would be reached soon[1]. J. McCarthy defined a machine as offering artificial intelligence if it behaved like a human being [MMRS55]. Branches like symbolic, statistical, embodied and emotional AI have been formed. As we know, today there does not exist an implementation that actually fulfills these expectations – however, intelligent systems are still required.

1.1 Heading Towards Intelligence

Back in 2000, Dietrich et al. discussed the future of modern automation and its influence on fieldbus systems [DFZB09, pp. 343-352]. For economic and ecological reasons, present-day office and public buildings are equipped with large numbers of sensor nodes. For example, the airport Frankfurt/Main includes as many as 200.000 sensor nodes [HMK+08, pp. 41-43]. Rising costs for integration and maintenance direct development towards configurable fieldbus connections. New strategies must be found in order to cope with performance issues regarding the amount of data to be processed and the expenses involved in managing the nodes in ad-hoc sensor networks. First steps in this direction were taken at the Institute of Computer Technology of the Vienna University of Technology. As a result, the Artificial Recognition System (ARS) project was started in 2003 [BDK+04, pp. 1219-1222] [PP05]. Dietrich et al. introduced the idea of mimicking the parallel organization of neural networks in fieldbus systems and the processing of sensor data [Die00, pp. 145-146]. Future building automation systems do not only process sensor data. They must perceive environmental events, realize their impact, anticipate potential dangers, and react adequately[2]. A surveillance system on an airport should be able to recognize suspicious actions – e.g. a suitcase

---

[1] "Machines will be capable, within twenty years, of doing any work a man can do" – by H. Alexander Simon [Sim65, p. 96]

[2] The term *adequate* does not only relate to find a solution to the given problem, but also to appropriately react related to specified real time constraints.

left on the floor – and inform the security staff. Additional actions like tracking the movements of certain individuals or locking doors with minimal consequences to normal airport traffic should be taken automatically. In contrast to a production line, the number of states is not foreseeable. No occurring event will match a previous one in detail. However, similarities between predefined templates[3] of an event and currently perceived sensor data, which represent the current external influences on the system, must be found. In order to cope with the amount of sensor data, as a first step, significant data required to deal with the current situation must be separated from insignificant one [Rus03]. This data are mapped to predefined templates. The next goal is to process the activated templates and compute an action handling process. Nature provides numerous systems that are able to fulfill these tasks. Although those capabilities are diverse, even natural systems considered to be of primitive intelligence are able to deal with their environment in an adequate and adaptive way. Hence, AI approaches try to copy these systems of nature regarding their behavior and structure.

Although this thesis deals mostly with smart control systems, it crosses over into the field of machine intelligence. The scientific community has not agreed on a uniform definition of the concept of *intelligence*[4], yet. There exist numerous definitions from different areas of research. Every single definition specifies the term for a certain domain but does not cover a wide range of application areas. According to the New Oxford Dictionary of English [Pea98, p. 949], intelligence is

"... *the ability to acquire and apply knowledge and skill*".

One of the numerous definitions in psychology states that

"... *a person possesses intelligence insofar as he has learned, or can learn, to adjust himself to his environment*" S. S. Colvin quoted by Sternberg [Ste00, p. 428].

The Artificial Intelligence (AI) point of view [Fog95, p. 1591] states that

"*Any system that generates adaptive behavior to meet goals in a range of environments can be said to be intelligent*".

The wording does not match in any definition. Nearly every problem statement dealing with intelligent systems comes up with a separate definition for system intelligence. However, they show similarities which can be summarized in the generic terms that the adaptability of an individual to the range of environments constitutes its intelligence. The other way of ap-

---

[3] Dietrich et al. define a template as a predefined pattern used as archetype or for comparison [DFZB09, p. 428].

[4] It is derived from the Latin word "intellegere": to understand.

proaching the question is to discuss the requirements that must be fulfilled to achieve intelligence. Pfeifer and Scheier present a list of frequently occurring terms [PS99, pp. 6-10]. This list includes *characterizing intelligence definitions, commonsense notions,* a *graduated property, thinking and problem solving, learning and memory, language, intuition and creativity, consciousness, emotions, surviving in a complex world, perceptual and motor abilities*. Amongst others, the ability to interact with the world and the requirement for emotions have met with a certain amount of acceptance in the area of Cognitive Science[5] (CS). Even though it is possible to specify a definition of intelligence, the question of its validation invariably arises. Apparently, the evaluation of whether an object is intelligent depends on the observer and is based on a subjective point of view. In addition, intelligent behavior need not always be the right behavior, and correct behavior not always intelligent. An interpretation would be to label behavior intelligent if the individual is able to explain the reason why it acted the way it did. Again, the observer must evaluate if the machine's description is intelligent or not. This problem is a typical "frame of reference issue" which is controversially discussed within the AI community. Generally, according to the generic definition of intelligence above, the requirements for intelligence are evaluated by the way a system deals with a specific situation and must be defined for any new scenario. The human being is said to be the species with the highest known level of intelligence – although it is high on complexity too, regarding the brain functionality. Hence, a number of approaches exist for trying to merge theories of neuroscience – neuropsychology, psychology, neurology – in operational systems. Thereby, researchers aim to achieve human-like mind functionalities. A large part of these projects end in a "shopping for solution"[6] problem. As the basic models from neuroscience lack coherence, different models and theories are combined in an attempt to fill the gaps. Often engineers design a system using theories from different scientific areas than their own without discussing the concepts with professionals from those areas. As a result, contradicting theories are combined and inconsistencies arise within the resulting model. Chapter 2 discusses this issue in detail. The ARS project tries to avoid this mistake, and breaks new ground in AI by using neuropsychoanalytic concepts. Neuropsychoanalysis *"... is the research field concerned with the correlation of psychoanalytic and neuroscien-*

---

[5] Cognitive Science is defined as an interdisciplinary field that combines findings from neuroscience, biology, psychoanalysis, artificial intelligence, computer science, philosophy, and psychology to study the cognitive and information processing functions of the mind [DFZB09, p. 429].

[6] In this context, shopping for solution relates to the procedure of combining different theories without taking care of their compatibility.

tific terms and concepts" [DFZB09, p. 425]. This definition results in a specification for the term neuropsychoanalytic concept.

Definition 1: In this work, the term *neuropsychoanalytic concept* refers to psychoanalytic and neuroscientific concepts that are attended by the neuropsychoanalytic approach.

M. Solms – neuropsychologist and psychoanalyst – is one of the main figures in the neuropsychoanalytic movement [ST02]. Neuropsychoanalysts work on combining findings of neuroscience and psychoanalysis[7] into one consistent model. Neuroscience provides knowledge on the human brain structure. Within the last decades, technological developments like MEG[8] and PET[9] have established new possibilities in this area. Psychoanalysis provides models of the human mind's functionality. Although the mapping between brain processes and human mind functionality remains unclear, neuropsychoanalysts work on connecting both disciplines.

The topic of information representation touches neuroscience and psychoanalysis at different levels. The technical realization must cope with a number of questions on object representation, object associations, object recognition, and the *symbol grounding problem*[10]. According to D. Knuth the term information refers to

"... the meaning associated with data, the facts or concepts represented by data; often used also in a narrower sense as a synonym for "data", or in a broader sense to include any concepts that can be deducted from data" [Knu97, p. 637].

The term data is referred to the *"representation in a precise, formalized language of some facts or concepts, often numeric or alphabetic values, in a manner which can be manipulated by a computational method"* while a data structure is defined as *"a table of data including structural relationships"* [Knu97, p. 633].

Neural networks, logic approaches or the frame concept are popular concepts for knowledge representations[11]. They are known to be feasible constructs in information engineering in

---

[7] Psychoanalysis is a scientific discipline founded by S. Freud which is considered under the three aspects of methodology, therapy, and theory [Lap73, p. 410]. The scientific aspect define psychoanalysis as a group of psychological and psychopathological theories emerging from treatment and research [DFZB09, p. 427].

[8] Magnetoencephalography

[9] Positron Emission Tomography

[10] The symbol grounding problem discusses the question how abstract symbols obtain sense within the real world.

[11] For a distinction between knowledge representation and information representation see Section 1.3.

order to describe problems. Regarding bionic[12] information processing the human being is often used as an archetype. A common approach is to model declarative and implicit human memory. This model certainly has its value in neuroscience and some of the specifications are suitable for engineering as well. However, they hardly give evidence on the structure of their content, which is the topic this thesis focuses on. Even though psychoanalysis reaches its limits when discussing the question of data perception, it provides a description of data structures as processed by the human mind. A common issue within AI is the tendency to model memory as a functionally closed entity. The author agrees with the idea that memory, like perception or intelligence, emerges from an individual's sensory and functional setup and is not restricted to simple storage and retrieval tasks. Chapter 2 goes into more detail regarding this statement. One jigsaw piece pertaining to the emergence of memory is information and its representation. This thesis focuses on the engineering description of this concept and its evaluation in the context of the ARS model that defines a control unit based on human-like information processing.

1.2 The Neuropsychoanalytic Approach for Engineering Applications

As described above, the ARS project is rooted in the area of building automation systems. It developed from the Smart Kitchen (SmaKi[13]) project [SRF00, pp. 1-8]. The SmaKi is a kitchen, representing the prototype of a smart room that is equipped with a sensor network. Received sensor data are compared to predefined patterns and used to detect and handle safety-critical situations [BLPV07, pp. 1033-1038]. The ARS project itself forms the basis for spin-off projects at the ICT, like the SENSE (Smart Embedded Network of Sensing Entities)[14] project, and the PAIAS (Neuro-Psychoanalytically Inspired Automation System)[15] project. SENSE is positioned in the area of ambient intelligent systems [BVZ08, pp. 1092-1096]. The aim is to merge video and audio data, which are received from an adaptive and self-organizing sensor network, to reliable higher-level information. Like in the SmaKi, scenarios and objects should be recognized. First implementations are being tested in a sur-

---

[12] The science of bionics deals with the technical implementation of constructions and operations of biological systems [Nac02, p.1].

[13] Smart Kitchen project [Available: http://smartkitchen.ict.tuwien.ac.at/project/project.html Accessed: November 25th, 2010]

[14] European Commission funded project of the 6th Framework Programme, Embedded Systems

[15] Funded by the Austrian Science Fund (FWF) [Available: http://ars.ict.tuwien.ac.at/paias/ Accessed: October 28th, 2010]

Introduction

veillance system at Krakow airport. In contrast to SENSE, the PAIAS project deals with the processing of information, not its retrieval. Reliable information is evaluated and compared to a predefined knowledge base. On the base of the internal system state, the environmental situation and predefined knowledge, an action sequence is computed. PAIAS aims at modeling a human-like decision process to determine actions.

According to Palensky et al., the history of AI can be divided into four generations – symbolic AI, statistical AI, embodied AI, and emotional intelligence AI [PBTD08]. The former two imply the use of a bottom up methodology[16]. Representatives of symbolic AI work on a description of the world's knowledge in rules and logical relations. Adapted to statistical AI, artificial neurons are connected to a network in order to achieve functionalities of the human brain. As complex problems are not manageable by the use of a bottom-up design approach, engineers also use top-down design approaches[17]. Embodied AI predicts that a system body is required to achieve human-like intelligence, while emotional intelligence AI concludes the same for emotions. Proposed models often face the above described "shopping for solution problem". As stated in Dietrich et al. [DZ08, pp. 12-17], a 5th generation of AI must argue about common issues and admit similar mistakes – therefore, a true evolution of AI is required. The ARS project heralds the 5th generation of AI and shows a possible path for progress.

Neuropsychoanalytic concepts are used for designing a building automation control system. In order to avoid common mistakes, the conversion of neuropsychoanalytic concepts to computer science is done in cooperation with an advisory board of neuropsychoanalysts and psychoanalysts. Two branches are defined. One discusses the perception of sensor data, covered by neuroscientific theory, the second covers its computation – covered by psychoanalytic theory. The work of Velik et al., Burgstaller et al., and Bruckner deal with the perception and fusion of sensor data [Vel08] [BLPV07, pp. 1033-1038] [Bru07]. Zucker (né Pratl) et al. introduce a hierarchy to sensor fusion [PLD05]. Raw sensor data are combined into semantic symbols[18]. Velik attaches her work to this approach and introduces the term neuro-symbol. A neuro-symbol is a concept of semantic information combining different

---

[16] *"The functionality of existing modules are enhanced piece-wise in order to gain a new system."* [DFZB09, p. 419]

[17] Top-down design refers to "… a design method that starts its design process with the problem to be solved or the task to be committed. The designer tries to identify the necessary functionality in order to overcome the problem. This functionality is then further subdivided until existing solutions can perform subtasks" [DFZB09, p. 429].

[18] A symbol is defined as *"… an object, picture, or other concrete representation of ideas, concepts, or other abstractions"* [DFZB09, p. 428].

characteristics of information processing – neural characteristics as well as symbolic one [VLBD08, p. 49]. The essential part of this method of sensor fusion is the use of a hierarchical and neurologically inspired fusion process. In Velik's work the sensor fusion is not a process that occurs on the same layer, but instead is separated into three layers which may be extended in further work. The foundation for this approach is formed by neurologic and neuropsychologic theory of information processing. Velik's concept is described in more detail in Section 2.5. Up to now, the ARS project focuses on external perception – perception of the environment. Internal perception – perception of a system's internal state – is addressed by Velik et al. [VLBD08, pp. 561-580] but not discussed in detail.

The ARS decision unit implies principles of human mind functionality. A psychoanalytic model is used for its specification. This work covers information representation within the decision unit and therefore mainly deals with the psychoanalytic branch of neuropsychoanalysis. However, the topic is not fully covered by psychoanalysis and hence touches neuroscientific concepts too. The use of a psychoanalytic approach in CS is rather new, but there have already been discussions on advantages of an alliance for both areas. S. Turkle, professor of the Social Studies of Science and Technology at the Massachusetts Institute of Technology, discusses accordance in the development phase between psychoanalysis and AI [Tur89, pp. 241–268]. She states that AI and psychoanalysis share concepts like the integration of personal references into their theoretical concepts and AI may be able to realize and support psychoanalytic models. A. Buller introduces a concept for a robot controller, which is based on the psychoanalytic theory of psychodynamics [Bul02, pp. 17–20]. The basic pillars of psychodynamics are psychic tensions and the defense mechanism, conflicting mental processes and the association of thoughts, feelings, and wishes [Bul05, pp. 70-79]. Buller models a human-like memory for controller units for software agents. They build on the theory of procedural, semantic, episodic, and working memory. Buller reviews psychodynamics in terms of his concepts. Definitions like feelings, pleasure, conflicts, thoughts and tensions are specified in technical terms. As Buller introduces a bionically inspired memory system into his agents, this approach is discussed in detail in Chapter 2.

The reason for the rare occurrence of neuropsychoanalytic concepts in the field of computer science can be found in the controversy surrounding its own scientific background. However, many theories in the field of CS are based on psychoanalytic ideas. One of the supporters of psychoanalysis, W. Bucci, discusses in [Buc00, pp. 203-224] the need for a *psychoanalytic psychology* to enter and refine the field of CS. She states that mind-body interaction, unconscious processes, or dual processes of thought have their roots in psychoanalysis. Unfortunately, this idea is often antagonized by psychology and neuroscience. E. Kandel explains in his article on the biology and the future of psychoanalysis [Kan99, pp. 505-524] that psychoanalysis lacks a conceptual and experimental scope. He argues for a closer relationship between psychoanalysis and cognitive neuroscience. However, he states that *"...psychoanalysis still represents the most coherent and intellectually satisfying view of the mind"* [Kan99, p. 505].

Still the main point of criticism is represented by the subjectivity of studying the subject of interest – the human mind. In neuroscience, experimental results can be measured by evaluating the brain as a physical object. Psychoanalysis does not provide a similar possibility. S. Freud obviously based his theory primarily on neurology. Due to the insufficient technological equipment of the late 19th century, he had to rely on different methods of observation. The methodology of analysis makes the difference. In psychoanalysis, the human mind is observed by a person, which creates a subjective experience. M. Solms states that the different methodology of observation opens the door to the functionality of the psyche, to concepts like feelings, which cannot be measured objectively by neuroscience [ST02, p. 306] but influence a human being's behavior. Thus, it can be assumed that mind and brain do not form a dualistic system. The only possibility to observe these functions is offered by the subjective view of psychoanalysis. Neuropsychoanalysis searches for connections between both concepts and applies their advantages to a combined approach.

The question arises if a psychoanalytic model can be used for the design of an engineering application. During the 1960's and 1970's, when statistical AI saw its heyday, the use of behavioristic approaches was respected by the AI community. Machines were designed by modeling the behavior of human beings. In contrast to psychoanalysis, the behavioristic object of study was not the mind itself but the person's behavior. Behaviorism assumed that a person's environment forms the person's behavior. However, behaviorists deduced the functionality of the mind from the individual's behavior. The input, which represents the environmental situation, is correlated to the output, which represents the resulting action, and this correlation is formalized in statistical dependencies. The legitimation for its use in AI is its mathematical description. The complexity of the mind and the individual's internal state is disregarded. However, because of the human being's complexity, it is nearly impossible to design an adequate model of its functionality by observing its behavior only. It would be like trying to model the internal mechanisms of a photo camera only by observing the input – pulling the release button – and the output – resulting photograph, an example given by the computer scientist Iran-Nejad [IN87]. Naturally, to design a model of a system implicates a level of abstraction. The level of simplification influences the level of consistency with the original. Regarding the example of the photo camera, a behavioristic observation of input and output of a transistor results in a high-level of similarity to the original – provided that the schematic diagrams of the computer chips are known.

The branch of embodied AI is formed in the 1980's and is strongly based on behavioristic observations. It is based on the intuition that intelligent life requires interaction with the environment and therefore a body. Brooks introduced this movement with the subsumption architecture[19], a layered control system for a mobile robot, in 1986 [Bro86a, pp. 14–23]. He argued that behavior emerges out of sensorimotor stimuli. At the same time, scientists were investigating the role of emotions in the context of intelligent behavior. M. Minsky discusses the need for emotions in order to achieve intelligent machines [Min06]. The neurologist A. Damasio summed up that emotions are essential for planning and decision making processes. In addition he predicted that it is not possible to create animated life-forms that live and feel in the sense human beings do. Their characteristics likely depend on the *medium* in which they are realized and their neural design [Dam03, p. 129]. The author must state that the goal of the ARS project and this work is not to copy the human being but to model and to abstract some of his functionalities.

At first glance, connectionists should have the best chance to succeed in constructing emotional agents, following Damasio's statement. Only upon closer observation, both approaches are equidistant to the "creation" of feelings, as the term medium not only stands for a structure of neural network but also for the material and its characteristics. In general, computer scientists are bound to systems, made out of silicon. This raises the question which approach to follow in order to converge with reality without the use of organic material – an issue which the designers of neural networks must face. Biological neurons are described by artificial ones on a low-level of abstraction. They are connected to a network with the aim of achieving mind-like functionality. Unfortunately, the mapping between the neural brain structure and its functionality is unclear. Hence, a functional description of the mind itself is needed as the engineer is interested in the functions and not the brain structure itself. Neuropsychoanalytic concepts provide this description.

The embodied as well as the emotional approach are essential in neuropsychoanalytic concepts whose use in the area of engineering is additionally legitimated by the functional and

---

[19] R. Brooks introduced a control system for a mobile robot based on a hierarchical layer structure [Bro86b, pp. 14–23]. Each layer represents a task achieving behavior. The higher layers deal with more complex behaviours, subsuming the behavior of the lower layers – subsumption architecture.

in many areas coherent description of the human mind that it provides. This work uses these findings as foundation and incorporates them to the proposed model. Section 1.3 defines the methodology to accomplish this task.

1.3 Methodology

This thesis focuses on bionically inspired information representation for a decision unit for embodied software agents (see Definition 7 in Section 2.4.1). As discussed above, neuro-psychoanalytic concepts, psychoanalytic ones in particular, must be touched therefor. The proposed model must fit the mechanisms of information processing into the functional blocks of the ARS decision unit.

The feasibility study is executed in close cooperation with psychoanalytic scientists and represents step number one of the modeling process, which is discussed in Chapter 3.

Step number two deals with the description of the psychoanalytic model in technical terms and the closing of theoretical gaps for a complete technical description.

The fusion of the model of information representation with the decision unit represents the third stage. Besides the definition of data structures, a component labeled as *information management system*, which summarizes *information management functionalities* and a *data storage*, is introduced. Since decision unit and information management system are decoupled from each other, their compatibility must be a point of focus within the modeling process.

The *information management system* is additionally tied to a perception unit, which is based on neuropsychoanalytic theory and provides semantic data which is received from the sensor system. The intersection between both parts is analyzed and elaborated.

Fourth, the resulting model is reviewed regarding its consistency and compatibility with psychoanalysis.

The decision unit is inspired by psychoanalytic theory and designed following these basic premises [DFKU09, p. 100] [DZ08, pp. 12-17].

1. Theoretically, it is possible to model every psychic function.
2. Although problems exist in verifying the psychoanalytic model, it still represents the best way to deal with the problem of simulating the human mind.

3. The theory that the model is based on must include a complete model of the human mind. A mix of different theories where each defines some of its functions leads to inconsistencies.
4. Interdisciplinary work between professionals of both scientific communities is crucial for successfully advancing the project.
5. The interdisciplinary work must be organized in such a way that psychoanalysts and neuropsychoanalysts deal with the functional description of the model only, while engineers deal with a translation into technical terms and the implementation as well as verification in comparison to competing technologies. Hence there must be a clear differentiation between the modeling and the implementation phase
6. The modeling must follow a top-down design approach (see Footnote 17).
7. Regarding the data processing, a clear distinction between information flow and control flow must be integrated. This is a common trend in data processing in the area of information technology. In biological systems, this principle is implemented by the neuron: Incorporation of information processing is required for flexibility.

Within this thesis, the differentiation between *knowledge representation* and *information representation* is established.

Definition 2: *"Knowledge representation is the study of how to put knowledge into a form that a computer can reason with."* [RN03, p. 16]

Definition 2 gives a broad explanation of the term knowledge representation. Knowledge representation implies the structural organization of information that the system possesses knowledge. The knowledge is stored in a collection of formal symbols [BL04, p. 4] that form propositions about the world. These collections are also labeled as knowledge bases. This thesis not only deals with the structural definition of predefined knowledge but also focuses on the representation of received data as well as changes made to this data due to manipulations by the decision unit. Hence, to avoid misunderstandings the term *knowledge representation* is discerned from the term *information representation* in this work. This leads to definition 3 that is applied for this work.

Definition 3: *Information representation* summarizes the structural composition of data that is received by the internal and external sensor system and the information management system. Information representation excludes functionalities that are required to handle this data like search, activation, and manipulation mechanisms.

Search, manipulation and activation mechanisms are part of the information management module's functions and the decision unit (see Fig. 1-1). The information management module additionally forms the interface to the information representation layer. This leads to definitions 4 to 6 that are applied to this work.

Definition 4: The *information management system* combines the information management module and the information representation layer.

This generic term is used as it is left open if the information management system represents a simple *database management system* or a *knowledge base management system*. A knowledge base introduces reasoning that is realized in the ARS decision unit itself. However, it is possible to extend the proposed concept by a filter mechanism using reasoning even though this is part of future work.

Definition 5: The *information representation layer* is synonymous with a data storage.

Definition 6: The combination of information representation and information management system form the *information representation system*.

Although the defined premises aim at the modeling process of the decision unit, they must be applied to the information representation system as well.

Neuropsychoanalytic concepts extensively deal with information processing. In order to comply with Premise 3, it must be investigated whether they are feasible with regard to a technical model. This leads to research Hypotheses 1 and 2 that must be proved in this work.

Hypothesis 1: It is possible to apply neuropsychoanalytic concepts to a technical model for information representation and information processing.

Hypothesis 2: The considerations of the premises that are defined above lead to the demonstration of Hypothesis 1.

As shown in Fig. 1-1 sensor data enters the decision unit through the perception interface – inner and outer perception – and leaves it towards the actuator interface. In between the information is processed by the functional blocks of the decision unit. The black box represents a bundle of functional blocks and their connections. Specific modules are able to exchange information with the information management module that defines mechanisms for processing data in the information representation layer. A rough draft of this concept is proposed by Zeilinger et al. [ZPK10, pp. 708-714].

After the modeling process begins the implementation phase. It must be pointed out that there is a strong differentiation between the modeling and implementation phases. The modeling phase deals with the design of a technical model obeying neuropsychoanalytic requirements and boundary conditions without concentrating on the technology the system should be executed on. The implementation phase has the aim to map the given concept onto the available technology by the use of common engineering techniques. As a first step the concept is implemented in embodied software agents within a simulation of artificial life. Use cases are defined in order to test the system's behavior.

Hypothesis 3: The proposed model can be implemented to an embodied software agent and evaluated in a game of artificial life.

As the decision unit and the *information management system* are closely related to each other, their behavior cannot be observed separately from each other. In order to avoid the typical controversial discussions regarding specific terms, the requirement is not to produce intelligent but smart systems. Second, the smartness of a system is evaluated by its handling of a specific predefined situation by satisfying its needs in the best possible way. However, these parameters must be defined in detail for the test framework.

Hypothesis 4: The functionality of the information representation system can be demonstrated by use cases and only in combination with the decision unit.

As the result of this work, a bionically inspired *information representation*, feasible for the

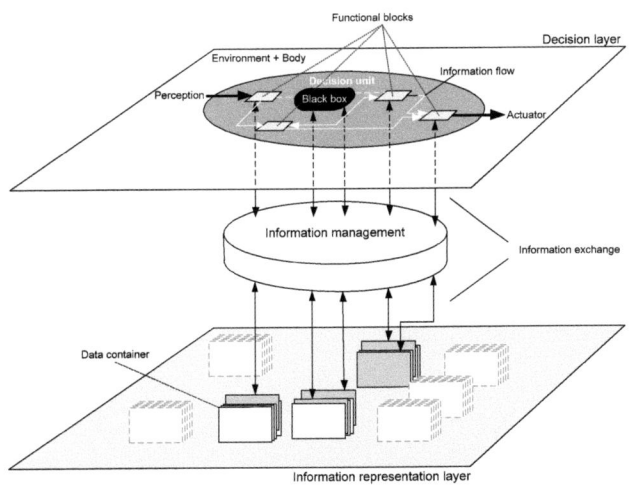

Fig. 1-1: Decision layer and information representation layer

use with the corresponding ARS decision unit, is realized. The integrated framework is named ARSi10[20]. The *information representation* is in the center of this work, even though the *information management system* is required for the control unit's functionality and must go along with defined data structure characteristics. The proposed *information representation system* should not be mistaken for a memory system, which, according to Section 1.2, is emergent and therefore cannot be. In addition, memory cannot be reduced to information processing. A learning mechanism is not implemented and information required for the decision making processes are predefined. Although the foundations for learning are implemented, the current work aims at transferring the psychoanalytic concept of data structures and information processing to engineering without the integration of learning mechanisms. Psychoanalytic theory is used as the theoretical background for the modeling process. To use this approach and transfer it to a technically feasible model poses the challenge in this thesis as this procedure is undertaken the first time. Despite ongoing discussions about cooperation between computer science and psychoanalysis (see Section 2.2), this is the first time that a technical model based on findings from both scientific areas has been formed as well as implemented. Hence, the author has had to familiarize himself with basic knowledge in psychoanalysis in order to be able to get an idea of the methodological differences between computer science and psychoanalysis, since only with this knowledge is it possible to work with psychoanalytic experts in order to transfer psychoanalytic terms and principles to a technical description. In a second step, open issues, which are not covered by psychoanalytic theory, must be verified and a way to introduce them investigated. Care must be taken that the defined solutions conform to the original psychoanalytic model.

Although the modeling process is extensive, the methodology used appears to be the only possibility of merging these sciences. It is important to follow this path in order to solve upcoming issues that are brought on by the increasing complexity of building automation systems and cannot be solved by a purely mathematical approach. A broad variety of related work regarding information representation in autonomous agents, evaluation methods, and neuropsychoanalytic findings regarding the interconnection between environmental and internal conditions must be investigated therefor. Different approaches that result in the proposed model are analyzed and discussed.

---

[20] ARSi10 for ARS implementation version number ten

2. Related Work

In Chapter 1 the 5th generation of AI is discussed. Below, we focus on the requirements for its realization and the current techniques that deal with the topic of this thesis. The influences of embodied as well as emotional AI to this work are discussed in detail on the basis of work by R. Brooks, R. Pfeifer, and T. Ziemke, to name but a few. Cooperation between the areas of psychoanalysis and engineering as well as their influence on AI are analyzed. In this context, the findings of S. Turkle, M. Leuzinger-Bohleber and R. Pfeifer are examined. The discussion focuses towards information processing and knowledge representation in control units for autonomous agents. Hence, two memory based control architectures, SOAR (State, Operator Apply Result) and ACT-R (Adaptive Control of Thought-Rational) are introduced. In addition, modeling and implementation techniques for knowledge bases that can be applied to the ARS model are analyzed. Frameworks to verify the proposed solution must be discussed and the neuro-symbolic data processing that prepares raw sensor data for the use by the bionically inspired *information representation system* is introduced.

2.1 Embodiment, Emotions, and Common Misunderstandings in Artificial Intelligence

In Section 1.2 the requirement of embodiment and emotions for the improvement of a system's behavior is discussed. Below, both approaches are analyzed related to the ARS concept and their use in autonomous software agents.

2.1.1 Embodiment in Autonomous Agents

Embodiment as a requirement for the development of human-like behavior has been widely discussed in the areas of neuroscience and CS).

A broad definition of the term embodiment refers to the ability of robots to

"... have bodies and experience the world directly - their actions are part of a dynamic with the world, and the actions have immediate feedback on the robots' own sensations" [Bro91b, p. 1227].

In the mid-80's R. Brooks started to focus on the system-environment interaction rather than the internal world modeling [Bro86b, pp. 14-23]. The introduced subsumption architecture represents the paradigm that intelligence emerges from several sub-components by interacting with the environment [Bro91a]. Brooks argues that intelligence *"... is determined by the dynamics of interaction with the world"* and that *"... only an embodied agent is fully validated as one that can deal with the real world"* [Bro91a, p. 155].

Pfeifer et al. define embodiment [PS99, p. 649] as

"... a term used to refer to the fact that intelligence cannot merely exist in the form of an abstract algorithm but requires a physical instantiation, a body. In artificial systems, the term refers to the fact that a particular agent is realized as a physical robot or as a simulated agent".

The term embodiment exists in different notions that are grouped by Ziemke into six categories [Zie03, pp. 1305-1310]:

- Structural coupling of the system to its environment that does not explicitly require a body
- Historical embodiment that results from interaction between agents and their environment
- Physical embodiment that requires physical instantiation
- Organismoid embodiment that restricts physical embodiment and introduces additional requirements of certain types of cognition and body abilities
- Organism-like embodiment or organismic embodiment that limits embodiment to organisms only
- Social embodiment that defines embodiment in the context of social interaction

By contrast, Núñez et al. categorize embodiment to three views called *trivial*, *material*, and *full* embodiment [Núñ99, p. 55]. Trivial embodiment gives a wide range covering the definition of embodiment as direct relation between the mind and the biological processes from which the mind emerges. The material embodiment view likewise claims that mental functionality emerges from biological processes. In addition, cognition is seen to be a decentralized phenomenon that deals with the complexity of real-time body-world interactions. The view of full embodiment combines trivial as well as material embodiment but additionally defines the body to be involved in any agent activity. It forms the basic activity of perception to thinking. Ziemke's categorization defines the basic requirements focusing on the realization of the agent's body and its environment. Nunez' definitions investigate the term embodiment regarding the connection between mind and the underlying physical processes as well as different hierarchical levels of the implication of embodiment. For further considerations it is assumed that *embodiment* requires a body that enables the agent to experience the world directly. Regarding Ziemke this accords to *physical embodiment* and assumes that the agent body is equipped with a sensor and actuator system.

Pfeifer et al. claim that embodiment forms the foundation for intelligence is the trivial meaning of the term, while the more concrete meaning relates to the physical and the information theoretical processes [PIG06, pp. 783-790]. They summarize the influence of embodiment to the principles of robot design in comparison to conventional control paradigms:

- Reduction of costs in terms of less computation
- More energy efficient control systems
- Enables temporal correlations and higher-order regularities and therefore form the basis for effective learning algorithms
- Introducing information structure to sensor data which results in the possibility to categorize input information

The last two points are basic and essential abilities as well as crucial for this work. Pfeifer et al. state that improvements in the agent design result from considering the agent as a whole, rather than its control unit only [PIB05, p. 99]. This automatically incorporates embodiment to the design. Pfeifer et al. claim that embodiment always requires the interaction with a real physical world system [PI03]. In addition the importance of embodiment in the area of *information representation* is claimed by Dautenhahn et al., who state that embodiment *"... is only the physical basis of cognition but a necessary condition and point of reference for perceptions and memory"* [DC96]. This states one of AI's basic problems that is the rapid identification of the area of interest by the agent as well the adaptation to environment that is continuously changing by appearance and properties of located objects and events [PLOS08, pp. 76-87].

In contrast to Brooks, Pfeifer does disagree with behavior-based control principles, but conforms to one that is completely based on sensorimotor coordination. This concept simplifies the mapping of sensor information to perceptual categories as due to the sensorimotor coordination, information structure is introduced into the sensor data. The agent's behavior emerges out of the association between received sensor data and the actuator control. This corresponds to the point of view of psychologists and cognitive scientists like S. Harnad who states that the

"... things in the world come in contact with our sensory surfaces, and we interact with them based on what that sensory-motor contact affords" [Har05, p. 20].

The *Braitenberg Vehicles* [Bra84] are one of the first models that imply a sensorimotor concept. The behavior of these vehicles, named after V. Braitenberg, emerges out of direct connections between the systems sensors and actuators. The exposure of light results in different speeds of movements. More light triggers an increase of speed. Darkness results in immobility.

In their Artificial Mouse (AMOUSE) experiment, Bovet et al. [BP05a, pp. 324-330] show a realization of this attitude in its purest form. AMOUSE's behavior develops on the base of associations between sensor and actuator modalities, weighted by a simple realization of the Hebbian law. Especially the emergence of a behavior despite the temporal difference between the action and an "award" is worth mentioning. A closer look to this experiment regarding the defined data structure is given in Section 2.3.

2.1.2 Emotions in Autonomous Agents

The approach of embodiment generally focuses on the body-world interaction and the body's configuration. The neurologist and neuropsychoanalyst A. Damasio denounced the approach to focus on external interaction between the body and its environment only. He argues for additionally arguing the interaction between the body and the brain [Dam98, pp. 83-86]. As the human being's emotional system was said to interfere logical rational thinking for a long time, emotions had been widely ignored in CS even though scientists like Galatzer-Levy claim that logic is maybe needed for playing chess but intelligence is essential for surviving [GL09]. When the emotional system attracts interest in neurosciences again[21] and in connection with the human being's intelligent behavior, CS started to take a closer look at emotional mechanisms[22]. Even though A. Damasio's claim that adequate rea-

---

[21] While at the beginning of the 20th century, the term emotion was relevant in scientific work it lost impact later.

[22] H. A. Simon released a paper on "Motivational and emotional controls of cognition" in 1967. This publication introduced the emotional approach to CS but was not influential initially. Its relevance increases at the end of the 80's and the beginning of the 90's.

soning does not work without emotions [Dam94, p. 191] is doubted by representatives of the scientific community of engineers [Slo04, pp. 128-134], emotions are widely seen as essential mechanism in the functionality of the human being within the neuroscientific community. Damasio assumes from the loss of emotional and intelligence capabilities due to the damage of certain brain areas that emotions are required for reasoning [Dam94, p.61]. Sloman argues that only because a state occurs as side effect of an operation that is essential for intelligence, it cannot be concluded that this state triggers intelligent behavior. He doubts that emotions form the foundation of intelligence and claims that they emerge from mechanisms which are important for intelligent behavior, as a side effect. In contrast, Piccard points out that there may exist intelligence without emotion but every actually known intelligent live form possesses emotions [Pic99, pp. 134-137]. Even though this is no evidence that intelligence is triggered by emotions, she states that in order to understand intelligence it is important to go on investigating emotions, respectively mechanisms which trigger them. This view has won attention in the area of CS. Apparently there are different opinions dividing the scientific community regarding the question if emotions influence intelligent behavior. However, it is a current opinion in AI that emotional systems are worth a closer look in order to design sophisticated control systems.

Damasio equates emotional mechanisms with any mechanism that serves the homeostasis of the body. The homeostasis accords to the regulation of body integrity and its internal balance. Heartbeat, hormonal levels, or body temperature must be kept near optimum levels. Damasio introduces three categories of emotions – background emotions, primary emotions, secondary emotions [Dam03, pp. 43-46], while another psychologist and neuroscientist Panksepp defined the basic mammalian emotional action system. These innate actions include seeking, fear, lust, care, panic, and play [Pan05] and associate an environmental situation with an individual's reaction. Emotions that show more complex control abilities of the individual are defined as complex emotions respectively as secondary emotions. However, numerous different arrangements for emotional categories have been defined and no one is identical to any other. As the investigation of the different systems is not the focus of this work, they are not discussed in detail. Different concepts of emotional systems have evolved that differ in detail but agree on a common base. The emotional system is claimed to be an evaluation system for the current situation, which enables the individual to react on uncommon situations. As this work is based on neuropsychoanalytic concepts, further definitions are constructed in respect to them. Dietrich et al. define an *emotion* [DFZB09, p. 421] as a

"... *psychic evaluation of contents of perception based upon memory traces*".

This work is based on the definitions given in [DFZB09] and ensuing publications. As memory traces describe and represent stored information in the mind (see Section 3.1) this given definition accords to an evaluation of the current and already experienced situation. Before going into detail on the technical realization of emotional evaluation systems, specific terms must be introduced.

According to neuropsychoanalysis, unbalances of the homeostasis result in bodily stimuli. These bodily stimuli trigger drives that are defined as psychic representatives of homeostatic unbalances (see Section 3.1, [DFZB09, p. 420]) which are formed by affects and drive contents. The drive content conforms to the instinctual aim and represents the activity that results in a decrease of the bodily stimuli. There exist a number of psychoanalytic affect theories. Further constraints follow the definition in Section 3.1.

Damasio defines the terms *pleasure* and *pain* to be a *"... constituent quality of certain emotions as well as a trigger for certain emotions"* [Dam00, p. 76]. While pleasure is associated with positive emotions, pain is associated with negative ones. In this way, coincidences to the psychoanalytic theory of affects can be seen. Pleasure, displeasure, and pain show similarities. According to psychoanalytic theory, pleasure and unpleasure[23] only exist within the psyche as result of bodily stimuli. Damasio [Dam00, p. 71] explains that pain and pleasure are results of bodily stimuli. Emotions and pain or pleasure have the same stimuli as origin but are different. Rather emotions are associated with pain and pleasure. Emotions are more complex than drives as well as pleasure and pain. Drives, pleasure and pain invoke emotions, a coincidence with the psychoanalytic definition of affect. Within the last decade, the influence of these theories in CS has grown.

Parisi, similar to Damasio, points out that robotics has generally concentrated on the interaction between an organism's nervous system and its environment [Par04, pp. 325-338] while the interaction between the nervous system and the internal environment has been ignored. He suggests the reproduction of the inside of the organisms' body in order to improve their understanding. Parisi labels the second type of interaction with the term *internal robotics* while he called the first one *external robotics*.

Cañamero discusses the use and the understanding of emotions in the context of autonomous robots [Cañ05, pp. 445-455]. Starting in the late 90's she has dealt with emotion systems in agents and introduced an autonomous creature (Abbott), situated in a 2-dimensional world, whose control unit is based on Brook's subsumption architecture [Cañ97, pp. 148-155]. One creature (Abbotts) consists of numerous agents (Abbott). The creature is ad-

---

[23] Unpleasure is a psychoanalytic term that is used for the expression of inner-psychic displeasure.

vanced by adding new agents. This approach is similar to the iterative process in the subsumption architecture. As an aim the creature should dispose of certain learning and problem-solving capabilities. It must experience certain phases of an organism's life. At the first stage, it accords to a newborn. Hence, according to Cañamero, the creature is strongly driven by "motivational states" that accord to triggering of actions due to bodily needs and basic emotions[24]. Cañamero differentiates between emotions – fear, anger, happiness, sadness, boredom, and interest – and motivations – aggression, cold, curiosity, fatigue, hunger, self-protection, thirst, and warmth. An imbalance in the homeostasis evokes a drive that serves as stimuli of motivations – e.g. increase of blood sugar invokes hunger. In Cañamero's approach an emotion influences the motivational as well as bodily state of an Abbotts. Regarding the implementation of an emotional system to autonomous robots, she defined four questions that must be discussed. First, there exist numerous emotion theories. Their scope must be investigated as well as the question how they can be combined should be discussed. Second, it must be figured out which mechanisms underlie the emotion system and how they influence perception and action. Third, which aspects of the chosen emotion system can be implemented in agents and fourth, a way must be found to measure respectively quantify emotional states [Cañ05, pp. 445-455]. These questions can be applied to the development of a control unit, respectively of an agent and must be faced when dealing with interdisciplinary research.

T. Ziemke et al. [ZL09] have based their research on the integration of emotions in an embodied cognitive-affective architecture for robots. The project is part of the ICEA (Integrating Cognition, Emotion and Autonomy) project. Similar to the ARS project, ICEA brings together knowledge from different areas of research. Different to ARS the scientific community consists out of neurophysiologists, computational neuroscientists, cognitive modelers, and engineers. The project aim is to model and to implement a cognitive system architecture, integrating autonomy, cognition, and emotion by modeling different brain structures on different levels of abstraction. Two premises form the foundation for the research. First, emotions and biological regulatory mechanisms are essential for the development of high-level functions, and second, artificial cognitive system architectures can be equipped with models of these mechanisms. Starting with *low-level* mechanisms – e.g. biological regulation – and ending up in *high-level* functions like learning or emotional decision making. In

---

[24] Cañamero defined basic emotions as *"peripheral and cognitive responses triggered by the recognition of a significant event"* [Cañ97, p. 148].

Related Work

the context of the ICEA project, Ziemke et al. introduce a concept of emotions. The term *emotion* is defined as [ZL09, p. 104]:

- Closely related to embodied cognition
- Based on a homeostatic regulation process
- A principle of organization for behavioral and cognitive mechanisms, used in organic brains and robotic cognitive architectures

Ziemke et al. base their models of an emotional system upon the theories of A. Damasio. Hence, the introduced terms are different to psychoanalytic inspired definitions that are the foundation of this work. In Ziemke's case, the term *affect* is a general definition of drives, motivations, emotions, feelings, and moods. They define an *affect* as any bodily impulse that is transferred to the mind and any signal that is invoked by them in the brain. Ziemke et al. propose a work in progress enactive/embodied cognitive-affective architecture which is strongly based on Damasio's work but additionally implies other psychological, neurological, and neurobiological approaches [ZL09]. The model introduces internal and behavioral organization which is achieved on three hierarchical levels that accord to reflexes, motivations and drives, feelings and emotions. As this work remains in progress, no experiences on the compatibility of the different theories are available.

AMOUSE, which is mentioned above, integrates a reward-punishment system [BP05b, pp. 2272-2277] that is used to evaluate the situation and actions which lead to the situation. The reward-punishment system has been introduced to couple a reward/punishment with a specific action. In so doing, Bovet et al. are able to associate an action with its time-delayed consequences. Pleasure and pain are applied to the sensor system by negative and positive stimuli. Following the definition of pleasure and pain by Damasio the reward/punishment system in AMOUSE can be compared with this theory, even though the term emotion is not explicitly discussed.

On the contrary, C. Breazeal explicitly introduces an emotional state to the robot *Kismet* [Bre02] in order to investigate human system interaction. The aim is to conceptualize a sociable[25] robot by combining findings from different scientific communities like infant social development, psychology, ethnology, and evolution. The aim is to design a system that physically, affectively, and socially interacts with humans. Kismet is a robot head that is

---

[25] Sociable robots are *"... socially participative "creatures" with their own internal goals and motivations"* [Bre03a, p. 169].

situated in the world and is disposed of facial expressions that change the body posture, gesture, gaze direction, and voice. Facial expressions and sounds should reflect Kismet's current "emotional state". Breazeal argues that *"... if the robot's observable behavior adheres to a person's social model for it during unconstrained interactions in the full complexity of the human environment, then we argue that the robot is socially intelligent in a genuine sense"* [Bre03b, p. 168]. The crux of the matter is that a person is needed to interpret Kismet's behavior as well its emotional state. Kismet disposes of a set of drives that are to engage people, to engage toys, and to occasionally rest. They are influenced by stimuli resulting out of a homeostatic concept. The drives are directly mapped to facial expressions by an emotion system. An emotional reaction includes:

- Event
- Evaluation of the event by affects
- According expression by the use of face, voice, and posture
- Evaluation of available actions which invoke a behavioral response

In Breazeal's approach emotions refer to particular computational processes that actually occur in the system. The observer interprets the resulting gestures as specific emotional states. However, because only a human being is able to interpret this emotive response as emotional states, it can be doubted that the system itself disposes of emotions. The only part within this interaction disposing of emotions is represented by the observer who is high on social competence and social intelligence. Palensky et al. argue [PPC09] that a machine must be able to use an emotional system for organizing its behavior. Facial gestures represent only some features of the possibilities that emotions would permit. Even though Kismet shows amazing possibilities to perceive and interpret sensor data to specific patterns, it cannot be said to be emotional or socially intelligent in any way. In addition, the example of Kismet stresses the question if a system can be described as humanoid robot only because its appearance is similar to a human being or it interprets human behavior. Even though the human body is important in terms of embodiment it does not identify a human being. The functionality of the mind should be the first step to be modeled in order to design a humanoid robot with an adequate body as a foundation.

Modeling bionic inspired systems often results in mixing up different scientific theories. Generally, theories in neuroscience focus on specific points of interest. Hence, considering the whole system, a huge area persists unnoted. As the system does not work by partial implementation, the remaining gaps must be examined and filled by the use of contradicting theories leaving a technical but useless model. This causes in the lack of full-fledged models on the one hand and the flippancy of technicians using theories without having the appropriate expertise. A predecessor of the current ARS model, described below – see Section 2.2 – is affected by this concern. The model is based on psychoanalytic and neuropsychoanalytic ideas which do not contradict each other but turned out to be incompatible. For further work it is tried to find a theory covering large areas of the given problem. The remaining gaps must be filled in close interdisciplinary work with experts from both sides and not by engineers only. This paradigm has been applied to the design of the *ARS model 3.0* that is discussed in Chapter 3.

Summarized, embodiment and the integration of emotional mechanisms tend to be a way in AI to advance current control systems. Scientists hope to gain a reduction of complexity, an increase of robustness, or new effective learning processes on the one hand and a control mechanism that allows the system to adapt itself to uncommon situations on the other hand. Questions on the agent's body configuration turn up and emotion theories and their implementation must be discussed therefor. For the last point, Wehrle [Weh01] stresses the possibility that the implementation of predefined emotions lacks on grounding as their definition is influenced by the engineer's meaning of emotion and not by the meaning that evolves out of a physical and social interaction with the environment. However, emotions are widely seen as innate and strongly connected to the body. Hence, they must be predefined by the designer of the physical body. Regarding the ARS project, neuropsychoanalytic concepts take a homeostasis and a body for granted and hence can be tied up to the embodied and emotional concept for the use in a control unit.

2.2 Psychoanalysis meets Artificial Intelligence

Psychoanalytically-inspired control systems are rarely found in AI. Several reasons, already listed in Section 1.2, have prevented engineering and AI from its utilization. Even though scientists like S. Turkle or R. Pfeifer have investigated the psychoanalytic approach for engineering applications, the ARS project transfers psychoanalytic concepts to computer scientific use for the first time.

Turkle discusses possible overlaps between AI and psychoanalysis and a way in which both areas can benefit from each other [Tur89]. At first sight, both theories track different goals. While psychoanalysis "*...explores the mind to discover the irrational*" [Tur89, p. 246], AI is based on rational designs. However, Turkle claims that both overlap in the propagation of subjective reflection [Tur89, p. 244]. As example she lists a chess move where intelligence is derived from the engineer's personal knowledge. The technical problem is solved by the engineer asking himself which mental and physical actions he would set to handle the situation. However, subjectivity as it is introduced by Turkle represents only a small part of the area that psychoanalysis deals with. The main part of psychoanalytic theory deals with unconscious[26] psychic processes that are generally not accessible – except by therapeutic methods. An important area of psychic mechanisms is ignored in case attention is only focused on processes that the individual is able to reflect on. Turkle claims that the psychoanalytic object relational approach and emergent AI show promising coincidences [Tur89, p. 247]. In contrast, information processing AI is not feasible for a model of the mind [Tur89, p. 252] because intelligent behavior follows from fixed rules. In case there is no rule defined that can be matched to the current situation the system breaks down. Contrariwise, the brain continues functioning. Turkle states that emergent AI, which is based on agent societies, handles this issue [Tur89, p. 252] as it does not store the knowledge of agents but the relations in between. It is not important what agents know but only their place in the network. This approach is similar to the theory of artificial neural networks.

As an example she introduces the perceptron[27] in the form of an agent. Perceptrons are connected to a network in order to achieve emerging functionalities. This procedure follows a bottom-up design approach. Turkle states that the theory of object relations can be matched to the network of perceptrons. She claims that agent societies deal with concerns that are treated by psychoanalysis like internal relational conflicts and inconsistencies. However, Turkle does not form a technical model on the base of psychoanalytic theory. She only tries to map two scientific theories without dealing with psychoanalytic concepts in detail. In particular, she establishes a theory and tries to map it to a psychoanalytic background. She additionally ignores that psychoanalysis extensively deals with information processing which is stated in [LBP02] and forms the foundation for this work. Furthermore, her essay ignores one of the main advantages that psychoanalysis provides for computer science – a functional description of the human mind.

In 1996, Rodado and Rendon [RR96] analyze the interconnections between AI and psychoanalysis and the possibility for mutual assistance. They encounter similarities between S. Freud's work and connectionism. They refer to the very beginnings of psychoanalysis when Freud based his theory of neurological assumptions. However, Freud detached the essential

---

[26] Dietrich et al. specify the unconscious as *"... processes and functions of the human mental apparatus that the subject is not aware of. It represents the main part of the psychic processes"* [DFZB09, p.429].

[27] The perceptron represents the prototype of an artificial neuron and relates to a hypothetical nervous system [Ros58].

part of his work from this early phase and introduced a functional model of the human mind that clearly differs from connectionism.

Additional investigations towards merging psychoanalysis to CS and AI have been done by investigating concepts of information processing. In 2000, Dietrich et al. discussed further developments in the area of building automation [DS00, pp. 343-350]. They claim that fieldbus systems show coincidences with the mammalian nervous system in terms of distribution and parallelism of information processing. Dietrich et al. prolong a new point of view on building automation systems that result in heralding the 5th generation of AI [DZ08, pp. 12-17]. The base for the new approach forms the hierarchical processing of sensor data and the decision making on the base of psychoanalytic principles. Both are discussed below in detail.

M. Leuzinger-Bohleber and R. Pfeifer conduct a dialogue between psychoanalysis and CS regarding memory processes [LBP02, p. 3]. They confirm the theory that memory is a function of the whole organism. It is embodied and hence, emerges out of a sensorimotor coupling. In addition, it always has a subjective aspect – information about stored experiences – as well as an objective aspect – neural patterns on the base of sensorimotor interactions. Their idea is to combine clinical psychoanalytic theorizing of early memory with current findings in CS. Their work shows the difficulties of interdisciplinary work as well as the opportunities which it presents. However, the results of their dialogue have not found further usage in CS and even less in engineering, yet. A computer scientific realization has not resulted from their thoughts.

This is true for the influence towards psychoanalysis by computer science. R. M. Galatzer-Levy investigates how AI can support psychoanalysis [GL88] . He proposes a model based on an AI algorithm supporting psychoanalysts by simulating the working through[28] process. However, the realization of this method was not followed up.

Even though investigations have been done for the use of psychoanalytic concepts in computer science, besides the ARS project, implementations are claimed by A. Buller only. As discussed in Section 1.2, Buller claims to implement the psychoanalytic concept of psychodynamics to control units for software agents [Bul02, pp. 17-20] whose key concepts are based on *psychic tension* and *defense mechanisms*. The agents are designed for autonomously exploring the environment, goal acquisition, and the planning/execution of actions related to objects of interest. Actions are triggered by a tension that evolves out of discrepancies

---

[28] Working through is a common process in psychoanalytic therapy dealing with overcoming of defensive mechanisms [Lap73, p. 123].

between four patterns of realities that are the *perceived, desired, ideal,* and *anticipated* one. In order to handle this situation the individual sets actions to reduce this tension. *Pleasure* results out of the discharge of this tension. This does not match with Damasio's definition who specifies pleasure as feeling. Three types of robots are based on first experiments with tension-driven behavior, called Neko, Miao, and Miao-V. While Neko is a physical robot, which implements dear-, excitation-, anxiety-, and boredom-related behavior, Miao and Miao-V are simulated agents that additionally include a hunger-related behavior. Neko and Miao include basic functionalities. Their task is to roam the environment regarding a maximum of pleasure. Miao-V's control unit is enhanced by abilities on the base of pleasure-related sensorimotor experiences. At first the robot produces random sounds and moves, invoked by specific increasing tensions. If certain moves and sounds result in a pleasure signal, sensorimotor connections are reinforced. This is similar to Bovet's AMOUSE even though in that case pleasure-related experiences do not exist.

Above approaches to combine the areas of psychoanalysis and engineering are discussed. All of them, except the ARS approach, lack on a realization of their concept. S. Turkle proposes a link between the psychoanalytic object relational approach and emergent AI. However, this link is identified as the attempt to map two different sciences, rather than to define a new technical model. In addition, she disregards that psychoanalysis bases on information processing. Leutzinger-Bohleber and Pfeifer author various interesting articles regarding a cooperation of both sciences on the topic of memory processes. Their ideas have not been realized yet. The same applies to Rodado and Rendon who mistakenly mapped Freud's theory to connectionism. Galatzer-Levy tries to introduce AI to psychoanalysis. His idea sticks to a theoretical elaboration as well. Only Buller implements the psychoanalytic concept of psychodynamics to autonomous agents. However, he tends to mix different theories in one model, respectively maps defined functions of the model to psychoanalytic principles. Cooperation between experts of both sides, the engineering and the psychoanalytic one, is ignored. Summarized it can be said that the use of psychoanalytic findings in CS is widely ignored although there exist theoretical concepts. The ARS decision unit is the first realization worldwide that is fully based on a psychoanalytic model. As psychoanalysis extensively deals with information processing it gain higher interest among a broader audience in the CS community in future.

The ARS project copes with the challenge of designing computer-systems that are able to make decisions based on experiences in dynamically changing environments. The system must extract relevant information out of the current situation and must set appropriate actions. The ARS project introduces a hierarchical view on the human mind. Even though this approach is investigated below in more detail the research basics as well as an overview of the first published model are given here. While the idea of a new start in building automation was introduced by Dietrich et al. in 2000 [DS00, pp. 343-350], the foundation to the ARS project was formed in 2003. C. Tamarit Fuertes [Fue03] introduced the perceptive awareness model (PAM) that extends the ISO/OSI (International Organization for Standardization/Open System Interconnection) model and aims at processing high amount of data in the area of home and building automation. G. Russ [Rus03] focused on the development of a situation recognition system that is able to deal with proactive operational actions. The filtering of data that is significant for a situation forms the focus of this work. Both theses form the foundation for further ARS approaches that also concern the subject matter of perception [BLPV07, Bru07, PLD05,VLBD08]. This branch of the ARS project was called ARS-PC (ARS-PerCeption). Contrariwise, B. Palensky [Pal08] and R. Rösener [R07] work on a first prototype for the ARS decision unit, which is called the ARS-PA (ARS-Psychoanalysis) model. Both branches, the ARS-PC and the ARS-PA are merged today.

In Fig. 2-1 a draft of the ARS-PA model is presented. It is based on the neuropsychoanalytic approach. The sketch shows the division into environment, body, and brain as well as sensor and actuator modules. Hence, the idea of embodiment is implied. The internal system state is considered and affects the evaluation of the current situation and therefore upcoming decisions. The decision making is based on two sub-modules labeled as *Pre-Decision* and *Decision*. The *Brain* receives information from the environment, and the system's homeostasis or respectively the internal state. Sensors and actuators serve as interfaces to the environment. The actuators have direct influence to the environment as well as the internal state. Regarding Fig. 2-1 no difference between the information flow and the control flow is drawn. The *Pre-Decision* module corresponds to the psychoanalytic idea of the Id (see Section 3.3) and accounts for low-level processes that are invoked by drives and basic emotions. Due to information from the so-called image memory, which is triggered by specific perceptual information, a reactive action is invoked. The triggering is influenced by the intensity of a possible inhibition signal from the decision unit and by the type of basic emotions. Basic emotions are mapped to a specific behavioral tendency. Images characterize objects or situations in the environment. The invoked basic emotions are additionally forwarded to the decision module.

As the *Pre-decision* module accords to the psychoanalytic Id, the decision module accords to the psychoanalytic definition of the Ego. It is divided into *Complex emotions*, *Decision making*, *Desires* and *Acting-as-if* modules and processes data from the *Working memory*

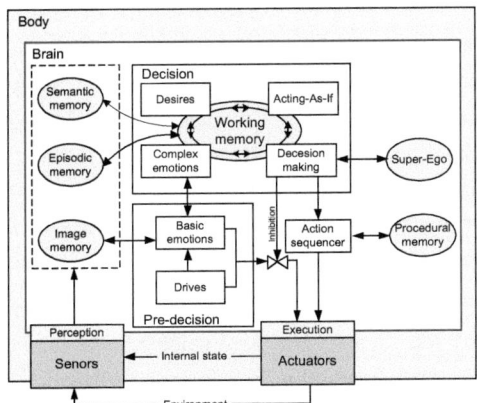

Fig. 2-1: ARS-PA model [Pal09, p. 202]

which in turn receives data from the *Episodic* as well as the *Semantic memory*. The decision making process leaves out the reactive action trigger in case the *Pre-decision* unit cannot invoke the *Execution* unit. The *Working memory* actively receives information from and provides information to functions of the decision module. Both types of memory are needed to provide sufficient information for the decision making process. A draft of the information system is discussed in [DGLV08, pp. 621-626]. While *Semantic memory* contains factual knowledge about the world, *Episodic memory* manages knowledge about subjective experiences. In order to advance further decision making processes, it should be possible to fall back on experiences and knowledge about unalterable facts like laws of physics. While the semantic knowledge stores factual knowledge, the Super-Ego hands over knowledge on social norms to the decision making process. Thereafter a high-level action is triggered in the action sequence. The action flow is loaded from the procedural memory while changes are saved to it. The execution module invokes the actuators that influence the internal state and the environment. Afterwards the control circle restarts.

The ARS-PA model shows a first approach to merge engineering with neuropsychoanalytic concepts. It is inspired by findings released by Solms and Turnbull [ST02] and ongoing work. The model is tested in a game of artificial life that defines groups of software agents controlled by different versions of the ARS-PA model. The behavior boost of the model depending on its implementation level as well as to an if-then rule-based model is discussed. Simulation runs comparing the ARS-PA model to other AI decision units are not done. The ARS-PA model forms the foundation of this thesis and ensuing work in the ARS project.

Related Work

However, it implies issues that have been addressed above and contradict the design paradigms in Section 1.3. First, the ARS-PA model does not divide information flow and control flow, a premise listed above and frequently used in system design. Second, even though the designing paradigm was to use non-contradicting theories for filling the gaps that are consigned by the neuropsychoanalytic approach, incompatibilities emerged. Gaps were generally filled by engineers. Based on gained experiences during the modeling process the design procedure changed. This results in a further development of the ARS model introduced by Dietrich et al. [DFZB09, pp. 56-64] and Zeilinger et al. [ZDML08, pp. 259-264] which result in a further draft of the ARS decision unit that is adapted to the findings in Chapter 3.

The fact that different communities have different types of scientific methodology is an issue that is an opportunity too. Their methods to reach certain aims differ the same way as descriptions and definitions do. In addition, psychoanalytic theory is not based on rules and standards and a consistent axiomatic system[29] as it is common in natural sciences. The effort to reduce scientific communities to a common denominator increases with the gap between them. Computer scientists, psychoanalysts and neuropsychoanalysts who cooperate with each other deal with this fact. However, exactly these different views open the door to new perspectives that result in new concepts for handling a given problem. CS adopts the requirement for embodiment and emotions from neurosciences in order to get closer to the goal of intelligent behavior. In addition, neuropsychoanalysis and psychoanalysis provide concepts for developing a functional model of the human mind to the computer society. However, this requires a change in the way of thinking from the outset. Turkle tries to change her perspective but just maps available theories to each other [Tur89]. This does not result in the advantage that is implicated by a perspective change. She does not relieve new information and ideas to develop a new technical model. Then again, a perspective change may be hindered by unknown issues. Regarding the discussed ARS-PA model the perspective change results in the knowledge that the modeling process must be adapted and restarted. However, this must not be seen as lost time as these are important lessons that are the foundation for research.

2.3 Information Representation in Autonomous Agents

The representation of world knowledge and its use for decision making and action planning is one of the basic questions in the area of AI. Below, this question is discussed for the area

---

[29] Defined by a set of axioms (a statement or proposition which is regarded as being established, accepted, or self-evidently [Pea98]).

of autonomous embodied agents. An overview of knowledge representation techniques and their realization in terms of data structures and knowledge bases is given. The topic is discussed with respect to its differentiation into two oppositional approaches, which are represented by the *logic* and the *anti-logic* group. The fusion of both approaches and their use in autonomous agents is analyzed by models and example implementations of R. Brooks, Ho et al., and Pfeifer et al., to name but a few.

2.3.1 Knowledge Representation Techniques

As defined in Section 1.3 *information representation* is distinguished from knowledge representation. However, techniques for modeling knowledge bases are applied to the *information representation system*. In the history of AI, a number of concepts for knowledge representation have been developed. Lifschitz et al. categorize these concepts to the *anti-logics* and the *logics* [LMP08]. The *logics* map knowledge to formal logic with various syntaxes while representatives of the *anti-logic* group argue that it is unfeasible to write down the whole world knowledge [LMP08, p. 67]. Both are also known as *neats* and *scruffies*. The *neats* have based all their theories on mathematical descriptions [RN03, p. 25]. In contrast, *scruffies* realize their concepts and afterwards evaluate their functionality. They generally ground their work on empirical knowledge. For them, common sense cannot be written down in logical rules.

First-order and propositional logic form the foundation for the *logics'* concept. Both show restrictions to the representation of world knowledge. Propositional logic is rather limited in order to describe complex content in a simple way. First and n-th order logic expand propositional logic by objects, relations, and functions. They assume that the world is represented by objects that are connected to each other. This factor leads to the categorization of objects within an ontology. Groups and sub-groups of objects are formed which inherit attributes from their super-group. Therein a big issue of first order logic is placed as it restricts the use of default values. This leads to a problem in the description of exceptions. A common example is the ostrich or penguin example. Both belong to the super-group of birds but cannot fly. In addition, first-order logic does not allow cross associations between different groups of objects. Hence, optional logics have been developed; respectively already existing ones have been expanded. Default logic deals with reasoning by default, temporal logic deals with temporal relations, description logic enhances the formulation of object attributes, and modal logic extends the first order logic to inference on knowledge.

Alternative to logical sentences, semantic nets are used to describe logical causalities and for formalizing super-group and sub-group dependencies in the form of directed graphs. It has been widely discussed if semantic nets are a form of logic with the result that in case a semantic net is based on well-defined semantics it is claimed to be a form of logic [RN03, p. 350]. Semantic nets are provided with graphical tools and a number of efficient algorithms that assist in the description of a knowledge base, the categorization and referring of nodes. Their components are represented by nodes and arcs. While nodes describe individual objects, concepts, and events, arcs represent the relationships in between. They define binary and non-binary relationships and mark inherited nodes. The expansion of the World Wide Web resulted in increasing use of semantic web technologies. This process contributed to the development of ontology languages that are also used to model and specify semantic nets. Standards like the Resource Description Framework (RDF) [InetRDF], the Resource Description Framework Schema, and the Web Ontology Language (OWL) [InetOWL][30] are widely used for a declarative specification of web services and used for the description of ontologies, concepts, concept properties, and logic relations in the area of AI. RDF describes the resources while OWL is used as modeling language. Related to these standards, a variety of Extensible Markup Language (XML) [InetXML] based languages have been formed, which are attuned to demands in AI and are used to represent knowledge in a structured way. They not only express logic sentences formed on common logic but also extended logics. One example is the Rule Markup Language that defines inferential-transformational tasks in XML and provides a concept for the use of forward and backward rules in XML [BTW01]. Paschke et al. [PB09] give an overview for reaction rule languages that define concepts for detecting, responding, and reasoning over events.

The *anti-logics*, respectively *scruffies*, argue for a different concept of knowledge representation. In contrast to the formal logic that has advantages for restricted system domains, the anti-logic approach aims towards a common sense description. They doubt that the logic approach is able to do so as not all common sense reasoning is deductive [LMP08, p. 70].

The era of embodied AI proposes a number of approaches that accord to the *scruffies*' arguments. With the idea of embodiment, the focus of attention is moved away from its knowledge representation towards the interaction of the system with its environment. R. Brooks internalized this concept in the subsumption architecture – see Section 1.2. S. Bovet and R. Pfeifer follow the same approach. The system's sensor modalities are associated due to the activation by the perceived environment. A close look at this approach is given in

---

[30] RDF, OWL, and Resource Description Framework Schema are defined by the World Wide Web Consortium (W3C)

Section 2.3.3. In addition the area of neural networks is part of the *anti-logic* group. The modeling of brain structures by the use of neural networks in order to achieve mind functionality shows best why the term *scruffy* stands for these concepts. Representatives of the logic approach criticize that the *scruffies* trust to chance to achieve a satisfying behavior of the system. However, exactly this part of the concept is claimed by them to be the only chance to reach intelligent behavior. Intelligent behavior emerges out of the interaction with the environment and not by the definition of world knowledge only. The expanding area of genetic algorithms shows similar effects.

Above the area of semantic nets is mentioned that is dedicated to the logic approach but is positioned at the border to the group of anti-logic concepts. The same is true for the *frame* approach that is proposed by M. Minsky [Min75] and is based on the theory of semantic nets. However, it is identified as scruffy approach. Summarized, the use of a well-defined semantic is the difference between the scruffy and the neat approach. Regarding the frame approach, M. Minsky defines a frame to be a data structure for the representation of situations and objects. The basic difference between semantic nets and frames is the additional dimension in the representation of knowledge. In contrast to the concept of nodes semantic nets include additional property structures in frames which define sub-frames or events. As semantic nets, frames follow the object-oriented approach that simplifies the realization by object-oriented programming. They define individual objects or situations (individual frames) but can also be interpreted as templates for object classes (generic frames) [BL04]. An example for a special type of frame is the *script* that defines the temporal relations between frames. A sequence of frames that is bound by scripts form a scenario.

Even though *neats* and *scruffies* support contradicting theories both do not exclude each other as several realizations are based on both concepts. Cognitive architectures like SOAR [LNR87] and ACT-R [AL98] merge formal representations and rules in order to create new data blocks that contain sensor input as well as current goals (see Section 2.3.2).

In ARS there is a strong differentiation between control flow and information flow. This has influence on the *information representation system* design and modeling techniques that are used for this step. The ARS project does conform to the *scruffy* approach by implying embodied concepts and on the opinion that it is not able to give a complete description of the world in logic relations. However, plans must be defined which hardly works without a logical formalization. Hence, concepts of *neats* and *scruffies* are introduced to the ARS control unit (see Chapter 4) as it is done for the cognitive architectures SOAR and ACT-R.

2.3.2 Memory Based Control Architectures

The State, Operator Apply Result (SOAR) architecture, introduced by J. Laird, A. Newell, and P. Rosenbloom [LNR87] and the Adaptive Control of Thought-Rational (ACT-R) architecture [AL98], introduced by J. R. Anderson and C. Lebiere, belong to the group of so-called cognitive architectures that are developed to define a model of the human cognitive apparatus. SOAR and ACT-R are the basis for state of the art control units in the area of cognitive architectures. Both are designed to achieve the same goal as the ARS control unit. The basic mechanisms and structures, similar to those in human cognition, are integrated to robot control systems. The concepts not only cover higher cognitive processes but deal with the area from sensor stimuli to actuator control as well. The central element of both models is their memory system. ACT-R and SOAR are based on production systems. They contain patterns for data structures in the form of frames that define associations between conditions and actions in the form of IF-THEN clauses. If the current input matches a pattern, respectively a condition, then an associated action is triggered. These rules are labeled as *productions*.

Concepts, which are applied to agent control systems, are discussed in the section below. SOAR does not differentiate between different types of memory regarding their structure, search control, or memory operations. This contrasts with ACT-R that is inspired by the multi-store model theory. The multi-store model was introduced by R. Atkinson and R. Shiffrin [AS68] and became the basic memory model in different scientific disciplines like neurology, psychology but also neuropsychoanalysis [ST02, pp. 154-160]. The key element is the division of the memory systems to separate memory structures and operations. The human memory structure is categorized by time to short-term memory, working memory, and long-term memory. Further research refined these categories by the type of content and sensor modality. For example, E. Tulving distinguishes between episodic and semantic[31] memory [Tul72]. However, there exist numerous additional categories like iconic, short-term visual, or flashbulb memory. A summary is listed by Pfeifer [PS99, p. 506].

SOAR is a physical symbol system as the system manipulates symbols in order to reach the defined goal. Symbols describe abstract concepts in the form of patterns. The SOAR system's behavior is defined by its goals and its knowledge about its environment [New94, p. 55]. Primarily, SOAR is defined as cognitive architecture. As it is a cognitive model of the human mind it theoretically should approximate human cognitive mechanisms. This in-

---

[31] Episodic and semantic memories form the declarative memory. While episodic memory stores experiences, semantic memory contains concept-based knowledge unrelated to specific experiences [ET01].

cludes memory characteristics like short-term and long-term mechanisms. However, SOAR implements mechanisms that are only required for the system functionality. None that is implemented in order to achieve the imitation of specific biological processes only [New94, p.309]. Hence, all cognitive characteristics emerge from the architecture and do not result from mechanisms that are introduced on purpose to achieve these characteristics. Newell et al. merge the functionality of their SOAR architecture to memory characteristics [New94, p.164]. Fig. 2-2 shows the SOAR memory structure. The arrows show the information flow between the different modules. It is differentiated between *long-term memory*, *working memory*, *perception*, and *motor system*. The perceptual sensor system receives information about the environmental state (arrow 1) and forwards these information elements to the *working memory* (arrow 2) that holds the current goal state. In SOAR it is possible to hold several goal states in parallel. The *working memory* is temporary and contains data elements that are necessary in order to compare perceived data with productions. As the system receives elements from a dynamically changing environment, the *working memory* serves as buffer in order to stabilize the information load. In addition it is a bus that interconnects all memory modules. The *long-term memory* is a production system that compares productions with elements that are held in the *working memory*. If these elements match with defined productions, they are written to the *working memory* or removed from it (arrow 3 and arrow 4). In contrast, the *motor system* translates control information to actuator control data (arrow 7). The stream back to the *working memory* (arrow 6) contains feedback on current *motor system* processes [New94, p. 197]. Goal-based problems are converted to productions and stored in the *long-term memory* (arrow 3). This conversion is called *chunking*. Chunking is a process of learning from experiences as new productions are formed and added to the *long-term memory* in case a problem is solved.

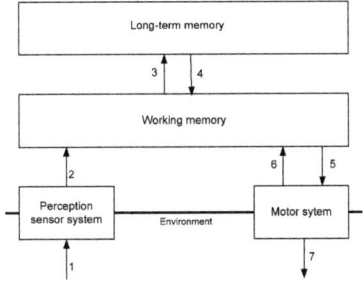

Fig. 2-2: Memory concept in SOAR [New94, p.195]

Related Work

In contrast to SOAR, ACT-R is based on a memory model that is inspired by the multi-store model. Fig. 2-3 sketches the ACT-R architecture. Since the release of ACT-R 1.0 a number of revisions have been introduced, however, the basic structure persists. Especially the division between declarative and procedural memory is still maintained in ACT-R 6.0 [InetACTR]. Anderson and Lebiere claim that this differentiation is backed up by neuroscientific research results [AL98, p. 21].

In Fig. 2-3, three memory modules are identified which are labeled as *procedural memory*, *declarative memory*, and the *goal stack*. The current *goal* represents the focus of attention and controls these modules. In contrast to SOAR, ACT-R concurrently allows only one goal state. Like in SOAR, chunks and productions represent the basic data concept in ACT-R that data structures are based on. They are stored in the declarative memory, and are described by frame-like patterns that contain pointers to their category and content. There exist two types of chunks. Object chunks represent the encoded perceptual object while goal chunks represent goals and facts. As in SOAR, productions describe rules for the manipulation of chunks. In addition they define the knowledge that is required to search through the problem space. They are stored in the *procedural memory* and do not differ regarding the type of chunks. In case the focus of attention changes, the current *goal* initializes a conflict resolution process. Productions regarding the current goal are sent to the *procedural memory* (arrow 1). Stored productions are compared with the current *goal*. The selected production triggers an action (arrow 2) and requests information from the *declarative memory* (arrow 4) that is realized by an associative weighted network that is formed out of rules and perception. The triggered chunks influence the current *goal* (arrow 9). The *declarative memory* receives chunks from the environment (arrow 8) and the current *goal* (arrow 10). Related to these input parameters a so-called production compilation process initializes

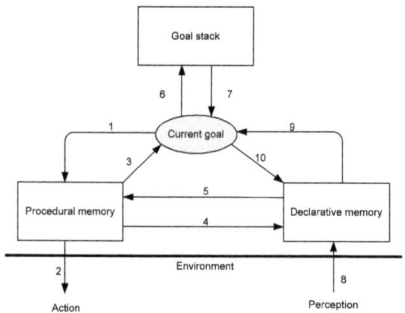

Fig. 2-3: ACT-R architecture [AL98, p. 11]

the creation of new productions. They are sent to the *procedural memory* (arrow 5). Depending on incoming information a transformation of the current goal is initialized (arrow 3). The current goal is sent to (arrow 6) or retrieved from the *stack* (arrow 7). ACT-R additionally introduces buffers to the architecture in order to limit resources for sensor processing. This is only done in order to simulate specific biological mechanisms. As discussed above this methodology strongly differs from SOAR.

Newell raises points of criticism regarding ACT-R [New94, p. 29]. From his point of view the ATC-R theory is mathematically not traceable. ACT-R is manageable only in straightforward tasks. Both, ACT-R and SOAR imply production systems and are strongly based on memory structures. The uniform character of SOAR – no differentiation between the different types of memory, search algorithms, and data structures – is different to ACT-R. Learning mechanisms are available for both systems. While SOAR uses chunking in the long-term memory, ACT-R differentiates the learning method with respect to the memory system. Procedural knowledge is acquired by correspondence with the input while declarative knowledge is defined by rules and perceived data. In contrast to SOAR and ACT-R the ARS model is not based on a memory structure approach. Mechanisms are derived from neurology, neuropsychoanalysis and psychoanalysis and are applied to a technical model; they are not mapped to them. Neither SOAR nor ACT-R assume embodiment for their functionality. This contrasts with control structures that take a body as requirement (see Section 1.2) like it is done for the subsumption architecture. The subsumption architecture is a reactive architecture and does not store any scenarios and experiences. Rules for data manipulation are introduced to every layer of the architecture. However, several models expand the subsumption architecture by a memory structure as is discussed in Section 2.3.3.

2.3.3 Information Representation Concepts in Autonomous Agents

As discussed in Section 2.3.2, SOAR and ACT-R represent a group of control units in CS whose functionality is strongly based on their memory structure. The control units discussed in this section realize alternative concepts. Some of them, as the ARS model (see Section 1.3), implement a knowledge base that is functionally decoupled from the decision unit. Another approach is based upon pure sensorimotor coupling that requires embodiment.

Related Work

Multi-store Model Inspired Memory Concept

A sophisticated realization, inspired by the theory of multi-store memory, is proposed by Ho et al. [HDN03, pp. 182-191]. There it is focused on the realization of an agent that dynamically reconstructs its experiences at run-time [HDN06, p. 26]. Ho bases the agent control structure on the reactive subsumption approach but extends the original [Bro86b, pp. 14-23] by a multi-store memory concept (see Fig. 2-4). This extension contradicts to the subsumption architecture's theoretical foundation. There it is intended that the system's behavior is a result of the sensorimotor coupling without the requirement of experienced situations. In contrast Ho et al. merge the embodied with the emotional AI approach as they introduce an internal system state. The integrated memory structure enables the provision of extra-sensory homeostatic information that influences the agent's current and future actions [HDN08]. Ho integrates a homeostatic and environmental state to software agents whose actions rely on stored information. As in the ARS project, Ho et al. strongly rely to interdisciplinary work covered by scientists from CS, computer science, and psychology. During design of the memory structure they cope with typical issues that rise by transferring scientific theories to different areas of research. Ho argues [HDN08] that due to a lack of granularity regarding the description of specific parts in the theory of memory details have had to be supplemented in the final concept. The approach is interesting for the ARS model as well, as the knowledge structure is based on the frame approach, which is an option for the *information representation system*. Hence, Ho's model is worth a closer look.

Similar to ACT-R the memory concept is based on the multi-store model. First, it is focused on the episodic memory. Fig. 2-4 shows the control structure that is introduced by Ho et al. [HDN03, pp. 182-191]. Input data is received from virtual sensors by detecting objects, landforms, and temperature. Internal variables like glucose, moisture, energy, and body temperature form the homeostasis and must stay within certain limits. In case a homeostatic level exceeds its limits, memory elements are triggered that influence the chosen behavior.

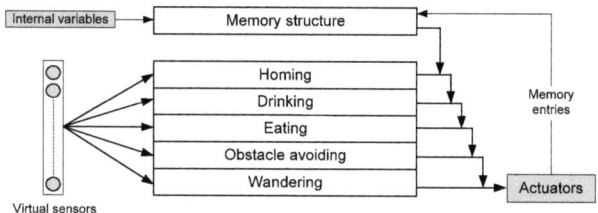

Fig. 2-4: Ho's agent control structure [HDN03, pp. 182-191]

The actuator module sends a new record back to the memory structure that implies the current environmental as well as homeostatic state. All records are temporally ordered and form the foundation for reconstructing episodes. Later the memory structure is extended by components for short-term and long-term memory [HDN05, pp. 573-580]. The short-term memory contains a finite number of memory entries that are formed out of the agent's current state which is identified by direction, location, perceived objects, and the distance it has covered since the last event. The recall of information is triggered by an exceeded threshold of internal variables which initializes a search for a similar memory entry – trace-back mechanism. In case of successful search, all actions up to the specific memory entry are undone. In theory, this leads the agent to the starting point where it can interact with the required object.

Long-term memory records are *temporally* ordered by *event reconstruction* and *filtering and ranking* processes. Every record represents an experienced situation and is identified by a *match key*, a *search key*, a *priority key* and an *optional condition key*. The *priority key* defines the way a situation affects homeostatic levels. Depending on their current state, the record ranking is introduced by the *event filtering and ranking* process. The record with the highest priority is defined as *key-record* and starting point for the *event reconstruction* process. Following a forward and backward search along the timeline, a record is searched that matches the current situation. The frame structure of a record holds three identifiers that specify current location, resources, and certain constraints. In case the required record is found, all actions are rolled back or reversed until the *key-record* is reached.

Elsewhere, Ho et al. introduce an interesting add-on in the form of a communication interface to their model [HDNB04, pp. 361-370]. The agent receives information from others without having experienced the same situations before. It must be able to interpret the others' knowledge although it may differ from their goals, intentions, and motivations. According to L. Steels, different memories are aligned by social interaction [Ste03].

The designed model is realized into software agents and tested within an artificial-life simulation. The agent must deal with its environment and internal requirements. Its basic demand is to set actions that let it survive. The success of the different models is evaluated by Ho et al. [HDN08]. The life span of the agent or a group of agents is used as evaluation criteria.

Volitron

Volitron is an agent whose control structure is based on a psychoanalytic approach that has few aspects in common with the theory which is introduced to the ARS project. Unlike Ho, Buller et al. have based their agent controller on two completely different theories [Bul02, pp.17-20]. Ho et al. introduced the neuroscientific multi-store model to the computer scientific subsumption architecture. Otherwise, Buller et al. merge the neuroscientific multi-store concept with the psychoanalytic theory of psychodynamics.

Buller et al. model five different memory types labeled as *perceptual representation* system, *procedural memory*, *semantic memory*, *episodic memory*, and *working memory*. Except for the *working memory* all memory components contain static information. Four reality types are introduced in order to evaluate the current situation (see Section 2.2). The *semantic memory* contains knowledge about the *ideal reality*, *perceived reality*, and *desired reality* while the *working memory* includes the *anticipated reality* as well as *functionalities* for processing memes. Volitron's data structures base upon information fractals that are labeled as *memes*. Memes of satisfaction as well as dissatisfaction are formed due to differences among the reality patterns. *Working memory* manipulations invoke motility functions.

It is assumed that the interaction between memes reduces upcoming tension and balances the system. Although they are triggered by perceived signals their processes are fairly unobservable like those in a neural network. Even the overall approach is influenced by psychodynamic theory, regarding information representation, the system is based on a concept developed by engineers. The resulting technical concept is mapped to different types of memory.

Here some points of criticism must be mentioned in the context of this work. Buller et al. introduce psychological concepts to a psychoanalytic theory. Their compatibility is doubted by the author and contradicts Premise 3 in Section 1.3. Furthermore, functions and data storages are mixed up, even though their concepts are different. This is avoided for the ARS model as the decision layer and the information representation layer (see Fig. 1-1) are separated.

ARS-PA Approach

As described in Section 2.2 the ARS-PA model includes a memory structure that implies a working, an image, a semantic, a procedural, and an episodic memory (see Fig. 2-1). The first four, whose underlying functionality is summarized in Section 2.2, are partly implemented [DGLV08, pp. 621-626]. The episodic memory must be discussed in more detail regarding the *information management system* that is proposed in Section 3.4. Even though both models differ in major parts the organization of episodes in the ARS-PA model serves as foundation.

As neuropsychoanalysis, amongst others, integrates memory concepts, the ARS-PA model contains a memory model similar to that of Ho et al. The *episodic memory* facilitates the decision making process by the implication of past experiences. The impact of an event to the agent is strongly influenced by the current emotional state. This approach is based on the work of A. Baddeley [Bad97]. Before the ARS-PA episodic memory is discussed in detail the terms *situation, template image, event, scenario,* and *episode* must be defined with respect to their use in the ARS project.

A *situation* is defined as array of information that characterizes the current state in which the agent remains. This term comprises an internal and environmental state. A *template image* is a predefined pattern that describes a situation. As claimed by Zucker (né Pratl) [Pra06, p. 22], an image of the real world corresponds to the inner perception of the outer world. In parallel the term abstract image has been introduced that has the same meaning. However, in current work the term template image is preferred (see Section 3.2). An *event* is an enclosed incident that specifies a particular situation [Tul83, p. 37]. Regarding the ARS-PA approach the *event* is characterized by *template image* matches, *emotional states*, and *actions* [DGLV08, p. 623]. A *scenario* is a sequence of events defined by a state chart. The states represent the current situation. The term *scenario* is different from the definition that is introduced in Section 3.2 where it is differed from acts. Perceptual images are compared with template images. The match between stored and perceived information is calculated out of the overlap of the perceptual and a template image. This result is used in the decision making process. The transition of one scenario state to another is triggered by an event that belong to a finite number of episodes which are stored in the *episodic memory*. Scenarios require predefined *template image* matches for state transitions. Events that occur but do not belong to the *scenario* are stored in an episode of the scenario. The scenario state transition and the match between scenarios and episodes are shown in Fig. 2-5. It must be outlined that Fig. 2-5 sketches the definition of an action plan in the ARS-PA model. It does not represent the functionality of the human brain that works in an asynchronous way and cannot be com-

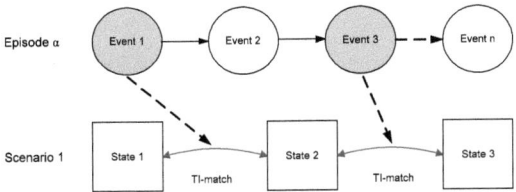

Fig. 2-5: Scenario state transition in the ARS-PA model

pared with a state machine. Also the representation of a scenario in terms of states is simplified and done with respect to the implementation.

Events that represent episode α and are required to fulfill the Scenario 1 are highlighted in grey in Fig. 2-5. The retrieval of certain events is defined by its impact factor, which is labeled as salience. The salience declines with time by following an exponential gradient. This feature simulates a forgetting process and avoids an ever-increasing number of identified events. Regarding the ARS-PA model, only events are retrieved. If they belong to episodes, previous and succeeding events are fetched from memory. This mechanism is similar to the one proposed by Ho. Simulation results show a slight improvement in the behavior of agents that contain the episodic memory [DZLZ08, pp. 621-626].

Similar to the ARS-PA model, the ARS model 3.0 (see Section 3.3) must store information as well. However, the ARS-PA model's memory structure is not adopted as this would result in inconsistencies with the multi-store model inspired concept. Hence, a psychoanalytic approach is used instead of the neuropsychoanalytic concept instead. The concepts *images* and *scenarios* still appear in the proposed model, even though their structural composition goes along with another theoretical concept.

AMOUSE

Above, agent controllers are discussed that are based on the multi-store memory concept and therefore explicitly define a memory structure. The subsumption architecture is already introduced as a concept that originally does not rely on a memory structure but only bases its behavior on the system-environment interaction. This is also applied to the concept introduced by AMOUSE.

The control system of AMOUSE represents the idea of embodiment in its pure form. AMOUSE is realized in a Khebera robot and was designed at the ETH Zürich for studying biological models of rodent behavior [FAD+04, pp. 114-122] in cooperation with biologists and neuroscientists. While the original controller architecture is based on the subsumption approach, Bovet et al. go one step further and introduce a *flat* control architecture [BP05a, pp. 324-330] [Bov06, pp. 525-533]. S. Bovet and R. Pfeifer discuss a robot control architecture whose behavior only relies on its sensorimotor coupling. In contrast to agent architectures like ACT-R, SOAR, or the subsumption architecture, they aim to

- rely on homogeneous[32], nonhierarchical, sensorimotor coupling

---

[32] No distinction is made between sensor and motor modalities.

- and abstain from basic modules or layers including any kind of function
- or preprogrammed skills.

A sensorimotor control system that leaves out any hierarchies is a foundational difference to the ARS model. Any modality is represented and implemented at the neural level of a sensor or motor system. They are fully meshed with each other. Correlations between simultaneous activities in any pair of modalities strength the connection between them. This procedure results on the base of a Hebbian learning rule.

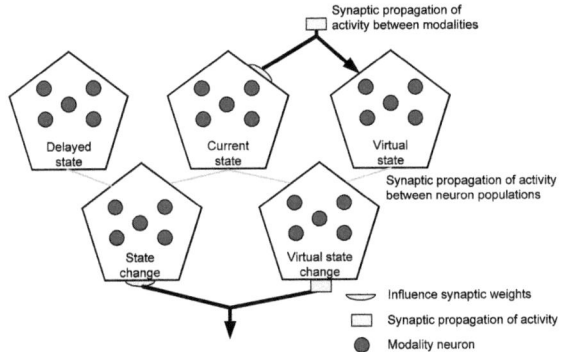

Fig. 2-6: AMOUSE modality

Fig. 2-6 shows the design of one modality that consists of five neuron populations. They are named *Current State*, *Delayed State*, *Virtual State*, *State Change*, and *Virtual State Change*. The *Current State* represents the current activity of the associated sensor or motor system. The *Delayed State* represents the temporal delayed *Current State*. The difference between both is saved into the *State Change*. The *Virtual State* represents a nominal condition of the modality. In combination with the *Current State* it results in the *Virtual State Change*. The state change and the current state are used to adapt the synaptic weights between the modalities. The arrows in Fig. 2-6 outline the synaptic propagation from the virtual state change of the current towards the virtual state change of the connected modalities. It is shown that AMOUSE is capable of developing behaviors that are not preprogrammed but emerge due to the interaction with its environment [BP05a, pp. 324-330]. After an initial phase, the robot associates different modality states with each other. For example, a visual flow is linked to the turning motion. AMOUSE develops certain behaviors like following an object without having an internal representation of an object, goal, orientation or desire. The experiment shows that an embodied robot is able to create abilities based on the interaction with the world. These abilities are strictly related to its sensorimotor modalities. In [BP05b, pp. 2272-2277], Bovet et al. discuss the temporal dependency between an action and a temporally delayed award. They claim that an agent must not possess a memory in order to relate clue and reward. AMOUSE is able to decide between a correct and a wrong move on the base of getting a reward or a punishment at the end of the act.

Bovet et al. claim that behavior *"... is only produced by the propagation of neuronal activity across the different modalities, modulated both by the cross-modal correlations learnt by the robot from its own experience, and by the robot's perception of the actual environment"* [BP05a, p. 326].

The achieved results are impressive as the robot is able to accomplish tasks without predefined knowledge but only by forming weighted connections between the sensor and motor modalities. In addition it shows the principle of embodiment in agent technologies at its very basics. However, it raises the question if this architecture is sufficient for more complex and conflictive tasks. Even though Bovet shows the emergence of insect navigation strategies in [Bov06, pp. 525-533] a wide gap to higher functionalities still remain. In addition the sensor and motor modalities are connected in a fully meshed network, whose complexity rises with the number of sensors and motor actions.

Above, four representatives of state of the art agent controllers and their memory structures are discussed. The selection starts with multi-store inspired structures that are merged with different control architectures and ends up with an approach that shows the theory of embodiment at its very basics. Except AMOUSE which gives an example of pure sensorimotor coupling, all approaches are based on on symbolic information processing. For AMOUSE control and memory structure is merged and emerges out of the system-environment interaction. It becomes manifest in the form of weighted associations between the different modalities and neural groups.

As in AMOUSE the ARS model does not explicitly integrate a *memory*. Memory-like behavior emerges from the *information representation system* and the decision unit even though it cannot be explicitly assigned to a specific functionality. This conforms to the theory of emergent memory (see Section 1.1). In contrast, Buller and Ho et al. explicitly introduce memory components to their concepts which are inspired by the multi-store concept.

Ho et al. deal with the two of the best researched multi-store memory structures – the episodic and the semantic memory component. Unfortunately, the approach lacks in knowledge about the structural composition of memory components and does not provide a uniform and consistent foundation for all of them. From the author's point of view, memory is not a construction kit where components can be chosen at will. If memory structures are not considered, important concepts and functionalities are lost. Even though Ho et al. design their model in interdisciplinary work with scientists from non-engineering areas, the lack on required knowledge about the memory structure leaves space open for the interpretation of computer scientists. This leads to a model that does not have a lot in common with the human memory itself. To the author's mind this reduces the multi-store model's usability for taking it as foundation for realizing human-like memory.

In contrast to Ho et al., the ARS model 3.0 clearly divides into information processing and information storage. Both parts are based on different backgrounds and must not be seen on the same layer. Buller et al. additionally mix inconsistent theories without consulting experts in these areas. On the one hand they include psychoanalytic pillars like defense mechanisms and drives to their concept. On the other hand they fill the remaining gaps with self-created functionalities and a multi-store theory inspired storage solution. Buller's definitions partly differ from those, specified in the ARS project even though they are both based on psychoanalytic concepts. For example, Volitron's defense mechanisms become active under certain circumstances while in the ARS model they are active all the time representing the system's homeostasis. In addition they specify the term conflict as a result of contradicting wishes. Follwing psychoanalytic concepts that are applied to ARS, conflicts already exist between drives that in turn form the foundation for wishes.

The ARS model is based on neuropsychoanalytic concepts. Their technical descriptions are harmonized in cooperation with neuropsychoanalysts and psychoanalysts in order to avoid inconsistencies. The distinction between information flow and functional units is reflected in the separated discussion of *information representation* and *information processing*. Information storage and functionalities are clearly decoupled from one another in order to avoid mixing different principles. The result is a model of human-like mind processes that covers a wide range of information processing like actuator, sensor, and planning functionalities.

2.4 Evaluation of the Information Representation System

Every system must be undertaken a performance evaluation. The framework as well as a quantifiable objective evaluation must be defined. In Section 1.1 this subject is already touched regarding a control system's *intelligence*. The same issues turn up for the evaluation of the ARS control unit. Regarding this work, it must be discussed how an evaluation of the overall system as well as single components can be arranged.

2.4.1 Entering Artificial Worlds

Regarding emotional and embodied AI, new concepts are integrated and tested in agents. A common approach is to design embodied autonomous software agents before applying the concept to real world applications. It is particularly used when implementing an embodied and emotional evaluation concept to a system. This procedure results in higher flexibility for adapting the environment where the agent is placed into and the possibility to test the system functionality without the need to take care of mechanical issues. An agent at its very basic definition is an object that is equipped with sensors through which it perceives its environment and influences the environment upon its actuators [RN03, p. 32]. Its task is completed on the basis of a program.

The term autonomous refers to the absence of direct control from human beings [PB07, p. 90]. Dietrich et al. define a software agent as *"... a software program, capable of acting on behalf of a user or another program"* [DFZB09, p. 417]. Implicating the discussion on embodiment in Section 2.1 leads to the definition of an *autonomous embodied software agent* used for this work.

Definition 7: An autonomous embodied software agent is a software program that accomplishes its tasks in the absence of direct user control by interacting with its environment. For this it uses sensors and actuators which are part of its body.

It is widely discussed by the CS community if a software agent can be embodied. Pfeifer et al. claim that the interaction with a real physical world is required [PIB05, p. 1]. The complexity of the environment forms the abilities of the agent to the same degree as the complexity of the sensor and actuator system. Pfeifer defines the term real world and opposes it to a virtual world [PB07, pp. 91-92]. According to this definition the real world possess following characteristics:

1. Acquisition of information takes time
2. An agent possesses only limited information about the world
3. Acquired information contains errors
4. The world is not defined by discrete states which results in the lack of clearly defined actions which must be executed in a particular state
5. Agents execute different actions simultaneously
6. The world is dynamic and induces time-pressure to the agent

This list raises the question if it is possible to cope with these requirements in a simulated world. Formal worlds like they are known from chess would fail. Nevertheless, it is possible to satisfy requirements 1, 2, and 6. If a simulated agent is equipped with sensors it must be assured that it operates on perceived sensor information. Placed in an environment the agent must fulfill specific tasks. The world can also be equipped with a certain dynamic. Requirements 3, 4, and 5 require discussion. Due to the error rate of physical components, the sensor data contains errors. Hence, the agent must deal with inconsistent or wrong information. It is possible to induce randomized errors to the sensors. A failure model must be predefined. Configuring a complex environment equipped with numerous and different objects and agents the chance is reduced to a minimum that the current state has already occurred. Depending on the complexity of the environment a simulated agent can be forced to execute different actions simultaneously. Even though a simulated world can never meet the complexity of the real world it can be approximated. In contrast, it is far easier to simulate the behavior of agent groups as no additional cost is incurred with a rise in the number of agents. It is widely discussed in the CS community if this approach really meets the requirements for embodiment. Summarized, three requirements must be kept.

First, the environment must be configured with a certain kind of complexity. Second, a physics engine must be integrated in order to allow physical interaction between the objects. Third, the agent possesses only information about objects within the sensor range in order to avoid full knowledge about the world. The ARS implementation meets these requirements as it is proposed in Chapter 4.

The idea is to design an environment where the agent depends on its abilities for fulfilling tasks without getting assistance from outside the world. The prototype of an agent-based social system is related to M. Toda's *Fungus Eater* thought experiment [Tod82]. The fungus eater is an autonomous agent that is sent to the fictive planet Taros. It cannot be remote controlled. Hence, it must survive in its own microcosm[33]. The fungus eater is sent there with the instruction to collect uranium ore which it gets rewarded for. To survive the robot must consume fungi that grow separated from the uranium ore. Hence, on occasion it must interrupt its mission in order to move to the fungi sources. Toda integrated the opportunity for conflicts in his experiment. The autonomous robot must decide between getting rewarded by collecting ore but simultaneously losing power, and collecting fungi which saves its life

---

[33] Here, a microcosm is a closed problem that consists out of numerous mutually dependent sub-problems [Tod82, p. 102].

but keeps it away from rewards. Toda extended his experiment with the considerations of more than one fungus eater roaming within the environment and that it is equipped with emotions. The scenario of diverse agents placed in a world is similar to the test-bed of a game of artificial life. A game of artificial life is an environment which focuses on the social interaction among agents [DFZB09, p. 417]. There exist a number of platforms which are designed for the integration of games of artificial life.

2.4.2 Multi-Agent Simulation Platforms

When designing games of artificial life, available simulation platforms can be used. The number of feasible simulation platforms can be limited by considering the given requirements that derive from the following criteria:

- The world setup
- Physics engine
- Software license
- Reusability
- Computational performance

The world setup corresponds to attributes like world size or number of agents and objects that are placed in it. Even though the computational performance is related to this point it should not be limited to it. As long as the simulation must not fulfill specific time constraints, the lack on computational performance is made up by hardware performance or more time consuming test runs. However, especially by simulating a high number of agents, the scalability is an important factor as performance limitations result into large time-delays. As stated by Pfeifer et al. embodiment needs a physical interaction with the world [PIB05, pp. 1-6]. Hence, embodied agents must be placed within an environment that underlies physical principles. Physical interaction is approximated to the real world by a physics engine whose selection must be considered in a decision for a simulation environment. The software license under which a platform is released is another criterion for choosing a simulation platform like it is done in [TH04]. The question is if an adaptation or extension of the source code is required. The software license defines the access to the source code as well as the legal restrictions and procedures for releasing a code that is based the simulation platform. In addition, the code's reusability depends on the programming language that is used for writing the simulation platform's code. Further development depends on the period of vocational adjustments for programmers as well as the size of the community behind the project. This number strongly depends on the quantity of programmers and therefore on the chosen programming language. Traditionally, object-oriented languages like Java or C++ provide the best chances for continuing development. In addition to their wide use, object-oriented languages assist in programming agents as they have characteristics with objects in common. The main difference between both concepts is that objects are considered passive, while agents have their own thread of control [Ode02, p.42]. Even though their similarities are discussed in the community, it is undoubted that agents are an evolution of objects. The same is true for agent programming that evolves out of object-oriented programming but is less common.

In case the project lacks further development and the community support changes its direction, the code-reuse is made easier by porting it to another framework. Berryman compares agent-based modeling toolkits [Ber08]. The evaluation criteria are constituted with flexibility, documentation, facilities, analysis, speed, adaptation, self-organization, and networked causality.

Deutsch et al. used the simulation tool AnyLogic[34] for an agent-based simulation [DZL07, pp. 1021-1026] [DZLZ08, pp. 1086-1091]. Even though tools discussed below show high performance gains, in this case a tool is needed for a rapid prototype design [DZLZ08, p. 1086]. AnyLogic supports Java and therefore a chance is given to port the written code to other simulation platforms that come with Java support – assumed that the use of AnyLogic data structures are avoided. Tests have shown that the scalability of AnyLogic is limited. Hence, tools providing higher performance must be used in this thesis.

Railsback et al. reviewed the simulation platforms NetLogo, Java SWARM, Object C Swarm, Repast, and MASON (Multi-Agent Simulator of Neighborhoods… or Networks… or something…) towards their development priorities and directions [RLJ06]. In addition sample models test implementation complexity as well as platform execution speed. These platforms are chosen for comparison as they are commonly used in multi-agent simulation design. SWARM, Repast, and Mason provide standardized software design tools [RLJ06, p. 612]. They enable dynamic scheduling which releases the simulation from fixed time steps. Hence, actions are generated and scheduled during runtime. MASON, SWARM, and Repast do not allow rapid prototyping as their complexity precludes such usage. In contrast, NetLogo follows a different development strategy.

---

[34] Developed by the company Xitek

Related Work

NetLogo is based on the Logo programming language[35] and provides a high-level development platform. It is designed for the use on different levels of education. Even though this aim may suggest that NetLogo is not usable for scientific usage, Railsback et al. discussed it as they are able to run their implementation samples on it. They mention NetLogo to be used for the prototyping of models that are later on implemented in low-level platforms [RLJ06, p. 630]. Even though, NetLogo is free of charge the source code is not available for third party programmers.

SWARM implements the concept of describing the simulated world as a swarm. It is one of the first so-called agent-based modeling and simulation platforms launched in 1994 [MBLA96]. A swarm is a group of objects that carry out actions. Every swarm can implement a swarm of lower hierarchy, which executes actions that are scheduled in the swarm at a higher level. In addition SWARM implements the concept of differing between the model itself and a virtual observation framework that can be used to experiment with agents. Repast is developed on the University of Chicago with the focus towards the simulation of social behavior [MN05]. In contrast to SWARM, which uses own data structures for representing objects [RLJ06, p. 616], Repast is available in pure Java, .NET, and Python forms. The Java version of SWARM suffers from low execution speed in comparison to the objective-C version [RLJ06, p. 631]. In contrast, the objective-C version suffers from specific flaws of the objective-C language like weak error handling, and no garbage collection. R. T. and C. Hoffmann compared SWARM and Repast among others [TH04]. They evaluate the simulation platforms by means of

- General criteria like their license, documentation, support, user bases, and future viability
- The support for modeling, simulation control, experimentation, project organization, ease of use, communication, and installation
- Support for modeling options like number of complex agents, inter-agent communication, nesting of agents, agent population, networks, dynamic structure change, and management of spatial arrangements

Even though SWARM and Repast come up with similar results, Repast has slight advantages in support and licensing while SWARM has a larger community. Especially the lack on documentation of Repast's core is one of the main criticisms of Railsback et al. [RLJ06]. Except for NetLogo, the discussed simulation frameworks generally suffer from

---

[35] Functional programming language that is based on Lisp

this issue. MASON is a Java library and released in 2005. It aims towards high performance, handling a large number of agents and crowded simulation environments. [LCRPS04, pp. 517-527]. However, Railsback claims that it is only useful for experienced programmers [RLJ06]. In addition a simple physics engine is provided which is compatible with the MASON library. In network causality MASON outpaces the other platforms [Ber08]. Berryman compared agent-based toolkits with those that are specifically adapted to battlefield applications [Ber08]. The simulation platforms are tested by a simple test framework that simulates a simplified battlefield. For this simulation setup the results show slight differences between the frameworks even though RePast, SWARM, MASON, and NetLogo are the leading candidates.

Neither Railsback et al. nor Berryman nominate one platform as clear winner. The results must be handled with care as the test samples are simplified. Advantages in speed that a platform provides by using own data structures changes the simulation outcome and do not turn up for other scenarios. For the area of scientific multi-agent simulations, the reviews show a tendency to Repast, SWARM, MASON, or NetLogo. The chosen platform crucially depends on specific project requirements but also on further development by the different communities.

2.4.3 Agent Performance Evaluation

In order to test the control unit of an autonomous embodied software agent, it is implemented in a game of artificial life [HDN03, pp. 182-191] [Bul02, pp.17-20] [DZL07, pp.995-1000] [DZLZ08, pp. 1086-1091]. When agent and simulated world are realized, the performance of the agent must be evaluated.

A possible way to evaluate the agent performance is the evaluation by a test person like it is done in the case of Kismet, which is discussed in Section 2.1. Even though Kismet is a robot that acts in the real world, the evaluation concept can be mapped to an artificial environment. An impartial person evaluates the behavior of the agent. However, the result requires subjective monitoring. In order to get significant results a certain number of samples are needed in order to allow a statistical evaluation. Hence, performance evaluation through clear defined quantifiable aims is preferred.

Ho et al. create an artificial dynamic world that proposes a certain complexity due to its configuration including a variety of objects [HDN03, pp. 182-191]. A number of different resources and areas with certain characteristics are introduced. The agent disposes of a certain amount of energy that must be refilled from time to time. Hence, it is forced to roam the world and find resources. The agent's task, which is also the performance indicator, is to survive as long as possible. In particular, Ho et al. test the performance of their realized memory structures. Different implementations are compared with each other and verified regarding the survivability of agents.

A similar approach is adopted by Deutsch et al. for the Bubble Family Game [DZL07, pp. 1021-1026]. The Bubble Family Game is applied to evaluate the ARS-PA model. Unlike Ho et al., Deutsch et al. do not evaluate the single agent but a team of agents of the same kind. The teams differ by the revision of the implemented ARS-PA decision unit that are evaluated by the team survival rate. Defined use cases focus on the social interaction between team members which is supported for using social interaction. In this case energy sources that must be eaten by two agents simultaneously are spread over the landform. Elsewhere, agents that implement the ARS-PA decision unit compete with agents based upon an if-then rule-based decision unit [DZLZ08, pp. 1086-1091]. With this evaluation approach the advancement between different developmental steps is elicited.

Evaluations generally lack on comparing different control-units within the same test framework. The reason for this condition can be summarized to three causes.

First, nearly every project team designs a simulation environment on its own as most are closed for the public. In addition, the agent controllers are generally not designed for the environment but the other way round. Hence, agent decision units must be adapted to the given input parameters, and the agent body. RoboCode [InetRC] is a simulation environment where attendees program a control unit for a predefined simulation framework. The designed bots compete against each other in a tank simulation. As this simulator is intended to deepen the knowledge in Java programming language, the environment and body setup is rather limited. Second, the development effort for realizing a reference system exceeds the resources of an average-sized research team. Even though numerous concepts are published, it still takes a certain amount of programming effort to implement control units of an adequate quality that are based on different principles. Third, already existing concepts are designed for different objectives and considerations which implicate the environmental, body and task setup.

Above, possible evaluation approaches and their realizations are discussed. The preferred approach depends on the project requirements and the provided expenses. In this thesis the *information representation system* is evaluated by the agent's behavior that changes in dependence to the different levels of extension. The ARS project makes the developed simulation platform available to third parties as testing suite for verifying different scientific control units. The simulation environment itself must provide a multi-agent platform as the

ARS control unit must support system-environment interaction. A further project aim is to test the developed system in comparison to a human being. However, this goal is not covered in this work.

2.5 From Sensor Signals to Neuro-symbols

This chapter gives an overview on related work in the area of CS and AI with respect to this thesis. Thereby, the processing of raw sensor data to actuator commands within the ARS decision unit is the central topic.

The work in the ARS project is separated into two areas. One deals with the decision unit itself. Section 2.2 gives an overview of the ARS-PA module. It is strongly inspired by neuropsychoanalytic concepts and incorporates the idea of an embodied agent. In addition, it introduces a body with an internal state. Chapter 3 deals with its successor that is based on neuropsychoanalytic concepts as well but also applies purely psychoanalytic theory that better matches design requirements. Both process information about the internal as well as external state. The sensor signals are merged to semantic symbols that are forwarded to the decision unit. This part is mainly inspired by neuroscientific concepts and represents the ARS-PC model that is condensed to the sensor and actuator module in Fig. 2-1.

The process of merging sensor signals to semantic symbols is discussed by Bruckner, Zucker (né Pratl), Velik et al, and Burgstaller et al. [Bru07] [Pra06] [VLBD08] [BLPV07]. As discussed in Section 1.1, a main challenge for future building automation control systems is the handling of the data flood due to an increasing number of sensor nodes. Hence, incoming data must be filtered and merged. The control unit itself deals with only a fractional amount of the original data stream.

Zucker (né Pratl) [Pra06] introduces a concept for processing incoming sensor signals along a hierarchical structure. This concept is based on knowledge of human perception that is inspired by neuroscientific and neuropsychoanalytic theories. The idea is to merge relevant data to semantic symbols and outsource overhead. The result should be used for scenario recognition in order to identify safety-critical situations.

Zucker (né Pratl) et al. introduce three hierarchical layers [PP05, pp. 55-62]. All of them represent a specific type of symbol – micro symbols, snapshot symbols, representation symbols. Fig. 2-7 shows the hierarchical layer structure of the ARS-PC model, their corresponding symbol types and their connection. Micro symbols are located on Layer II of the hierarchical structure and are formed by raw data. They represent characteristic features in sensor information such as shapes, edges, or sound snippets. A group of micro symbols is merged to a snapshot symbol (see Layer III). The snapshot symbol represents the momentary perception of an event or an object. All snapshot symbols together form the currently perceived representation of the world and influence the representation symbol (Layer IV). Micro symbols and snapshot symbols are formed whenever a change in the internal or external state is perceived. In contrast, representation symbols exist for a longer time and include the system's recalled knowledge of the past as well as the information that is given by the snapshot symbols. By combining all three symbol types, a scenario symbol is created that stands for the detection of a specific scenario. The representation symbols form the input for the decision layer that represents the topmost layer (Layer V) in the ARS-PC layer structure.

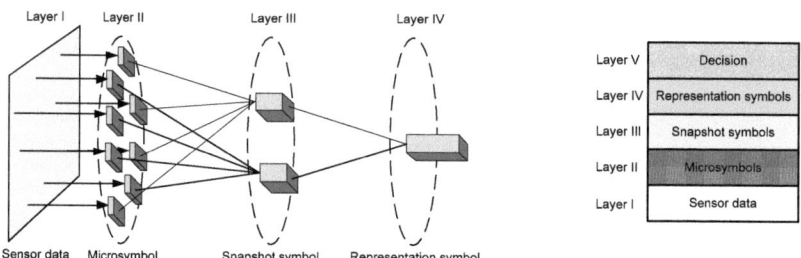

Fig. 2-7: ARS-PC hierarchical layer structure

ARS-PC: *ARS-PerCeption*

At this point [BLPV07, pp.1033-1038] tied in and extend the abilities of the system for scenario recognition. They introduce an emotional evaluation of semantic symbols for detecting safety-critical situations. For example, the SmaKi serves as test platform for the proposed concept. A variety of sensor arrays serves as input for the system. Motion detectors, pressure sensor fields, shock detectors, distance sensors, and cameras are the basis for defining micro symbols. The example scenarios for this test environment are *a meeting of people*, *a person who is making coffee*, and *a person placing objects within the kitchen*. Possible safety-critical scenarios are in case a person falls down on the floor or a child is located within the room while the stove is heated and no grown up is in sight.

Velik bases her work [VLBD08, pp. 657-662] on Zucker (né Pratl) et al. [PP05, pp. 55-62] and Burgstaller et al. [BLPV07, pp.1033-1038]. She focuses on the design of a technical model for human-like perception and uses neuroscientific and neuropsychologic concepts as foundation. In contrast to former work, the introduced concept not only follows the symbolic approach but also tries to combine it with the theory of neural networks. As a result the term *neuro-symbol* is created. Neuro-symbols are information processing units that carry attributes of neural and symbolic information processing with them [VLBD08, p. 50]. In contrast to neurons, neuro-symbols have properties and a specific perceptual meaning that is formed by perceptual stimuli. Neurons follow the black box mechanism. The *neuro-symbolic* approach uses a hierarchical concept of sensor fusion and differentiates between the *sensor* layer, *feature* layer, *sub-unimodal* perceptions layer, *unimodal* perceptions layer, and the *multimodal* perception layer. The concept allows a bidirectional information flow between the layers as well as the idea of knowledge based learning by example and neuro-symbol activation. This knowledge need not to be stored in the neuro-symbolic network but can be also stored in layers of higher abstraction. Knowledge that is used by the decision unit influences the neuro-symbolic network as well. This is an unsolved issues and an objective for future work. This thesis does not deal with them but provides a foundation for a future integration. Velik focuses on the perception of the environment. Perception of the physical body and the homeostasis is addressed by Velik et al. [VLBD08, pp. 657-662] but not discussed in detail.

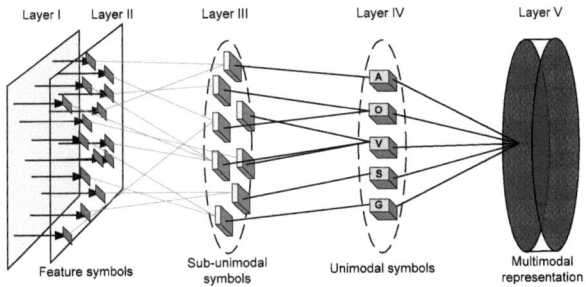

Fig. 2-8: Neuro-symbolic data processing

A: *Acoustic;* O: *Olfactoric;* V: *Visual;* S: *Somatosensory;* G: *Gustatory*

Fig. 2-9 and Fig. 2-8 give an overview of the proposed design. Raw sensor data approaches the perceptual system (Layer I). The feature layer processes data to feature symbols (Layer II). Burgstaller and Zucker (né Pratl) [BLPV07, pp.1033-1038] , [PP05, pp. 55-62] equate feature symbols with micro-symbols. The first two layers are inspired by theories on the information processing mechanisms in the primary cortex. *Sub-unimodal* (Layer III), and *unimodal* layer (Layer IV) define the information processing mechanisms in the secondary cortex [Vel08, p. 67]. The last stage that forms multimodal representation is mapped to the mechanisms of the tertiary cortex (Layer V). As in the ARS-PC model, the decision layer (Layer VI) is located at the top of the hierarchy. In contrast to the primary cortex layer, the

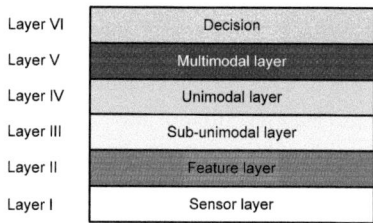

Fig. 2-9: ARS hierarchical layer structure; Layer I to V defined in [Vel08, p. 67]

symbols in the upper layers do not have a topographic structure. Every feature symbol sources from one type of perceptual sensor modality – visual, acoustic, somatosensory, olfactory and gustatory perception. The *sub-unimodal* layer merges the feature symbols to a *sub-unimodal* symbol. It is required as it is possible to get information from two sensors of one modality on the same perception – e.g. a human being's vision.

However, in case no redundant information about the similar perception is received, *unimodal* symbols are identical to *sub-unimodal* symbols. *Unimodal* symbols represent the current informational state of one sensor modality. In Fig. 2-8 they are labeled with A (acoustic), O (olfactory), V (vision), S (somatosensory), and G (gustatory). At the *multimodal* layer, the *unimodal* symbols are merged to *multimodal* symbols that trigger the scenario recognition. *Unimodal* and *multimodal* symbols form the input for the ARS decision unit and the foundation of the ARS information processing.

Summarized, the perceptual part of the ARS model merges sensor signals to semantic symbols through a layered model of perception. It forwards neuro-symbols to the decision unit that forms the most abstract layer. While the lower layers are inspired by neuroscientific principles, the decision unit is based on psychoanalytic theory.

2.6 Outcomes

Chapter 2 discusses possible research efforts facilitating the development of automation control systems capable of handling future demands. Common and alternative approaches used for the solution of this problem are discussed and analyzed by focusing on information processing.

As discussed in Section 2.1, recent developments in the area of embodied and emotional AI suggest a system-environment and system-internal state interaction in order to realize a situated system. This conforms to neuropsychoanalytic premises that view a body and its emotional aspects as the foundation for reasoning.

It is a common approach to use neuroscientific findings in system design as biological mechanisms show high effectiveness in areas that are under investigation by CS. However, the suitability of the various theories must be verified. Two main issues are identified below.

First, theoretical foundations are used which provide solutions for specialized problems but ignore associated questions. Concepts based on differing theoretical principles are therefore combined and lead to inconsistencies in the developed solutions. Other approaches have a theoretical model available that covers wide areas of a problem statement but are hardly practicable for engineering system design without running the risk of losing the advantages of a bionic approach. Systems, which are based upon the multi-store model concept, are inspired by bionics even though it is questionable if their theoretical foundation does not leave too much space open for technical interpretations. This issue is discussed in Section 2.3.3. The behavioristic description of memory structures requires a functional interpretation by the system engineer that leads us to the second issue. Regarding this first problem, the conclusion can be drawn that the use of bionic principles in engineering requires a *holistic functionally described model* as foundation.

Second, the conversion of a theoretical concept between different sciences must never be done without at least one scientist from each area. Otherwise, the expertise is missing that guarantees the transfer without missing important points of a theory. As the human mind is strongly based upon information processing, disregard of the neuroscientific findings or their interpretation by nonprofessionals in this area is unacceptable in the author's point of view. In Section 2.3.3 this issue is discussed using the example of psychodynamically inspired autonomous agent control. Moreover, Section 2.3.2 discusses memory based control structures whose mechanisms and behavior are compared to processes in biological systems. In the author's point of view the transfer of scientific findings to different research fields must be accompanied by intensive *interdisciplinary* efforts. Without these, it is of little or no value.

Both requirements are explicitly addressed in the development of the ARS model. Neuro-psychoanalytic principles cover the perception of sensor data up to the functional description of principles of the human psyche. In between a link is provided that describes the hierarchical aggregation of sensor data to semantic symbols as it is discussed in Section 2.5. An additional advantage of this approach is the strict differentiation between the functional description and the definition of the information flow, which facilitates its use for technical applications. Requirement number two incorporates interdisciplinary work that results in an

Related Work

iteratively developed technical specification.

From the author's point of view neuropsychoanalytic principles provide a foundation for the conversion to a technical model, which incorporate a holistic concept up to a level where no alternatives can be found. This conversion cannot be realized without interdisciplinary work, but is also dependent on the design process itself.

These processes are discussed in Chapter 3, where they are described based on the proposed *information representation system*. Upcoming questions like the interface definition between the functional modules, the mapping between neuro-symbols and psychoanalytically inspired data structures, as well as the design of an information representation module that manages the information exchange between reasoning and decision layer are solved. The implementation of the achieved model is discussed in Chapter 4 and evaluated in Chapter 5 based on the findings in Section 2.4.

3. Concept and Model

Below, concept and model of the proposed *information representation system* is discussed. It is based on the theoretical background given in Chapter 2 and the interdisciplinary work between engineers and psychoanalytic scientists. Psychoanalytic terms are prepared in order to use them in a technical model. The chapter focuses on the *information representation* and its combination with the decision unit but discusses the information management system as well. Resultant questions are the conversion of perceived data to proposed data structures, their usage in dependence to the different process types as well as the generation of action commands. The information exchange inside the decision unit must be rethought and the question must be answered if the access points between *decision layer* and *information management system* can be coordinated with psychoanalytic concepts. In addition, *information management module* functionalities like activation and retrieval of stored data structures are discussed.

3.1 Psychoanalytic Terms and Technical Definitions

Below psychoanalytic terms as well as terms inspired by psychoanalysis are defined and discussed with respect to their use in a technical model. They are required as foundation for the explanation of the ARS decision unit, the definition of the interfaces, and the modeling of *the information representation system*. This procedure has its source in the missing axiomatic system in psychoanalytic conception (see Section 2.2, p. 24). Natural sciences must form their theories on self-consistent axioms; their existence is a fundamental prerequisite as argued by Whitehead and Russell [WR10]. The absence of this foundation in psychoanalysis confronts it with arguments not to belong to natural sciences. An example for the conceptual conflicts that arise out of this circumstance is discussed based on the term *affect* below. Its ambiguous definition allow different interpretations and therefore as many descriptions in technical terms. These uncertainties are disallowed in natural sciences and are avoided for the technical definitions at which this work is based.

Drive

In Section 2.1 the term *drive* is introduced. Palensky specifies the term as the key for the connection between physiology and psyche [Pal08, p.68] in accordance to Freud's definition [Fre15a, p. 122]. In this context, physiology is represented by the homeostasis. Hence, the drive is the psychic representative of a homeostatic unbalance [Fre15b, p.111] that evolves out of physiological stimuli that are represented as *affect* and *drive content* in the psyche. W. Mertens states that *drives* are the key to form subjective memory content [Mer98, p.86].

Drive content is a non-psychoanalytic term that is introduced during the modeling phase in order to summarize the drive components: *drive source*, *drive object*, and *drive aim*. It represents the quality of a drive and is internally mapped to a mesh of *thing presentations* (see below). The affect is a quantitative dimension and is mapped to the temporal change of the drive's intensity. The data structures are discussed in detail below.

The *drive source* represents the homeostatic unbalance that triggers the drive [DFZB09, p. 57-58] and therefore a psychic demand. The *drive aim* is to decrease this demand. The aim can be reached by a use of the *drive object* for reducing the bodily need. *Drive source* and *drive object* are represented by a *thing presentation mesh*. The *drive aim* is not explicitly arranged in a data structure as it is implicitly introduced into the functional description of the decision unit that always tend to set actions which decrease the bodily demand.

According to Lang, psychoanalysis does not differentiate drives in dependence to the organ at which they originate but by their *drive content* [Lan10, p.59]. It is distinguished between constructive and destructive content. Any representative of a destructive content has a constructive opposite. Each of one group forms a pair together with one of the other group. Nourish, repress, sleep, breath, and reproduce are representatives of constructive content while bite, deposit, kill, regress, disintegrate or halt belong to the destructive group. They are called *pairs of opposite* [Fre72, p. 71]. As these terms are less important for the proposed model, the reader is referred to Lang for more detail [Lan10, p. 59].

Memory trace

As stated by Laplanche, a *memory trace* defines the way events are established in memory [Lap73, p. 138]. Regarding the technical realization, Dietrich et al. specified memory traces to be a psycho-physiological concept of representing memories in the psyche [DFZB09, p. 424]. Any new information forms a memory trace that serves as pattern for upcoming perceived data. In case a perception matches a memory trace, the memory trace is activated and forms thing presentations, word presentations, or affects. These psychic data structures are connected by *associations* that are defined as data structure in the technical definition. The memory trace is a pattern for psychic data structures. Hence, memory traces and psychic data structures should not be mistaken for each other. It is mentioned here for the sake of completeness as it forms the base for all psychic data structures. However, it is not discussed further as it does not introduce any additional principles that are feasible for the modeling and implementation process.

Thing presentation

Thing presentations belong to the group of three atomic psychoanalytic data structures. Affects and word presentations complete this group which is extended by *associations* for the technical specification. As mentioned above, presentations evolve out of activated memory traces but must not be mistaken for them [Fre15c, p. 178]. The term thing presentation (TP) is defined to be the representation of a thing [Lap73, p. 445]. Dietrich et al. define the TP as the psychic representation of an object's sensorial characteristics in the form of acoustic, visual, olfactory, haptic, and gustatory modalities [DFZB09, p. 426]. This is not a psychoanalytic definition. It is specified in order to deduce the psychoanalytic term to a technical feasible one. Though this definition concentrates on the perception of a physical object, as well as bodily and organic signals. Hence, the definition by Dietrich et al. is expanded to the representation of homeostatic stimuli. According to Koukkou and Lehmann [KL98, p. 319], motion sequences like running, talking, or eating are identified as behavioral patterns. These sequences must be trained and repeated until they migrate from declarative to procedural knowledge. Regarding the proposed model, the behavioral patterns are identified in terms of TPs. Summarized, *TPs* represent environmental, bodily and homeostatic information as well as automated motion sequences. TPs do not possess any logical structure.

[Mer98, p. 75] states in accordance to Freud that memory content is stored in classification of its occurrence in temporal contiguity (temporal coincidence), similarity or their accessibility to secondary processes. The last characteristic deals with the association with word presentations and is discussed below. Temporal contiguity and similarity define two types of associations between TPs. Regarding the technical model, the term *thing presentation mesh* (TPM) is introduced and describes connected TPs. The term TPM is introduced to the technical model only and does not occur in psychoanalytic theory.

Word presentation

Dietrich et al [DFZB09, p. 429] defined the term in accordance to Laplanche [Lap73, p. 445] with respect to the technical model. A *word presentation* (WP) is the description of an object by the use of a set of symbols. In case of human beings this set is represented by verbal expressions. However, it is not limited to language. The alphabet, logic relations, or hand gestures also belong to this group.

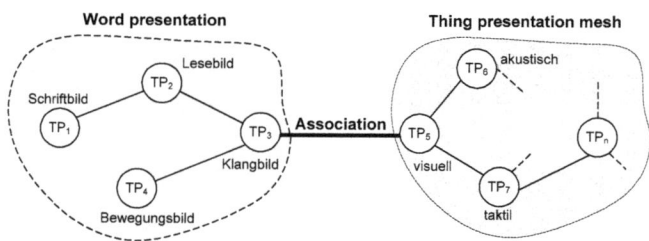

Fig. 3-1: Association between word representation and TPs [Fre91, p. 121] – original definitions are in German and translated below

TP: *Thing presentation;* Schriftbild: *Visual image for script;* Lesebild: *visual image for print;* Bewegungsbild: *Kinesthetic image;* Klangbild: *Sound image;* akustisch: *acoustic;* visuell: *visual;* taktil: *tactile*

In Fig. 3-1, Freud's view on the connection between *TP* and *WP* is shown [Fre91, p. 121]. In the beginning, a word presentation is formed out of visual images for script and print, kinesthetic, and an image of sound. Regarding the technical model, these components of the word presentation are represented by TPs too. In Fig. 3-1 the word presentation is linked to the TPM (object representation) by an association between the visual thing presentation (TP_5) and the sound image (TP_3). Fig. 3-1 shows the original sketch. However, the associated elements are not limited to *sound image* and *visual* TPs.

A word presentation merges a TPM to one symbol. The *meaning* of the word presentation, respectively the consequences of the object to the individual and the environment remain within the TPM. In contrast to the TP, word presentations allow logic and temporal relations that enable them to form acts and action plans (see Section 3.2.2). As described above, word presentations are represented by at least one TP. Definitely, it is assigned to the TP that represents the sensory perception on the word presentation like the visual stimuli that is triggered by the typeface of the letter "A". In addition, it is assigned to the TPM that represents an object – e.g. the object "can". The sensory information about the object does not intersect with that of the word presentation. Both are associated through the word presentation only.

Even though the letter "A" is associated by its word presentation with the object representation of "can", their TPMs are not associated with each other.

All knowledge originates from external perception [Fre23, p.23]. A TP is formed by subjective sensory perception of an object that depends on the individual's sensory setup. Word presentations are a subject of cultural, linguistic, or environmental restrictions; they are aligned with the environment. Regarding language, this means that society and language prescribe the way a term is associated with an object, action, or behavior. This aspect contradicts to the cognitive scientific notion of the language of thought [Den87]. Regarding this theory everyone individually forms symbols that are used for the internal thinking process and are mapped to language. Hence, the thinking processes is not based on the same language as the spoken one which contradicts with psychoanalytic theory.

Affect

Regarding Freud, the term affect represents the quantitative component of the drive. In particular it describes the drive demand's intensity [Lap73, p. 37]. Related to the ARS model, this description accords to a quantitative measure of the homeostatic unbalance that is represented as absolute value of the stimulus intensity. In this case the term affect is equalized with pleasure and unpleasure [Fre98b, p. 410]. However, affect is a multifunctional term that is defined in different ways elsewhere [Fre20, p.7]. There, pleasure measures the temporal change of unpleasure that in turn defines the drive demand's intensity. This is one example of the confusion coming up in the translation of psychoanalytic terms to the area of computer science. Hence, the affect occurs in different forms with different units. This does not mean that there are deficiencies in the theory. It is not an issue in psychoanalytic usage but would be an issue for an engineering specification in case it is not handled.

For this work, the term affect is related to the second definition that equates it with pleasure. It emerges out of the variations in the homeostatic unbalances. Even though the homeostatic stimulus that results in the drive demand is seen as the basis for the affect, regarding the technical model the affect is defined as one of the atomic data structures. This is reasoned in the fact that affects are stored in the database while homeostatic stimuli are used for the drive generation only (see Section 3.3). In addition, affects are used to form more complex data structures like drives.

Association

In terms of the technical model, *associations* are introduced as the fourth type of atomic data structure. As mentioned above, associations are not defined as psychoanalytic data structures. However, for the technical realization they are seen as component in an information mesh as it is impossible to construct any kind of non-atomic data structure without their use. Associations are formed based on the content of perceived information (see below). They should not be mistaken for *relations* that imply logic dependencies and belong to the group of word presentations. Regarding the technical model associations are grouped into four classes. As summarized above, memory content is categorized due to temporal contiguity, similarity and accessibility to secondary processes. This classification is realized by associations that are differentiated by the following characteristics:

- The accordance of attributes between perceived objects
- Temporal concurrence
- Their description by word presentations

In addition the interaction with the drive object results in the change of homeostatic stimuli. Though, the resulting affects are connected by their drive source to the drive object. This connection is also formed by an association. This association is explicitly introduced in the technical model. In psychoanalytic theory its characteristics are not discussed in detail but implicitly assumed. Freud defined the term of facilitation [Fre00, p. 539] that describes the decrease in the resistance of an excitation due to a repeated perception. Even though, Freud developed psychoanalysis towards another direction, the term facilitation also turns up in his later work [Fre20, p. 26]. The decrease of resistance is mapped to an associative weight. Regarding the technical model, the weight of an association differs in dependence to the occurrence of its nodes. Even though this theory sounds similar to the Hebbian rules, the theories are in fact quite distinct as the types of nodes are completely different. While psychoanalytic theory introduces associations between semantic symbols, the Hebbian rules learn parameters in a neural net.

Primary process

Psychoanalysis differentiates between two psychic encoding mechanisms: the primary and the secondary process. Both summarize two basic groups of functionalities that can be completely separated [LP73, p. 396]. The primary process manipulates TPs and affects and follows the pleasure principle [ST02, p. 100]. This means that the priority by which information is processed depends on the drive demand without considering the current situation. Conflictive and contradicting information is not filtered out but processed in parallel [DFZB09, p. 426]. Primary processes do not deal with data structures that include logic relations. Hence, word presentations are not handled by them. Regarding S. Arieti, primary processes identify semantic symbols as similar if at least one of their attributes is identical – similarity becomes identity [Ari64, p. 52]. However, this contradicts with the idea that perceived information is complemented by experienced one (see Footnote 36) but not replace completely. The second theory is applied to this work.

W. Mertens claims in [Mer98, p. 84] that memory content is generally stored in dual encoding. This means that any memory content is encoded in TPs and word presentations. This enables the manipulation by primary and secondary processes. However, the type of manipulation is completely different

Secondary process

In contrast to primary processes, secondary processes must solve contradictions and conflicts in information. The secondary process structures information and puts it to temporal, local and logic dependency. Primary processed data structures are associated with word presentations. Once this association is formed, it cannot be changed by secondary processes anymore until the information reaches primary process based functionalities again. Secondary processes cover functionalities like goal decision making, planning, and the thinking itself. This type of manipulation requires logical structures, respectively word presentations. In contrast to the primary process, the secondary process governs the reality principle [Sol09, p. 118]. Environmental, cultural, and situational conditions are considered before demands are discharged. The satisfaction of demands does not aim towards a maximum of pleasure but implies given restrictions. Demand satisfaction is deferred or handled by substitute acts. Objects stay in the same process and are associated with each other only in case they own to the same context. They yield to local constraints and causality. Regarding the processed information, objects are only identical if all of their attributes concur. A process like thinking can be realized in the secondary process only.

The given definitions form the foundation for the proposed model. They technical feasible terms are applied to the modeling process in Section 3.3 and 3.4. Section 3.2 shows the technical conceptualization of the discussed psychoanalytic data structures that are the foundation of the *information representation*.

3.2 Technical Conceptualization of Psychoanalytically Inspired Data Structures

In Section 3.1 an overview of the psychoanalytic data structures as they are defined related to Freud's 2nd topographical model (see Section 3.3) is given. This is one big advantage re-

Concept and Model

garding the use of the psychoanalytic theory as it not only covers the functional description of the psyche but also provides a theory of the processed data structures. Open issues must be complemented in interdisciplinary work with neuropsychoanalysts and psychoanalysts. It is important that this is not done by engineers but in cooperation with psychoanalysts. In order to avoid a conflictive state with psychoanalytic theory, the solutions for open issues must be synchronized with the original theory.

3.2.1 Atomic Data Structures

In Section 3.1, the psychoanalytic description of the term *TP* is given. They are defined to represent external perception in the psyche. In addition, they originate from the homeostasis and specify the drive source. Regarding the computer scientific model, TPs tie up to the sensor interface and evolve out of neuro-symbols. As shown in Section 2.5 the decision unit receives unimodal and multimodal symbols as representatives of input at the sensor arrays. They represent the physical occurrence of a perceived object by means of *visual, acoustic, somatosensory, olfactory,* and *gustatory* sensor modalities. The somatosensory modality summarizes the *sense of touch* and *body sensations*. It is assumed that this information is explicitly mapped to an object. The decision unit does not only receive a list of neuro-symbols. It additionally relies on the information which neuro-symbols are associated. This assumption implies that the binding issue is nothing to be solved in the decision unit. It is already handled in the neuro-symbolization layers (Layer III-V in Fig. 2-9). Unimodal symbols accord to TPs related to the psychoanalytic term and are directly mapped to them. Multimodal symbols combine more than one sensor modality to a neuro-symbol. Psychoanalytic theory does not make a statement on a separation between a single and a group of TPs. As multimodal symbols by definition merge several sensor modalities, they are mapped to a

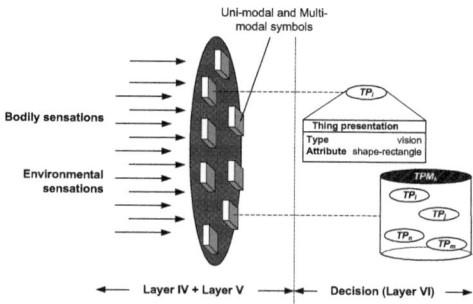

Fig. 3-2: Mapping of environmental- and bodily sensations symbols to TPs

TP: Thing presentation; TPM: Thing presentation mesh

mesh of TPs. This structure is already discussed above and introduced as TPM. Fig. 3-2 once again illustrates the difference between both structures. The simplest thing presentation (TP$_i$) is defined by the type of sensor modality from which it originates and an attribute value. In this case a TP of type *vision* represents a *rectangle shape*. For the sketched example, the TP represents a temporally independent neuro-symbol. However, scenarios, which are discussed below, may also take the place of the attribute value. They imply a temporal sequence of sensor input and are represented as uni- or multimodal symbols as well.

A TPM that is formed by environmental sensations represents a physical object. This simplification is assumed for the proposed model but does not inhibit an extension in future work. It is differentiated between three types of decision unit input in terms of environmental sensations, bodily sensations, and homeostatic state. Bodily sensations and homeostatic state source in the body but they must not be mistaken for each other. Bodily sensations are impulses that can be posted to specific body parts like organs or extremities. They correspond to nerve signals in a biological life-form. Homeostatic states represent unbalances in bodily systems that cannot be targeted to specific body areas. Hence, they are considered as overall picture for specific circulations. Examples for homeostatic systems are the blood- and the hormone state. In this work, both concepts are summarized in the term *bodily state*. Environmental sensations are defined by *visual, acoustic, gustatory, olfactory* and *tactile* information. The *somatosensory* modality is part of environmental and bodily sensations. Environmental- and bodily sensations are represented by TPs only. In this work environmental- and bodily sensations are summarized in the term *external perception*. Even though it is a point of discussion if the intensity of bodily sensations should be forwarded to the

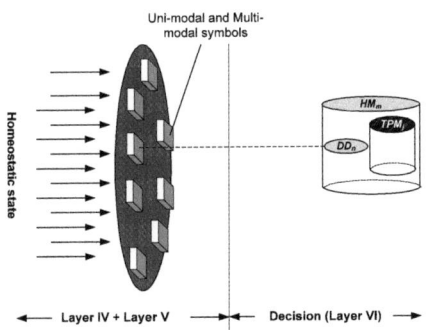

Fig. 3-3: Mapping of the homeostatic state to the HM

TPM: Thing presentation mesh; DD: Drive Demand; HM: Homeostatic mesh

decision unit, it is not foreseen in the neuro-symbolic layer and therefore not done in the proposed model.

The homeostatic state is mapped to TPs, which represent its source, and a scalar that corresponds to the unbalance in the homeostasis and therefore form the drive demand (DD_n). Both together form the *homeostatic mesh* (HM) that is shown in Fig. 3-3.

Summarized, two groups of TPs are defined. The first accords to the sensory representations, the other one defines scenarios like movements, handlings, basic abilities. All together form a TPM. Homeostatic states additionally introduce the drive demand as scalar. Together with TPM_j that represents the drive source, HM_m is formed. The set of external sensations and the homeostatic state forms the *perceptual image* (see in Section 3.2.2). Perceptual images are compared with stored *template images* (see below) that are retrieved from the database and used for further processing. An important part in the retrieval process is taken by *associations*. Like word presentations they are not retrieved through sensor information. However, they are formed on the base of input information and stored in the information representation layer. Associations connect data structures and define the set of information that is retrieved in case it matches input information. In Section 3.1, four types of associations are defined. Three of them originate from psychoanalytic theory and define the accordance of attribute between TPMs, the temporal concurrence of sensor information, and the link to word presentations. The fourth type represents the association to a tuple that defines the impact of objects to the homeostatic state. The *local* association between sensor signals is already done in the neuro-symbolic layer. TPMs include all TPs that are identified in one physical object (locally associated). Hence, the local association type is already introduced by TPMs. Associations between attributes are not solved in the neuro-symbolization layer. They are weighted associations between attributes and TPMs. While local associations are formed by the binding of sensor modalities in the neuro-symbolization layer, the attribute associations are already stored in the *information representation layer*.

Fig. 3-4 sketches an example for the use of attribute associations between TPs and TPMs. The TPs *shape rectangle*, *shape circle*, and *color red* construct the two objects *red circle* and *red rectangle*. Both are represented by TPMs. Every TPM consists out of a number of associations to its attributes, respectively the TPs by which it is formed. According to Fig. 3-4 TPs can be associated more than once to TPMs. The reason for this concept sources in the assumption that every *memory trace* is created only once in the memory. In case perceived information cannot be matched with stored one, new memory traces are formed. As stated by Freud, perceived information is associated to stored information [Fre08, p.544] and defines a new variation of data structure [Fre20]. We assume that perceived data which correspond in type and attribute is only stored once. In case two objects (TPM) are identified by the same TP they are linked by a weighted association. In reality perceived information is hardly identical to preceding one. The assumption still can be used as the human being's sensor system has been trained since birth. Perceived sensor data is mapped to trained templates that are activated and forwarded to the decision unit.

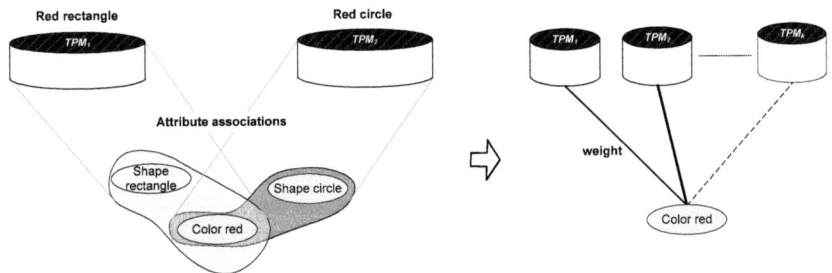

Fig. 3-4: Weighted associations between TPMs and their attributes

TPM: *Thing presentation mesh*

In case of Fig. 3-4, TPM_1 and TPM_2 contain the TP *color red*. On the right hand side the associations between the TP and a number of TPMs is shown. The different line widths mark the association weights that are formed in dependence of the number of coincidental occurrences of a pair of TPM and TP. Hence, various objects are triggered by the color red even though those things have nothing in common, except the color red. The proposed *information representation system* differentiates between class and instance attributes.

Class attributes are data structures that are essential for the physical definition of an object type while *instance attributes* can change with the object itself and are individually different. For example, the object *ball* implies a class attribute *shape sphere*. Its physical occurrence strongly depends on the attribute of type *shape*. Though, it can be associated with more than one attribute of type color. Hence, they are instance attributes as they do not have much effect on the object ball in case of ball.

This differentiation is done in order to put limitations on the change of predefined TPMs. It is introduced in order to identify object attributes as requisites or optional. In case the association weight between a TPM and one of its associated TPs reaches a specific strength, it is transferred to a class association. This is one of the possible learning mechanisms.

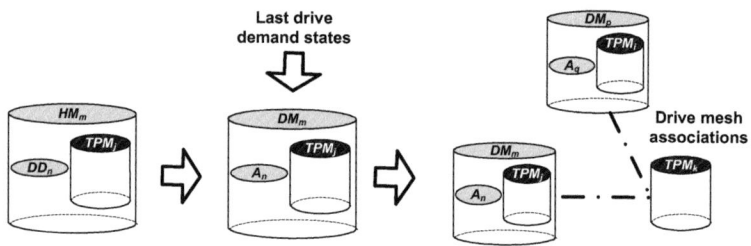

Fig. 3-5: Associations between TPMs and their DMs

TPM: *Thing presentation mesh;* DD: *Drive Demand;* HM: *Homeostatic mesh;* A: *Affect;* DM: *Drive mesh*

In Fig. 3-5 an association is introduced that links an object represented by TPM_k to tuples, which define the homeostatic impact of the object to the individual. The tuple is derived from HM_m and includes drive sources in the form of TPM_j. However, it does not contain a scalar that accords to the drive demand DD_n. Instead, it introduces the affect A_n that is derived from the temporal change of the drive demand (see Section 3.1). This tuple is labeled as *drive mesh* (DM). In ARSi10, DMs are only associated with TPMs that represent objects as their impact on the individual's homeostatic state. A single TP has a different meaning regarding the object with which it is associated. As shown in Fig. 3-5 TPM_k can be associated with several DMs (DM_m, DM_p) as an object can influence the individual in several ways. It is assumed that individuals have opposed experiences with one and the same object as these objects can have harming or satisfying effect depending on the way they are handled.

Fig. 3-6 shows the temporal association between the TPMs TPM_i, TPM_j, TPM_k. For ARSI10 it is assumed that temporal associations are formed between TPMs, TPs, and Template Images (TI). Temporal associations are sketched by doubled lines and associate contemporaneously perceived TPMs. Above, the term image is mentioned. It introduces simultaneity of

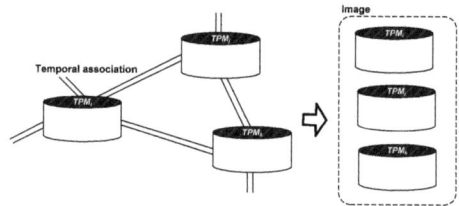

Fig. 3-6: Temporal associations of Thing presentation meshes

TPM: *Thing presentation mesh*

sensory information and therefore corresponds with the temporal associations. Hence, all data structures that are temporally linked are combined in an image.

In Section 3.1 a fourth association type is defined that connects primary data structures (TPs, affects and all data structure meshes formed out of them) with secondary data structures (WPs, acts). Word presentations are encoded related to the secondary processes characteristics and introduce logical relations and an organizational structure. This enables the model to evaluate perceived information by the use of rules and physical constraints. Word presentations are embedded in a set of signs that is predefined for this work. As discussed above, psychoanalysts assume that any memory content is stored in dual encoding. Hence, information is described by primary data structures on the one hand and secondary data structures on the other. Primary data structures are mapped to an infinite number of word presentations and the other way round. However, for ARSi10 the number is limited to a well-defined one to one connection.

Associations trigger the activation of connected data structures. Section 3.4 goes into detail regarding the conceptual activation and retrieval mechanisms. The discussed data structures form the information that is processed in the ARS decision unit and managed by the information representation module. In ARSi10 it is assumed that stored data structures are not changed during runtime. The system is said to imply the characteristics of a grown up whose actions are based on experiences that marginally change. However, the proposed concept anticipates an adaptation of data structures in future work.

Above the terms template and perceptual images are mentioned. They are data structures formed by combinations of TPMs, TPs, and TIs. They are strongly required for the information process mechanisms in the ARS model as acts are derived from them. In Section 3.2.2 they are put into context of the proposed data structures.

3.2.2 Images, Scenarios, and Acts

The discussed data structures specify from which kind of sensor modality they emerge and to which encoding type they are allocated. The basic questions are settled, however, the definition of images, scenarios, and acts remains. Psychoanalysis reaches its limits in this issue. Neuropsychoanalysis ties up to it and discusses some of these concepts in detail.

Solms and Turnbull [ST02, p.90] as well as Damasio [Dam94, p.97] discuss the terms perceptual images and mental images. Perceptual images source in sensor data from the *outer* – body and environment – and *inner* – decision unit – world and represent changes of the en-

Concept and Model

vironment and the organism. Rösener defines the perceptual image in technical terms [R07, p. 20]. There it is stated that the perceptual image is formed by sensory input and represents a snapshot of the external and internal system state. Images can contain other images. At least they contain symbols that are predefined and grouped regarding the context to so-called template images. As assumed by Rösener, template images are mentally created templates of experienced perceptual images [R07]. Damasio labels them as mental images and defines them as replications of patterns that have been experienced before [Dam94, p.97]. They can be adapted to plans for further acts. Educed from Damasio's definition, Rösener defines the abstract image in a technical system [R07, p. 20]. In her definition, an abstract image is used for a comparison during the reasoning process that does not contain any time dependencies and interprets the perceptual image. Both definitions are adopted in this work. Below the term *template image* (TI) is used instead of abstract image as it matches the current concepts in the ARS project.

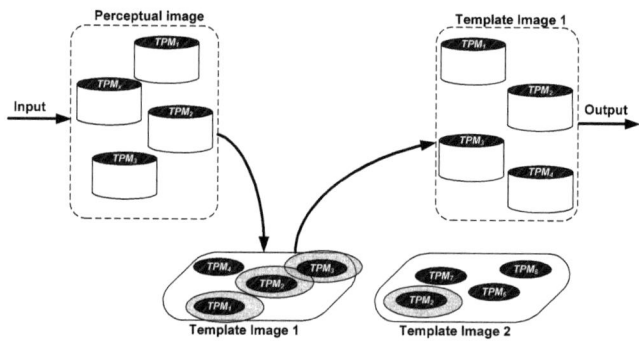

Fig. 3-7: Template image match

TPM: Thing presentation mesh

A perceptual image corresponds to the perceived environmental, bodily, and homeostatic state. TIs are stored patterns for perceptual images. Matches between perceptual and TIs trigger the templates and retrieve them for further processing. TPMs are temporally associated in case they occur in parallel. This corresponds to the image on the right hand side of Fig. 3-6. Hence, the psychoanalytic approach of contemporaneously associated TPMs is mapped to the TI approach. The ARS system only processes TIs. Information is filtered that is included in the perceptual image but not in the TI match. Contrariwise, fragmentary perceived data is complemented, as a perfect match of template and perceptual image is not required[36]. The internal image of the outer world incorporates subjective stored experiences [Mer98, p. 59]. Missing information about the world is complemented by stored knowledge [Köh98, p. 143]. The TI with the highest correspondence to the perceived data is retrieved. Fig. 3-7 summarizes this comparison process. An exception for the complete replacement of the perceptual image represents information that is highly dynamic and therefore cannot be stored to every template. Examples are position data or instance attributes. In case they occur, their corresponding image matches are retrieved and merged with the formerly retrieved TI. In Fig. 3-7 the perceptual image is formed out of four TPMs (TPM_1, TPM_2, TPM_3, TPM_x). It is compared to the TIs number one and two. As three of the received TPMs also occur in TI number one (TPM_1, TPM_2, TPM_3), while only one TPM turns up in TI number two (TPM_2), TI number one is activated. Even though *TPM_4* is not part of the perceptual image it is forwarded as output. Contrariwise, *TPM_x*, which is part of the perceptual image, is filtered out as it is not part of the selected TI. This is different for the exceptional case that is mentioned above. Images are formed by temporal associations between TPs, TPMs, and TIs as images can contain other images [R07].

Images contain only data that occurs at the same moment. They do not define any changes of sensory input and transitions of environmental and bodily states. Zucker (né Pratl) [Pra06] and Russ [Rus03] introduce the *scenario* as a sequence of images. Rösener adapts this definition to neuropsychoanalytic theory and renamed it to *episode* [R07, p. 23]. Regarding her definition, an episode is a sequence of a finite number, but at least two perceptual images which describe the differences between those images on a continuous timeline. The stored template of an episode is labeled as template episode. The term scenario is defined by her as an expected and predefined sequence setting of the test setup. Dietrich and Zucker specify scenarios as limited to duration of a few seconds [DZ08, p. 16]. Sequences of images that cover a finite time range are named *acts*. Scenarios as discussed by Dietrich are processed in the neuro-symbolic layer on a lower level of abstraction and are represented at higher layers as single TP. They represent procedures that are individually different like movements and the way movements are performed by the individuals. Acts are said to be processed in the psychic apparatus [DZ08, p. 17]. Rösener did not differentiate between episodes regarding the different layers of abstractions. Regarding the proposed model, the term episode is equated with the definition of acts. Scenarios are not discussed further as

---

[36] This accords to the claim that the human being processes only a small part of its sensory information and complements it with stored knowledge ([ST02, p. 155] [Rot92, p.317] [Mer98, p. 59]).

they are processed in layers of lower abstraction, respectively turn up as TPs in the decision unit.

For ARSi10 a sequence of images is equated to an act that is specified as a type of episode. As discussed above drives define the impact of an object to the individual. As drives define only consequences, the way this impact is triggered is defined in acts the way acts are represented in the ARS model must be synchronized with psychoanalytic theory.

Above the temporal order of simultaneity is introduced. Freud focused on chronological sequences [Fre98a, p. 292]. It is claimed that they can be handled by primary processes. In case of the ARS model this means that a sequence of images, respectively acts, can also be processed by primary processes. As primary data structures do not possess any logical structure, images can be chronologically reordered without respect to any logical limits. In addition, they are not mapped to a reference dimension in the form of real time. This means that the length of acts cannot be determined by primary data structures. The only temporal order is simultaneity and the differentiation between *before* and *after*. This is where word presentations come in. Temporal relations in the form of word presentations enable the mapping of actions and sequences to a period of time. M. Dornes stated by discussing D. Stern's theory of thought that, regarding psychoanalytic theory, the memorization of experiences does not run in their experienced time period [Dor06, pp. 134-135]. The experiences themselves can be mapped to real time. Secondary processes enable to imagine a change in the chronologic order of experiences and differ from primary processes in the way that this is done in accordance to logical, temporal, and physical rules. The generation of languages and symbols enables to visualize and change the reality [Köh98, p. 181]. These mechanisms are required to generate acts. Action plans, which are discussed by Lang in detail [Lan10, p.75], are formed by acts and require a time rating.

Fig. 3-8 shows the defined relation between acts and TIs. In this case the act consists of two TIs (TI_i, TI_k). TI_k varies from TI_i as it is reduced by TPM_5 but additionally contains TPM_8 instead of TPM_2. The two TIs that are ordered in time represent the primary data structural representation of an act. Both are connected with WPs (WP_i, WP_k). These WPs are not only ordered in a temporal sequence but also linked by a *temporal relation*. This relation enables the realization of a reference time. In addition, both word presentations are connected by an *action relation* that defines the way to proceed in order to reach a situation that corresponds to TI number two. This construct defines the secondary data structural representation of acts and can be composed out of a finite number of images. Fig. 3-8 shows an exceptional case of an act that is defined as *micro-act* in this work. A micro-act is the most basic act that contains only two images. One represents the initial situation (precondition) and one represents

Concept and Model

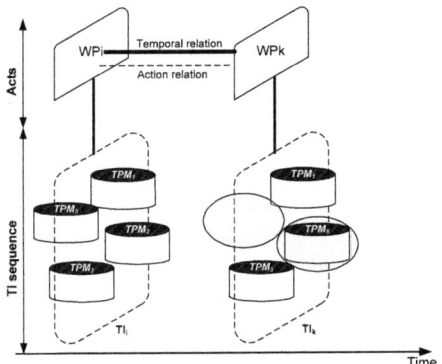

Fig. 3-8: Template images versus acts

TPM: *Thing presentation mesh;* WP: *Word presentation;* TI: *Template Image*

the outcome (consequence). The concept of a micro-act is identical to the one of a rule and is used in this way as well. Micro-acts are the atomic components for assembling new acts.

Summarized, images and acts are formed by atomic data structures. Regarding the technical model, it is assumed that images contain TPMs or other images. Images can be temporally ordered, even though this sequence can be changed without respect to logical and physical restrictions. Word presentations form acts in case they are connected with *temporal relations* or *action relations*. Temporal relations establish a reference time.

The defined data structures are processed in the ARS decision unit as well as in the *information representation management* unit (see Section 3.4). In the next section we focus on the ARS decision unit, its functionalities and interfaces as they are a prerequisite for the information representation and processing in ARSi10.

3.3 The Artificial Recognition System Decision Unit

The ARS decision unit design is based on a functional approach that uses the human being as archetype. It is inspired by psychoanalytic theory, respectively S. Freud's 2nd topographical model of the human psyche [Fre23]. The reason for the use of psychoanalysis is the functional description it offers. In Section 1.3, the top-down design approach is listed as Premise 6. Two basic design steps can be identified:

1. Starting from the most abstract view, the model is stepwise refined by dividing it into

Concept and Model

sub-modules with respect to their functionality.

2. The interfaces[37] between the described modules are defined.

3.3.1 Top-down Design Approach

Premise 4 in Section 1.3 is to form an interdisciplinary cooperation with psychoanalysts for realizing the modeling procedure. This methodology is introduced as experts from both sides, psychoanalysts and engineers in this case, are required to develop a consistent technical model. The next step, which is the implementation of this model, is carried out by computer scientists only. This principle applies to the modeling methodology of the *decision unit* and the *information management* unit. As shown in Fig. 3-9 the decision unit receives information about the current environmental and bodily state. The arrows I0.1 to I8.1 show this information flow. The labels are taken from Fig. 3-19 that lists the ARS decision unit at its highest level of detail. The raw sensor data passes Layer I to V of the ARS hierar-

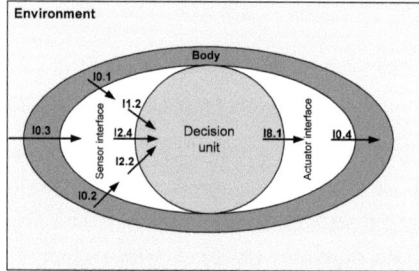

Fig. 3-9: Information flow through the decision unit – 5th Topological Layer

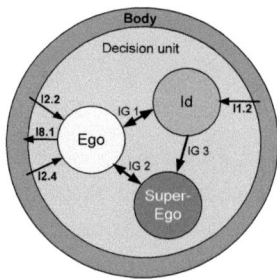

Fig. 3-10: Decision unit – 4th Topological Layer

I: *Interface*   IG: *Interface group*

chical layer structure (see Fig. 2-9). This information flow is shown in Fig. 3-9 by the interface I0.1 to I0.3. The sensor interface merges received data to unimodal- and multimodal neuro-symbols that are forwarded to the decision unit (Layer VI) through the interfaces I1.2, I.2.2, and I2.4. The perceived information is manipulated by the decision unit (see below) and forwarded to the output interface I8.1 where action commands are transported to Layer V of the ARS hierarchical layer structure. There, the de-symbolization process is started. Semantic symbols, that hold information about action commands, are processed to neuro-symbols

---

[37] An interface is the point of information exchange between linked modules

and afterwards separated to control signals for the corresponding actuator signals. I0.4 shows this final information flow to the system's actuators.

Fig. 3-10 indicates the division of the decision layer following Freud's second topographical model of the psyche. Three blocks are defined that are labeled as *Id*, *Ego*, and *Super-Ego*. Fig. 3-10 shows these blocks as well as the interfaces between them. The interfaces I1.2, I2.2, I2.4, and I8.1 mark the information flow between the outer world – environment and body – and the inner world – decision unit. The terms inner and outer world are traced back to Solms and Turnbull [ST02]. Both terms are investigated for their use in computer science by Zucker (né Pratl) [Pra06]. Transferred to technical terms, the psychic apparatus represents the decision unit. The Ego receives information about bodily sensations while the Id receives information about the homeostatic state. The arrows, named with IG1 to IG3 in Fig. 3-10, show the information flow between the psychic modules. The label IG stands for *interface group* and arranges interfaces, which are shown in Fig. 3-14, to groups. While the inner world information flow is a bidirectional one, the information flow between outer and inner world is unidirectional as the Ego sends actuator commands to the body. In the following sections the Ego, Id, and Super-Ego modules' functionalities are described following the top-down design approach.

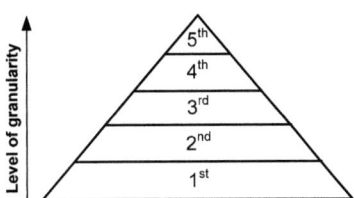

Fig. 3-11: Top-down structure of the ARS decision unit –ARS hierarchical Layer I-VI; the level of granularity is displayed by the surface area of the Layers 1 to 5.

As shown in Fig. 3-11, here five topological layers are defined. Their structure is different to those that form the hierarchical layer structure in Fig. 2-9 as every layer describes the same functionality, even though with a different level of detail. While the topological Layer 5 describes sensor layer (I) up to the decision layer (VI) in the lowest detail level, topological Layer 1 contains a description with a maximum of granularity and is shown in Fig. 3-19. Though, Layer I to V are covered by the topological view of the body in Section 3.3.2 while Layer VI describes the decision unit itself. There is no information exchange between the

Concept and Model

topological layers as they describe the same functionality. The different layers as well as the interfaces that are defined for the topological Layer 1 are described below. Lang proposed a prototype implementation of these modules [Lan10, pp. 101-112]. Table 3-2, Table 3-1, and Table 3-4 describe the formed interfaces and their content in detail. The interface definition process follows the usual method of describing the output interface (I8.2) first and then going step by step towards the input interface (I1.1). Hence, the type of information that is received by the actuators is defined first. At the end the sensor system input is defined.

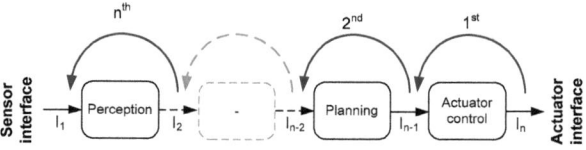

Fig. 3-12: Interface definition process

I: *Interface*

Fig. 3-12 sketches this process. The definition process is started at the actuator interface, labeled with I_n in the figure. Systematically the interfaces are defined up to interface I_1. Fig. 3-12 shows this methodology by a typical agent control system. It is divided to its functionalities perception, planning, and actuator control and leaves place for additional modules. The interface names are independent from those in the ARS decision unit.

3.3.2 Topological View of the Body

Before the ARS decision unit is discussed, its interfaces to the sensor system and homeosta-

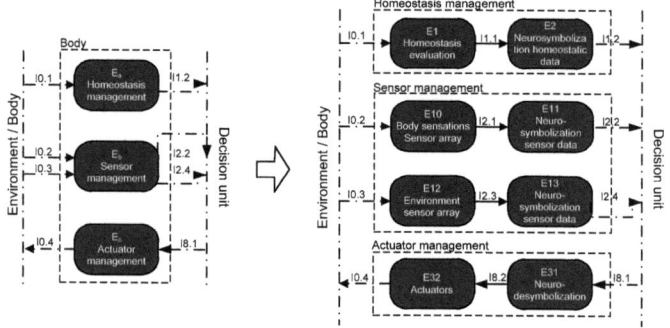

Fig. 3-13: Top-down view of the body

sis are described which represent Layer I to V in the ARS hierarchical layer structure. As shown in Fig. 3-13 the interfaces to the body are divided into three groups: homeostasis management, sensor management, and actuator management, which are labeled with E_a, E_b, and E_c. On the right hand side, they are subdivided to their core functionalities. The enumeration of the modules is taken from Fig. 3-19 where the ARS decision unit is presented at its highest level of granularity. The homeostasis management is divided to the modules *Homeostasis evaluation* and *Neuro-symbolization of homeostatic data*. The module *E1* merges raw sensor data, which is retrieved through I0.1, from the homeostasis to feature symbols. These symbols are delivered through I1.1 to *E2*. There they are converted to neuro-symbols by following the approach discussed in Section 2.5.

The sensor management contains two basic functionalities. One deals with the perceived environmental information while the other one deals with bodily sensations. *Body sensations sensor array* (*E10*) receives information about body sensations through I0.2 and passes them on to the *Neuro-symbolization of sensor data - body* (*E11*) through the I2.1. The *Environment sensor array* (*E12*) receives environmental information about the visual, acoustic, olfactory, somatosensory, and gustatory type through I0.3. These signals are for-

Interface name	From	To	Data type	Content
I0.1	Body	E1	Raw sensor data	Homeostatic state
I0.2	Body	E10	Raw sensor data	Bodily state
I0.3	Body	E12	Raw sensor data	Environmental state
I0.4	E32	Actuator	Raw data	Actuator commands
I1.1	E1	E2	Feature symbols	Homeostatic state
I1.2	E2	E3	Neuro-symbols	Homeostatic state
I2.1	E10	E11	Feature symbols	Bodily state
I2.2	E11	E14	Neuro-symbols	Bodily state
I2.3	E12	E13	Feature symbols	Bodily state
I2.4	E13	E14	Neuro-symbols	Bodily state
I8.1	E30	E31	Neuro-symbols	Actuator command and parameters – speed or duration of execution
I8.2	E31	E32	Feature symbols	Actuator command and parameters – speed or duration of execution

Table 3-1: Body interfaces

Concept and Model

warded through the I2.3 to the *Neuro-symbolization of sensor data – environment (E13)*. Parallel to *E11*, *E13* handles the neuro-symbolization of perceived sensor information. The I1.2, I2.2, and I2.4 form the connection between the body and the decision unit. The actuator management handles the information flow that is sent from the decision unit towards the system's actuators. The *Neuro-desymbolization (E31)* is responsible for the conversion of neuro-symbolic actuator commands to actuator control signals in the form of feature symbols. The *Actuator control (E32)* module handles these symbols and distributes them to the actuators. I8.1, I8.2, and I0.4 show the corresponding information flow.

Table 3-1 gives an overview of the interfaces that are listed in Fig. 3-13. Fig. 3-19 shows how the body modules fit in the overall view of the functional unit. It forms the interface between the environment and the decision unit that is discussed below. The 5th topological layer additionally defines the decision unit itself (see Fig. 3-9) that represents Layer VI in the ARS hierarchical layer structure. As its interfaces are discussed above and no additional functional divisions are introduced, the description is started at the topological Layer 4.

3.3.3 Fourth Topological Layer

Fig. 3-10 sketches the modular composition of the decision unit. Fig. 3-14 goes into more detail regarding the connection to sensor-, homeostasis-, and actuator management and the interfaces between Ego, Id, and Super-Ego. Below the modules' functionalities as well as the interfaces are discussed by providing insight to the originating psychoanalytic theory and its adaptation for engineering use.

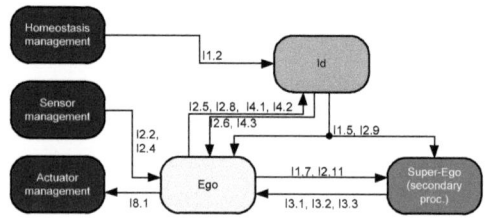

Fig. 3-14: Modular decomposition of the 4th Topological Layer

Id

Regarding psychoanalytic theory, the Id is the source of the psychic apparatus and is controlled by drives following the pleasure principle. From birth onwards it controls the human being's behavior. During the child's development, Ego and Super-Ego evolve and start to handle the Id's demands. The three modules form a control system that balances between the bodily state, the environmental state, and information that is aggregated in the past. Within the Id, conflictive, unorganized and contradictory processes are admitted. Hence, the Id's functionality is based on primary processes that have drives as result. Assumed that certain drives reach the Ego, they become organized and ruled by the secondary processes. The question if a drive is transferred to the Ego depends on the mechanisms of defense that evaluate the drive on its priority specific criteria [DFZB09]. This decision is influenced by perceived information as well as knowledge about social rules (see Super-Ego module), restrictions, and former experiences. Occurring conflicts between this information as well as drive demands are evaluated. If the access to the secondary processes is avoided, than the discharge becomes temporally inhibited or redirected by a substitute act.

Regarding the technical model, the Id provides the interface to the system's homeostasis. It receives information about the homeostatic state, processes it, evaluates it and passes it on to the Ego. In Sections 3.3.4 and 3.3.5 the Id is further divided.

Super-Ego

The Super-Ego is the counterpart to the Id. It manages rules on social demands and restrictions that are formed during life by the influence of culture and social environment. In addition, it not only handles restrictions but serves as a rewarding system too. This can come true in case an Id's drive is repressed due to the applying of a social rules or coping with social norms.

Regarding the technical model the Super-Ego represents a management for a database that contains information about system tasks, their preferred execution, and the execution of predefined scenarios. In addition, safety issues can be defined as restrictions. The Super-Ego receives information from the Ego on the Id's demands and the environmental situation. Dependent on this data the Super-Ego sends information about the preferred action handling to the Ego. Like in the Id, the data that is retrieved from the database can be conflictive and contradicting. The evaluation as well as the balancing process is done in the Ego module.

Ego

The Ego is the balancing component of the psychic apparatus. It mediates between the inner- and the outer world as well as Id and Super-Ego. The Ego receives information about the environmental conditions, the Id's demands and the Super-Ego's rules. Any external and internal sensor information passes the Ego (see Fig. 3-10). After processing this information it decides on a specific action that must be taken. It balances between the drive demands and the consequences of breaking rules and restrictions or awards on keeping them. The decision is converted to an action plan that is transferred to the actuator interface where they are interpreted as actuator commands. The Ego is responsible for the decision making as well as the organization of the mechanisms of defense.

The Ego is the most complex of the three modules. Its functionalities are mainly based on secondary processes. Lang described sub-divided Ego, Id, and Super-Ego on up to four layers and discussed their functionalities in detail [Lan10]. Below, an overview of the achieved sub-modules is given. The interfaces in between are adapted to the proposed model.

3.3.4 Third Topological Layer

On the 3rd topological layer, the decision unit is sub-divided as it is shown in Fig. 3-15. By analyzing the Id's functionality, three sub-modules are identified. They are labeled as *Drive management*, *Affect management*, and *Management of repressed content (E15)*.

Drive management and affect management

The drive management receives information about the homeostasis via I1.2. This includes information about the intensity of a bodily demand and the drive source. The module deals with the generation as well as the fusion of drives (see Section 3.3.5).

The second sub-module of the Id is the affect management. On the one hand it extracts the stimuli intensity of incoming data and turns them into affects. On the other hand it assigns affects to externally perceived data. DMs, which are retrieved from the *information representation layer* by the Ego modules, are merged with affects that are repressed by the mechanisms of defense. The result is forwarded to the *Super-Ego (primary proc.)* and the *Psychic mediator* modules.

Management of repressed content – E15

The *Management of repressed content* module deals with information that is repressed by the mechanisms of defense. The information is received through I4.1 and I4.2. Regarding psychoanalytic theory, information is repressed due to its incompatibility with moral and Super-Ego rules. Other possibilities are traumata or experiences that elapsed long ago. Repressed information can get through to the secondary processes by changing their structure, respectively by being connected with external perceived information that is received via I2.5 in the form of TPMs. Repressed information is split into its atomic components and added to incoming information. This manipulation enables drives to influence the decision making process, even though they are not able to reach the secondary processes in the first try. The

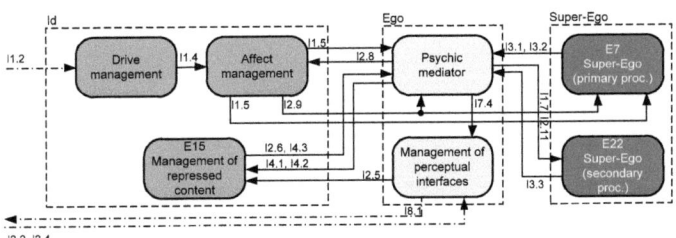

Fig. 3-15: Modular decomposition of Id, Ego, and the Super-Ego modules

ways atomic components are connected with each other depend on their type. An affect tends to connect itself to a TPM that is similar to the one it was connected before the separation.

For example, I4.1 delivers a repressed DM that contains the drive content *nourish* (see above). In *E15* the DM is split into its components. Now the affect is connected to a repressed object TPM (received through I4.2) that is connected to *nourish*. As a next step the repressed TPM is exchanged by a perceived TPM. The perceived TPM is received through I2.5 and selected by a best match. If the external perception does not forward any match, the object TPM, which is received through I4.2 and the affect, which is received through I4.1, remain repressed. Summarized it can be said that the chance for connecting two components with each other increases by the correspondence between the counterpart of the component and its predecessor.

The *E15* numeration of the module follows the functional description in Fig. 3-19. It marks the topological Layer 1. However, this does not mean that the module is not split up to separated functionalities in further work. *E15* is in charge of controlling the separation and remerge of perceptual information. *E15* forwards information by I4.3 and I2.6. Perceived raw data as well as repressed content is transmitted via I2.6 to the *Management of memory traces* module (*E16*). Interface I4.3 forwards formerly repressed drive content to the *Defense mechanisms for drive content* (*E6*). *E16* and *E6* belong to the *Psychic mediator* module (see Section 3.3.6). Table 3-3 gives an overview of the transmitted content and information type.

The Super-Ego is divided to two functional modules that vary in their basic processing type. The *Super-Ego (primary process)* operates based on the primary process principles while the *Super-Ego (secondary process)* is controlled by secondary processes.

Super-Ego (primary process)

The Super-Ego - primary process (*E7*) serves as basis for the mechanisms of defense that receive information about restrictions, bans, and awards regarding the current drive demands. Hence, *E7* manages the access and retrieval of rules that are represented by:

- Drives that are able to pass the mechanisms of defense
- The way drives must be changed to pass the mechanisms of defense
- Drives that must be repressed

The interfaces I1.5 and I2.9 provide the input to *E7*. Perceived TPMs on the one hand as well as DMs on the other are evaluated in context to rules and restrictions. Regarding the external perception, references to TIs are retrieved from the *information representation layer*. It is possible that TIs as well as their components possess associations to DMs. In case of the second possibility, the Super-Ego module evaluates the situation by the use of these DMs. The retrieved DMs are compared with the input from I1.5. In case of correspondence, the affect is taken from the stored DM and used as evaluation factor for the external perception or the homeostatic state. The result is forwarded to the *Defense mechanism for perception* (*E19*) by I3.2 and to *E6* by I3.1. *E6* and *E19* belong to the *Psychic mediator* module.

Super-Ego (Secondary process)

In contrast to *E7* the *Super-Ego (secondary process)* – *E22* – module manages rules, restrictions, and awards that influence functions following the secondary process principles. It receives word presentations including environmental and bodily state information via I2.11 and I1.7. Similar to *E7*, this information is evaluated regarding its conflicts with rules and restrictions. It retrieves acts from the *information representation layer* and uses *micro-acts* to evaluate the current situation. The current environmental state is compared to the precondition in micro-acts (see Section 3.2.2). The consequences in the retrieved micro-acts are compared with the current homeostatic state. Those which define a level of pleasure as consequence (positive or negative) and have an impact to the current state are forwarded to the *Decision making* (*E26*) module, which belongs to the *Psychic mediator* module, through I3.3. The Ego is subdivided into two sub-modules.

Psychic mediator and management of perceptual interfaces

The *Psychic mediator* module comprises inner psychic Ego functions that exchange information with Id and Super-Ego modules. It serves as the mediator between the Id demands and the Super-Ego rules and awards. In Section 3.3.5 it is discussed in more detail.

Concept and Model

The *Management of perceptual interfaces* forms the connection with the sensor system (see I2.2, I2.4) as well as the actuator control (see I8.1). It controls the interfaces between Ego and the outer world.

3.3.5 Second Topological Layer

The modules in the second topological layer are sketched in Fig. 3-16. The Super-Ego modules *E7* and *E22* are not divided further. Their functionality is restricted and focuses on the management of rules that are retrieved from the *information representation layer*. The Id modules *Drive management* and *Affect management* are divided to *Generation of drives* (*E3*) and *Fusion of drives* (*E4*) respectively *Generation of affects for drives* (*E5*) and *Generation of affects for perception* (*E18*). Table 3-2 summarizes the interfaces between the modules.

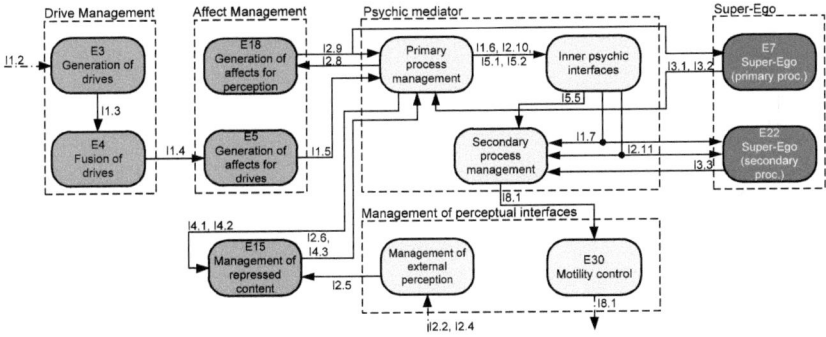

Fig. 3-16: 2nd Topological Layer

Generation of drives – E3

As shown in Fig. 3-16, *E3* receives information about the homeostatic state in the form of a neuro-symbolic structure via I1.2. Bodily demands are converted to drive components and drive demands. As discussed in Section 3.1 a pair of opposites forms the drive content that is deduced from the drive component. A list of tuples that contain the affect and the drive content are forwarded to *E4* by I1.3. The content of these tuples correspond to HMs. In Table 3-2 the drive demand is highlighted as it is not defined as atomic data structure but still processed in the decision unit.

Interface name	From	To	Data type	Content
I1.3	E3	E4	[{drive demand, TPM, TPM}]	Drive demands and pair of opposites
I1.4	E4	E5	[{drive demand, TPM}]	Drive demand and merged drive content
I1.5	E5	E6, E7, E9	[DM]	Perceived homeostatic state
I2.6	E15	E16	[{TPM, [{TPM, affect}]}]	Perceptual image and a associated repressed drive content
I2.9	E18	E7, E19	[TPM]	Template image on external perception
I4.3	E15	E6	[{affect, TPM}]	Repressed drive content and corresponding affects

Table 3-2: Id interfaces – square brackets "[]" specify a list of data structures while curly braces "{}" represent a tuple

Fusion of drives – E4

E4 receives its input via I1.3. It manipulates the information by merging the drive content counterparts. Together with the drive demand it forms the module's output that is delivered via I1.4 to *E5*.

Generation of affects for drives – E5

After the drive content opposites are merged in *E4*, here, the quantity of the drive demand is converted to an affect. As the affect represents the temporal change of the drive demand, its previous values are buffered. Now the concept of the drive is completed and is represented by its quantity in the form of an affect and a quality in the form of a TPM. The TPM contains the drive source. The affect is represented as scalar that ranges in the interval from minus one to one in order to cover experiences of unpleasure and pleasure. *E5* passes on a list containing these DMs to *E9* and *E6* via I1.5.

Generation of affects for perception – E18

E18 exchanges information with the *Psychic mediator* via I2.9 and I2.8. By I2.8 it perceives a list of tuples that contain TIs including the external perception. In addition the tuples contain a list of repressed content. A list of DMs, which is retrieved from the *information representation layer* in *E16*, evaluates the TIs by experience. The repressed content and the DMs are used to initialize a new evaluation of the received TPM. The new formed DM and the TPM form a pair that is sent back to the *Psychic mediator* via I2.9. The list of pairs represents the currently perceived situation that the system must deal with.

Regarding the Ego modules, the *Management of perceptual interfaces* is divided into *Preliminary external perception (E14)* and *Motility control (E30)*. The *Psychic mediator* module is divided into *Primary process management, Secondary process management* and *Inner psychic interfaces*.

Preliminary external perception – E14

The preliminary external perception receives information about the environment and bodily sensations in the form of neuro-symbols by I2.2 and I2.4. In *E14* this information is converted to primary data structures. The result is forwarded to *E15* via I2.5.

Motility control – E30

In contrast to the *Preliminary external perception* module, here a specific action plan is converted to a series of motility actions and mapped to neuro-symbols. Via I7.4 the generated action plan is received while the stream of neuro-symbols is forwarded to *E31* through I8.1.

Primary process management, Secondary process management, and Inner psychic interfaces

The primary process management and secondary process management modules contain Ego functions that follow the primary process principle, respectively the secondary one. This means that those following the primary process principle manipulate primary data structures, while the secondary one manipulates secondary data structures only. Both groups of modules are interconnected by inner psychic interfaces. Corresponding word presentations are retrieved from the information representation layer and forwarded for further manipulations.

3.3.6 First Topological Layer

Super-Ego and Id have already reached a specific granularity on the 2nd respectively the 3rd layer. Even though both modules can be subdivided to further modules, the actual description is sufficient for a prototype implementation (see Fig. 3-17). In contrast, the Ego must be refined further. The *Management of primary processes* module is divided into *Management of memory traces (E16), Fusion of external perception and memory traces (E17), Knowledge about reality (E9), Defense mechanism for perception (E19), Defense mechanism for drive content (E6), Conversion to secondary process 1*and *2 (E8, E21)*, and *Inner* perception of affects (*E20*).

Management of memory traces – E16

E16 compares raw perceptual sensor data and formerly repressed content, which is received through I2.6, with data structures stored on the *information representation layer*. A list of TIs, which can also be represented by single TPMs, is retrieved that is ordered with respect to the level of accordance between the templates and the perceptual image. TIs that match the perceptual image best are selected. Affects that are repressed by the defense mechanism are added to the perceived information in case they match the drive content. This process is discussed above for *E15*. A closer look on the retrieval process is given in Section 3.4. In case the perceptual image additionally contains dynamically changing data, data structures that match this information are retrieved from the data storage. They are linked with the main template by an instance association. New formed TIs, repressed content, and associated DMs are forwarded to *E17* via I2.7.

Fusion of external perception and memory traces – E17

The information that is retrieved from *E16* through I2.7 is merged. Formerly repressed content and DMs that are associated to the external perception are merged to a new homeostatic evaluation of perceived data. This information is forwarded to *E18* via I2.8.

Knowledge about reality (primary process) – E9

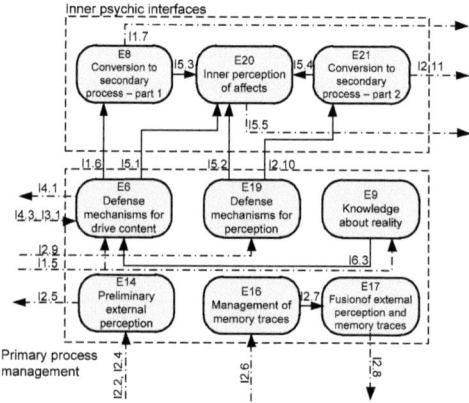

Fig. 3-17: Top-Down view of inner psychic interfaces and primary process management modules

E9 receives a list of DMs through I1.5. It is tested if they can be executed considering the system's abilities. This is required to filter unreal, respectively infeasible demands. The module's mechanisms are controlled regarding primary process principles. A list of DMs is retrieved from the *information representation layer* (see Section 3.4). These DMs have the same content (TPM) as those, which are retrieved via I1.5. *E9* evaluates the differences between affects that are retrieved from the database and the input parameters. If the result is negative, according DMs are deleted from the input. The remaining ones are forwarded to *E6* through I6.3. *E9* is required for the complementation of the psychoanalytic model. However, it is assumed that it can be merged with *E7* regarding the engineering model.

Defense mechanism for perception – E19

The input is received through I2.9 and I3.1. The interface I2.9 submits data in the form of TPMs and DMs. This information is blocked and not forwarded in case it gets in conflict with a Super-Ego rule. The impact of a Super-Ego rule according to the tuple of TPMs and DMs is received through I3.1 in the form of affects. If the conflictive potential between a rule and an information component is too high, the TPMs and DMs are sent back to *E15* via I4.2. Otherwise, the received information is forwarded to *E21* by I2.10. The initially associated affect that is replaced in *E18* is forwarded to *E20* through I5.2.

Defense mechanisms for drive content – E6

Similar to *E19* the principle of the defense mechanisms is applied to drives, respectively the drives' content. Interface I1.5 provides DMs that hold the homeostatic state. Through interface I4.3, formerly repressed drive content and affects are received. I6.3 provides filtered DMs while *E7* evaluates the incoming DMs and forwards corresponding rules and awards through I3.1. The defense mechanisms decide if the received data is redirected to *E15* via I4.1 or forwarded to the conversion to secondary process and inner perception. Interface I1.6 transmits the DMs while I5.1 transports their decoupled affects.

The *Primary to secondary transformation management* is split into *Conversion to secondary process* (*E8* and *E21*), and *Inner perception of affects* (*E20*) modules.

Conversion to secondary process (part one) – E8

The conversion to secondary process functionality is divided into two parts. The first one deals with DMs that are received by interface I1.6. In *E8* the drive content is linked to WPs that are handled by secondary processes. As secondary processes introduce logic relations, temporal sequences, and local constraints, the conglomerate of primary data structures are translated to WPs. Conflicts and contradictions between upcoming drives are solved. The result is forwarded to *E22* and *E23* through I1.7 in the form of a list of WPs and their according DMs. Primary data structures remain associated with secondary data structures. Via I5.3, a tuple of WPs and corresponding DMs is forwarded to *E20*.

Conversion to secondary process (part two) – E21

The mechanisms of this module are similar to those in *E8*. However, the processed information contains information about the bodily sensations and the environmental state that is received from the mechanisms of defense through I2.10. After corresponding word presentations are retrieved from the *information representation layer* and connected with the primary data structures, the result is forwarded through interface I2.11. Interface I5.4 forwards a tuple of DMs and WPs to *E20*.

Inner perception of affects – E20

First, affects, which are decoupled from their DMs by the mechanisms of defense, are received by I5.1 and I5.2. These affects cause unpleasure that cannot be redirected to a special drive content and therefore are interpreted as anxiety. Second, *E20* receives DMs and corresponding WPs via I5.4 and I5.3. *E20* calculates new affects for the received DMs by taking account of the level of anxiety. As a result, a list that contains new DMs and their associated WPs is passed on to *E29* and *E26* via I5.5.

Interface name	From	To	Data type	Content
I1.6	E6	E8	[DM]	Drive content that passed the mechanisms of defense
I1.7	E8	E22, E23, E26	[WP, DM]	Homeostatic state prepared for secondary processes
I2.5	E14	E15	[TPM]	External perception
I2.7	E16	E17	[{TPM, [DM], [DM]}]	External perception; associated homeostatic impact; repressed content
I2.8	E17	E18	[{TPM,[DM]}]	External perception with new homeostatic evaluation
I2.10	E19	E21	[{TPM, DM}]	External perception as well as corresponding homeostatic impact
I2.11	E21	E22, E23	[{WP, TPM}, {WP, DM}]	External perception and associated homeostatic impact arranged for the manipulation by secondary processes
I3.1	E7	E6	{[TPM], DM, affect}	External perception evaluated by the Super-Ego (affect) in dependence to the current homeostatic state (DM)
I3.2	E7	E15	[DM, affect]	Homeostatic state evaluated by the Super-Ego (affect)
I4.1	E6	E15	[DM]	Repressed homeostatic state

I4.2	E19	E15	[{TPM, DM}]	Repressed external perception
I5.1	E6	E20	[affect]	Affects that are decoupled from their drive content; resulting in anxiety
I5.2	E19	E20	[affect]	Affects that are decoupled from their drive content; resulting in anxiety
I5.3	E8	E20	[{WP, DM}]	Homeostatic state arranged for the manipulation by secondary processes
I5.4	E21	E20	[{WP, DM}]	Homeostatic evaluation of external perception
I5.5	E20	E26, E29	[{WP,DM}}]	Affective evaluation of the current state;
I6.3	E9	E6	[{DM}]	Drives that passed mechanisms of defense

Table 3-3: Primary process management interfaces – square brackets "[]" specify a list of data structures while curly braces "{}" represent a tuple

The block *Management of secondary processes* (see Fig. 3-18) is split into *Focus on external perception (E23)*, *Knowledge about reality (E25, E34)*, *Reality check (E24, E33)*, *Decision making (E26)*, *Knowledge base of stored scenarios (E28)*, *Generation of imaginary actions (E27)*, *Knowledge about reality (E34)*, and *Evaluation of imaginary actions (E29)*.

Focus on external perception – E23

E23 controls the focus of attention. It receives information about the current homeostatic state as well as external perception via I1.7 and I2.11. Even though, primary data structures are associated to the input, the secondary data structures are used for the evaluation. WPs that hold the homeostatic state are used to prioritize the external input. The individual's subjective experiences with the object (stored in the corresponding DMs) influence the ranking process. It can be verified which perceived objects are used to satisfy certain bodily demands. The priority is influenced by the intensity of a bodily demand and the level of satisfaction that can result from a perceived object. The attention is triggered to the objects that are rated with highest priority. Prerequisite for focusing on external perception is the control by secondary processes. The resulting list of prioritized WPs with associated primary data structures and their aimed homeostatic state is forwarded via I2.12 to *E24*. This combination of prioritized external perception and the influence on the homeostatic state are defined as *goal candidates*. In case external perception cannot be mapped to a current homeostatic state, it forms the goal on its own. Hence, information about external perception is not lost but remains unevaluated.

Concept and Model

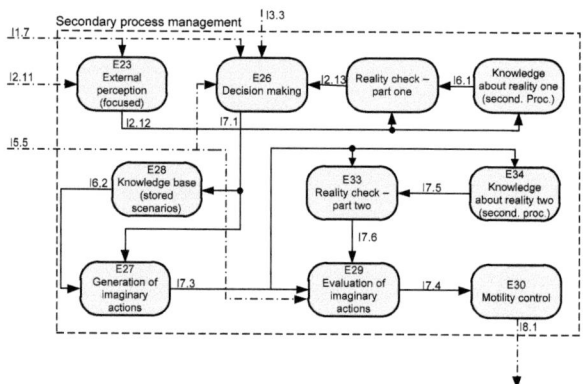

Fig. 3-18: Top-Down view of the secondary process management

Knowledge about reality (secondary process, part one) – E25

In contrast to the knowledge about reality module, which operates based on primary process principles, *E25* implies secondary process functionality. It receives information via I2.12 with a list of prioritized external perception. *E25* retrieves information from the *information representation layer* on rules (micro-acts) that are imposed by abilities, attributes, and actions which underlie physical and logical restrictions. Contrariwise to the Super-Ego rules, knowledge about reality is not influenced by social structures but by limits of the physical world and the own body. *E25* influences the reality check and as a consequence the decision making process. The retrieved *micro-acts* are forwarded to *E24* via I6.1.

Reality check – E24

E24 receives input via I2.12 and I6.1. The reality check deals with the synchronization between external perception that is prioritized by homeostatic demands and reality rules. The knowledge about reality is factored into the goal candidate priority. Hence, the goal candidates become reordered depending on the possibility to get accomplished regarding reality rules and their affect to the homeostatic sate. The resulting list is forwarded to *E26* through I2.13 and influences the decision making process. The information about external perception is kept as part of the list of goal candidates as it is required for the decision making and action generation process.

Interface name	From	To	Data type	Content
I2.12	E23	E24, E25	[{WP, TPM}, {WP, DM}]	A prioritized list of goal candidates (focus on external perception)
I2.13	E24	E26	[goal candidates]	A prioritized list of goal candidates including rules about reality
I3.3	E22	E26	[rule]	Super-Ego rules
I6.1	E25	E24	[rule]	Knowledge about reality rules
I6.2	E28	E27	[acts]	List of acts that end up in accomplishing the selected goal
I7.1	E26	E28, E27	{goal, [{WP, TPM}]}	Selected goal and external perception
I7.3	E27	E34, E29	{[acts], [{WP, TPM}]}	Prioritized list of acts and external perception
I7.4	E29	E40	[[WP]]	Action plans
I7.5	E34	E33	{[rule], [acts], [{WP, TPM}]}	Knowledge about reality rules
I7.6	E33	E29	[acts]	Prioritized action plans

Table 3-4: Secondary process management interfaces – square brackets "[]" specify a list of data structures while curly braces "{}" represent a tuple

Decision making – E26

E26 receives its input through I5.5, I3.3, I2.13, and I1.7. Through the interfaces I5.5 and I1.7 information about the current demands is received. In accordance to reality checked goal candidates (I2.13), Super-Ego rules (I3.3), the homeostatic demands (I1.7, I5.5), one goal is selected. *E20* sends a list of homeostatic demands to *E26*. Even though there is no goal candidate that matches a high prioritized homeostatic demand, it still can be selected as goal by the decision making process. Afterwards a scenario is retrieved that enables to reach an according object. In addition to the selected goal, information about the external perception is extracted out of the list of goal candidates and forwarded via I7.1 to *E28* and *E27*.

Knowledge base of stored scenarios – E28

The information that is received through the interface I7.1 triggers the act, which must be executed in order to achieve the goal. Therefore, micros-acts are retrieved from the *information representation layer* that are stringed together to acts that hold the current external state as precondition and the goal state as consequence. This can be reached by various

Concept and Model

mechanisms. Section 5.2 gives insight to the realization in ARSi10. The formed acts are passed on to *E27* via I6.2.

Generation of imaginary actions – E27

The current goal as well as information about the external perception is received through I7.1. A list of acts is received via I6.2. Acts are selected by selection requirements that are not fixed right now. For ARSi10 the crucial factor is the act length. Acts are converted to action plans and forwarded to *E29* and *E34* via I7.3.

Knowledge about reality (secondary process, part two) – E34

E34 implies identical mechanisms as *E25*. They only differ in their input parameters. The input information is used as search pattern in order to retrieve rules, which are imposed by reality, from the *information representation layer*. Reality check rules are forwarded to *E33* through I7.5.

Reality check (part two) – E33

Reality check part two evaluates the received information regarding the feasibility of the action plans in reality. Its mechanisms are similar to those of reality check part one. Acts that cannot be handled are removed. The others are ranked and forwarded to *E29* via I7.6.

Evaluation of imaginary actions – E29

E29 receives a list of action plans and external perception through I7.3 and a list of reality rules through I7.6. An affective evaluation of the current state is received by I5.5. These three branches form the selection requirements for one action plan. For their evaluation, the action plans are accomplished without triggering any motility control. This is inspired by the human being's process of thinking that is, according to Solms [ST02, p. 298], acting without setting actions. They are evaluated by considering the input parameters. Before the decision for one action plan is made, all possible alternatives must be analyzed. At the end, one action plan is chosen and forwarded to *E30* via I7.4. There the action plans are converted to actuator commands (see above).

Fig. 3-19 shows the ARS model at its current state. Section 3.4 discusses the interfaces to the information representation management module as well as its functionalities in detail.

Concept and Model

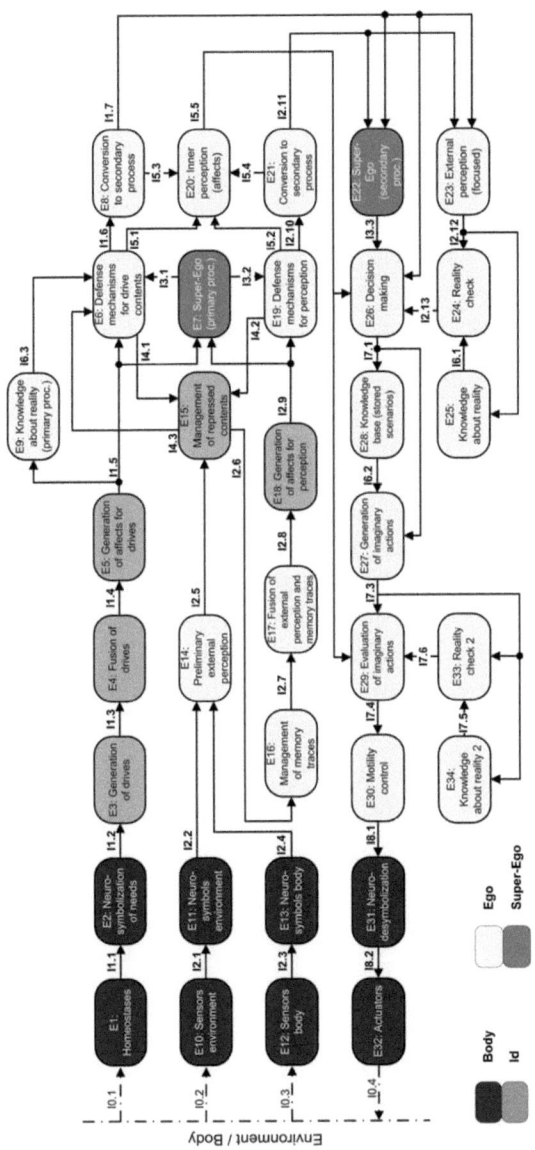

Fig. 3-19: Functional view of the Artificial Recognition System

Concept and Model

3.4 Information Representation Management

In Section 3.2 the psychoanalytically inspired data structures *thing presentation*, *word presentation*, *affect*, and *association* are defined. Any date that is exchanged among the decision unit modules is a combination of these atomic information components. While Section 3.3 discusses the information processing on the *decision layer*, the question remains unanswered how information is exchanged with the *information representation layer*. The *information management system* is not based on neuropsychoanalytic concepts. It is an auxiliary tool that handles stored knowledge and provides the interface between the decision- and the information representation layer. Therefore both layers must be loosely coupled as the information management system's functionalities must not influence the decision layer processes.

3.4.1 Information Management System

The information management system is separated into *information management module* and *data storage* (see definition 4 in Section 1.3). The *Information management module* provides functionalities that allow the decision unit to search data in and retrieve data from the data storage. For ARSi10 stored data structures do not change during runtime due to the absence of learning mechanisms. Any knowledge is predefined. Data structures can only be changed on the *decision layer*. A change of this factor is considered for future revisions. Fig. 3-20 sketches the information representation management module, which is functionally di-

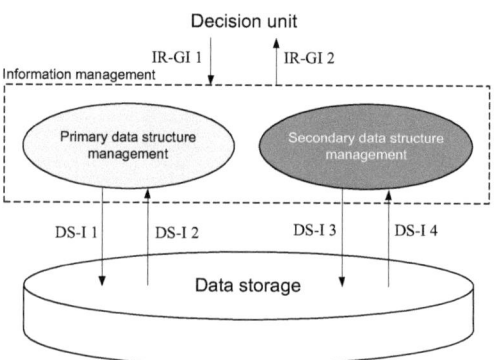

Fig. 3-20: Information representation management module

IR-GI: *Information Representation Group Interface*; DS-I: *Data Storage Interface*

vided into *Primary data structure management* (PDSM) and *Secondary data structure management* (SDSM). As the names imply each of them handles either primary or secondary data structures. Fig. 3-20 additionally shows the bi-directional information flow (*IR-GI 1*, *IR-GI 2*) between the decision unit and the *information representation management* module. The interface allows certain decision unit modules to retrieve stored knowledge. These modules are specified below. The interfaces between the information management module and the data storage are shown in Fig. 3-20 and labeled as DS-I 1-4.

The set of stored data structures forms the search space that is used for the search procedure. Search patterns that are retrieved via *IR-GI 1* from the decision unit are compared with the search space objects. Matches are retrieved to the decision unit, together with associated data structures. This implies an indirect activation of data structure, which is discussed in Section 3.4.2. The PDSM processes primary data structures and requires algorithms that are able to handle associative networks. The SDSM processes word presentations, logic relations and acts. Due to the different characteristics of primary and secondary data structures, PDSM and SDSM modules imply different types of search algorithms.

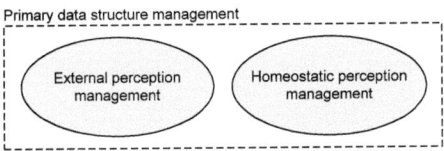

Fig. 3-21: Primary data structure management

The PDSM is divided into the *External perception management* module (EPM) and the *Homeostatic perception management* (HPM) module. Both are shown in Fig. 3-21. For example, the EPM handles the input from the module E16. The perceptual image in the form of TPMs, TPs, TIs is compared with stored templates. Contrariwise to the HPM module the search is not driven towards DMs. They are indirectly activated and retrieved in case they are associated with the search results. The HPM module searches through the set of DMs that are hold by the search space. This differentiation is a result that originates in the characteristics of the psychoanalytically inspired data structures but is not explicitly mentioned in psychoanalytic theory. For ARSi10 a detailed discussion about the type of search algorithm would exceed the limits of this work. For the realization of the proposed concept, shown in Section 4, the list search algorithm is introduced.

As mentioned above, not every decision unit module has access to the *information management system*. The interfaces between the decision unit modules and particular information management sub-modules are specified in the following. The *information management* module is represented by its modules *SDSM, EPM,* and *HPM*. Regarding the ARS decision unit there are nine modules identified that possess an interface to one of the three *information management* modules. The modules *E21, E16, E7, E8,* and *E9* have access to the *PDSM* module. While Fig. 3-21 summarizes the information flow to *IR-GI 1* and *IR-GI 2*, Fig. 3-22 shows a more detailed categorization. Their interfaces are labeled as *Information Representation Layer Interface* (*IR-I 1.x*). The modules *E22, E34, E28,* and *E25* have interfaces to the *SDSM* module (*IR-I 2.x*). Arrows in light grey mark sub-interfaces of *IR-I 1* while black arrows label sub-interfaces of *IR-I 2*. The return values contain matches for received search patterns as well as data structures that are associated with these matches.

Both Super-Ego modules, *E7* and *E22*, access the database in order to retrieve TIs or micro-acts. The primary process driven module *E7* forwards a search pattern that contains environmental and bodily information via *IR-I 1.1* to the EPM module. The EPM module searches for TIs that match the perceptual image and returns an ordered list of matches – ordered by their correspondence with the search pattern – to E7 via *IR-I 1.2*. E7 does not receive rules in the common sense. As primary data structures do not possess a logic and temporal structure the rules are not defined in the form of cause-and-effect chains. In this case, *E7* evaluates the retrieved TIs and their associated DMs by incorporating the current homeostatic state.

E22 exchanges information with the SDSM module. Via *IR-I 2.1* information about the external perception is sent to the SDSM. There, matching micro-acts are searched whose precondition matches the perceptual image. The result is returned to *E22* by *IR-I* 2.2. Further manipulation by *E22* is discussed in Section 3.3.

E9 sends an image of the current homeostatic state to the HPM module via *IR-I 1.3*. The HPM module starts a search for similar DMs. The similarity is indicated by the drive content. Found DMs are returned to E9 via *IR-I 1.4*.

E16 sends the perceptual image to the EPM via *IR-I 1.5*. There, it is searched for TPs, TPMs, and TIs that match the input. As it is possible that several data structures match the search pattern up to a threshold level, a list that is ordered by their match level is returned through *IR-I 1.6*. The threshold level must be predefined.

E8 and *E21* handle the association of primary data structures with secondary data structures. *E21* sends a list of TPMs (external perception) via *IR-I 1.7* to the EPM module. In return it receives the corresponding WPs through *IR-I 1.8*. Both, *E8* and *E21* send DMs to the HPM module through *IR-I 1.9* and *IR-I 1.11*. According WPs are returned through *IR-I 1.10* and *IR-I 1.12*.

Concept and Model

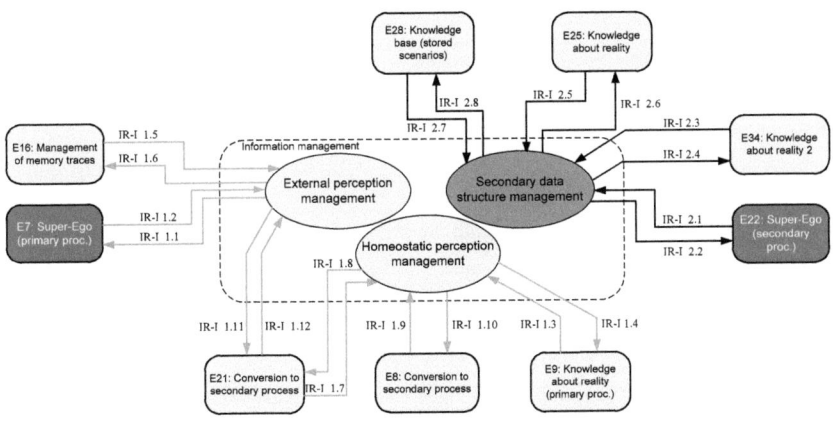

Fig. 3-22: Interfaces between decision unit and information management modules

Table 3-5 summarizes the interfaces between the decision unit and the PDSM module. The modules *E25* and *E34* have access to the SDSM module via *IR-I 2.5* and *IR-I 2.3*. E34 sends a prioritized list of goal candidates through *IR-I 2.3*. Activated acts and micro-acts are retrieved through *IR-I 2.4*. E34 picks micro-acts and forwards them to *E24*. The same is ap-

Interface	From	To	Data type	Content
IR-I 1.1	E7	EPM	[TPM]	Perceptual image
IR-I 1.2	EPM	E7	[{TI, [DM]}]	Template images and associated DMs
IR-I 1.3	E9	HPM	[DM]	Current homeostatic state
IR-I 1.4	HPM	E9	[{DM, [DM]}]	Corresponding DMs
IR-I 1.5	E16	EPM	[TPM]	External perception
IR-I 1.6	EPM	E16	[primary data structure]	An ordered list of templates
IR-I 1.7	E21	EPM	[TPM]	External perception
IR-I 1.8	EPM	E21	[TPM, WP]	External perception and according word presentations
IR-I 1.9	E8	HPM	[DM]	Homeostatic state
IR-I 1.10	HPM	E8	[DM, WP]	Homeostatic state and according word presentations
IR-I 1.11	E21	HPM	[DM]	Affective evaluation of externally perceived objects
IR-I 1.12	HPM	E21	[DM, WP]	Affective evaluation of externally perceived objects with according word presentations

Table 3-5: Interfaces between the decision unit and the primary data structure management module – square brackets "[]" specify a list of data structures while curly braces "{}" represent a tuple

Concept and Model

plied to *E25*, which sends action plans to the SDSM module via *IR-I 2.5* and receives reality rules by *IR-I 2.6*.

E28 requires access to stored acts and micro-acts that it gets by *IR-I 2.7*. A list of word presentations that describe the current goal state is forwarded to the SDSM module. Micro-acts, whose consequence corresponds to the goal state, are added to a list and returned to *E28* via *IR-I 2.8*.

Interface	From	To	Data type	Content
RI-I 2.1	E22	SDSM	[WP]	Current environmental and bodily state
RI-I 2.2	SDSM	E22	[micro-acts]	Rules for handling the current state
RI-I 2.3	E34	SDSM	[WP]	Goal candidates
RI-I 2.4	SDSM	E34	[micro-acts]	Rules that are applied to the current external state
RI-I 2.5	E25	SDSM	[WP]	Action plans
RI-I 2.6	SDSM	E25	[micro-acts]	Rules that are applied to the current external state
RI-I 2.7	E28	SDSM	[WP]	Goal
RI-I 2.8	SDSM	E28	[acts]	Acts whose consequence state match the goal candidates

Table 3-6: Interfaces between the decision unit and the secondary data structure management module – square brackets "[]" specify a list of data structures while curly braces "{}" represent a tuple

Table 3-6 summarizes the interfaces between the decision unit and the SDSM module.

The proposed *information management* unit provides the infrastructure for the information exchange between the *decision layer* and the *information representation layer*. As the unit's functionality is not based on psychoanalytic concepts it must be ensured that it is decoupled from the decision unit's functionality in order to avoid any disturbing influences. The search space, which completes the *information management system*, is read only during runtime. The concept for activating and retrieving information from the information representation layer must be resolved in Section 3.4.2.

3.4.2 Activation and Retrieval of Stored Data Structures

After defining the *information representation*, the retrieval mechanisms must be defined. The *information management* modules are differentiated with respect to the searched data structure type. They have in common that perceived information is mapped to stored templates. This process activates and retrieves data structures in respect to their associations. The retrieved data structures are returned to the *decision unit* via the interfaces defined in Fig. 3-22. The search mechanisms that are used to compare the search pattern with the appropriate templates are not discussed by psychoanalytic theory and therefore fully covered by the engineering side. The used type of search algorithm influences the overall system performance but does not limit the conversion of the psychoanalytic theory into a technical model. The HPM module searches for DMs, the EPM module searches for TPs, TPMs, and TIs and finally the SDSM module searches for WPs and micro-acts. Found pattern matches are added to the return list that is ordered with respect to the match level. Two groups of activation types are defined for ARSi10. They are discussed in detail by Zeilinger et al. [ZLM09, pp. 24-30] and are summarized below. The first group is divided to *indirect* and *direct* activation. The second group defines where the perceived information sources from and differentiates between *external perceptual* and *homeostatic activation* which were labeled as *internal* and *external* activation by Zeilinger [ZLM09, p. 28]. Due to changes in the nomenclature their labels must change. The first activation type influences the *information management* unit's functionality for ARSi10. The second one becomes important in case different activation mechanisms are introduced with respect to the data structure type. This is not applied to this work that therefore focuses on the first group of activation mechanisms.

Direct activation occurs in case the search pattern matches components that correlate with stored data structure templates. For example, in Fig. 3-23 received TPs and TPMs match stored items. As discussed above, data structures are only stored once and are used to form data structure meshes – TPs and TPMs form TPMs, TPs, TPMs, and TIs form new TIs while WPs are combined to acts. Fig. 3-23 shows the activation of TIs by TPs and TPMs. Three TPs (*color red*, *shape rectangle*, and *shape circle*) as well as TPM_l are directly activated by the search pattern. The thing presentations TP_y and TP_x are ignored. The directly activated data structures trigger data structures that are associated by *temporal* concurrence and *attribute* associations. This triggering mechanism is labeled as *indirect activation*.

In Fig. 3-23, TPMs and TPs are associated by *temporal* and weighted *attribute* associations. Data structures that are activated by the search pattern indirectly activate the TPMs *red rectangle* and *red circle*. The TPs *shape rectangle* and *color red* indirectly activate the TPM *red rectangle*. In addition, it is indirectly activated through the temporal association with TPM_l. In Section 3.2 it is defined that TPs are not directly associated with each other. They are associated through *high-level* data structures in the form of TPMs and TIs. For ARSi10 the activation of data structures is directed towards data structures at higher levels. TPs and TPMs activate TPMs while TPs, TPMs, and TIs activate TIs in case they are temporarily fully meshed. This activation process does not work the other way round as ARSi10 does not support *recursive* activation. TPMs do not activate TPs and TIs do not activate TPMs.

Concept and Model

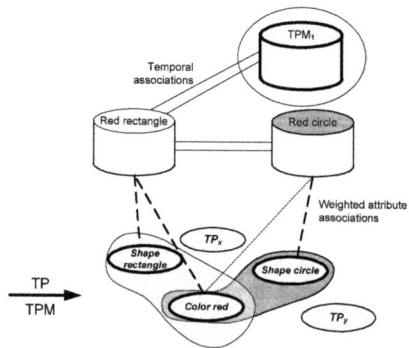

Fig. 3-23: Direct activation of TPs and a TPM

TP: *Thing presentation*; TPM: *Thing presentation mesh*

Taking the example of a tree, it can be said that the way from the root to the leaves is open but the way back is closed.

In Fig. 3-24 the open way is labeled as *activation direction*. These limitations are introduced in order to reduce the amount of indirectly activated data structures. Otherwise, indirect activation of data structures propagates to further activations that again activate data structures. Even though associations of *attributes* are weighted and the activation process is not infinite the amount of activated data structures increases rapidly in case the associative net is not correctly parameterized at startup. Hence, these uncertainties are avoided for ARSi10 that focuses on the activation of data structures at a higher level. TPs, TPMs, and TIs can be connected by *temporal* associations. The conglomerate of *directly* and *indirectly* activated data structures forms images of the current situation that activate TIs as is shown in Fig. 3-24.

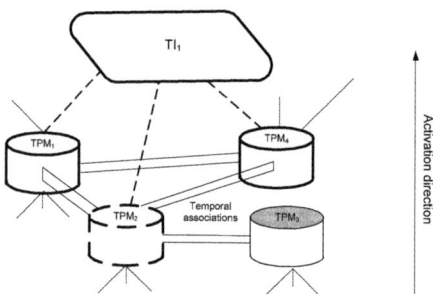

Fig. 3-24: Indirect Activation of TIs

TPM: *Thing presentation mesh*; TI: *Template image*

102

Perceived data structures are complemented and filtered out by stored TPMs and TIs. This accords to the assumption that perception is constructivist. This means that only a fraction of perceived information is processed (see Section 3.2.2).

While TPs, TPMs and WPs are activated in both ways, affects are only indirectly activated by the drive content (TP) with which it forms the DM. DMs in turn indirectly activate associated TPMs and TIs. This accords to [Dam03, p. 71] who claims that emotions trigger thoughts which normally cause them. This leads to and activation of data structures even though they were not part of the perceptual image. In Section 3.1 and 3.2 different groups of associations are introduced. Only *attribute associations* possess a weight whose intensity accords to the number of coincident and direct activations of both connected data structures. The association weight influences the indirect activation process. The match level between perceived and stored information initializes an activation potential that is transferred over the associative net. The stronger an association between two data structures is the higher is the chance that the indirect activation is propagated. This mechanism accords to a spread activation process (see Section 2.3). Associations of *temporal occurrence* are not weighted in the current version of the model. As the system does not contain a learning mechanism, all templates are predefined. They are selected by the match factor between the search pattern and the stored template.

So far we have focused on the activation of primary data structures. WPs can be activated indirectly and directly as well. Indirect activation is done by primary data structures that are linked to a WP by a *word presentation* association. Direct activation occurs in case the search pattern is formed by secondary data structures. This in turn leads to an indirect activation of acts and micro-acts. The activated data structures are returned to the *decision layer* via the interfaces shown in Fig. 3-22. In case they are returned within a list, the list is ranked with respect to their match level.

Section 3.2 focuses on the *information representation* in ARSi10 that must be synchronized with the information processing mechanisms in the *decision layer* which are discussed in Section 3.3. Psychoanalytic concepts form the foundation of the *information representation system*. The psychoanalytic concept of TPs, WPs, affects, and associations is introduced and transformed to engineering terms. They represent the atomic information components that are combined to data structures of higher level like TPMs, DMs, TIs, and acts. It is discussed which upcoming questions in the area of information processing are adequately covered by psychoanalytic theory and which areas of the technical model must be complemented by common engineering approaches. The last point applies to the *information management* module that provides the infrastructure to the *decision layer* for accessing the *infor-*

mation representation layer.

Summarized, Chapter 3 proves Hypothesis 3 in Section 1.3. The proposed data structure concept results into five assumptions that must be considered for the implementation.

1. Local associations are already realized by the binding of sensor data within the neuro-symbolic layer.
2. Attribute associations are held in TPMs.
3. Temporal associations are formed between TPs, TPMs, and TIs.
4. Temporally associated data structures are combined to TIs.
5. For ARSi10, association weights are not realized even though the concept incorporates them.

The decision unit contains interfaces to the *information management* module (see Sections 3.3 and 3.4.1) that is divided regarding the processed data structure types. This allows an adaptation of the modules' functionalities to requirements that turn up with specific data structure characteristics. For ARSi10 this affects the choice of the search algorithm that must be synchronized with the introduced activation mechanisms.

The considerations in Section 2.4 imply the use of an artificial life simulation to verify the outcome of Chapter 3. This follows the requirement for a system body that allows a *system-environment* and a *body-decision unit* interaction and supports the interdisciplinary work as it eases the introduction of neuropsychoanalytic findings to a technical application. Chapter 4 discusses the simulation environment as well as the implementation of the proposed model.

4. Examined Solution

Chapter 3 introduces concept and model of a bionically inspired *information representation system* to the ARS decision unit. The psychoanalytic concept of information representation and processing is introduced to a technical model. This chapter discusses its realization in embodied autonomous software agents. Thereby questions about the agent's characteristics, its environment and the interface to the ARS control unit come up. It must be answered how the *information representation* is realized and data structures are stored in search spaces and retrieved from there by keeping the requirements of the proposed model in mind. This step is done without support by neuropsychoanalytic expertise as the technical model is already defined and its realization is an engineer's job. The implementation of the decision unit's functionalities (see Section 3.3) ties up to the ARSi09 [Lan10] realization. Adaptations of the modules' functionalities are described due to changes in the interface definitions. The revised decision unit and the coupled information management system are merged and labeled as ARSi10 (ARS implementation number 10).

4.1 Simulation Environment and Embodied Software Agents

Section 2.4 discusses the possible ways of evaluating the proposed model. There it is decided to implement the ARS decision unit to a software agent and test it in a game of artificial life. The agent is provided with a sensor and an actuator system which enable a system-environment interaction. This meets the requirements in order to define the software agents as embodied (see definition 7, Section 2.4.1). As is discussed in Section 2.4, the simulation of an artificial world allows the specification of an environment and body of arbitrary complexity. Even though real world complexity will not be achieved (see Section 2.4.1), the variation of complexity levels and the possibility to factor out mechanical malfunctions and unplanned environmental changes is advantageous. The aim in introducing the bubble world simulator (BWsim) to the ARS project [DZL07, DZLZ08] is to allow the configuration of a complex and rapidly changing environment. Still it is possible to reduce the setting to a minimum in order to test certain agent abilities and behaviors. The agent body represents the interface between the simulated world and the decision unit. The basic set of sensors, actuators, and abilities is defined at the first step. This ensures the provision of sufficient information for the decision unit in order to accomplish the selected action plans. ARSi10 is realized in a multi-agent system (MAS) that are based on the Java programming language. Java is developed by Sun Microsystems that is owned by the Oracle Corporation [InetOra]. The BWsim embeds the MASON library to introduce multi-agent functionality. In Section 2.4.2 the MAS toolkits Swarm, Repast, and MASON are compared. The decisive factor for the use of MASON is its design that is focused on the simulation of large numbers of agents and therefore provides the required performance for doing so. Therefore, MASON exceeds the usage only for rapid prototyping. Even though the toolkit does not imply a physics engine in its source the programming community provides a library that can be used to simulate physical effects in two dimensional simulation environments. In order to extend BWsim to three dimensions, more sophisticated physics engines like the ODE4j (*open dynamics engine for java*) [InetOde] are available. The physical interaction is accomplished in only two dimensions. In addition, the MASON framework provides an interface to a 2-dimensional and 3-dimensional visualization. This makes it possible to monitor the agents' behavior. In addition an *inspector package* is included that provides monitoring tools, labeled as inspectors, for objects and their attributes. These tools assist in the debugging process of the agents' internal, sensor, and actuator systems.

As discussed in Section 3.3 the decision unit requires information about the external and the homeostatic state. This implies information about the environment and the body. The agent's body is equipped with a sensor system that detects external and homeostatic signals. The external sensor system handles *visual*, *tactile*, and *gustatory* stimuli in order to perceive the environment. Extensions to *acoustic* and *olfactory* sensor modalities are intended but not part of this work.

The bodily state is formed by *fast messengers*, *slow messengers*, and *body condition levels*. Their specification is inspired by the human body where information is transferred by the nervous system and the hormonal system. Fast messengers represent bodily sensations that are transferred without time loss between source and destination. They can be linked directly to their origin and contain information about the current position of actuators and body parts, as well as stimuli that originate from organs. Regarding the characteristics of the transport system, fast messengers correspond to a life form's nervous system. Contrariwise, the slow messenger system implies the characteristics of hormones. Slow messengers do not influence the control unit only for a moment in time as it is done by fast messengers. The level of a slow messenger rises over time – measured simulation steps – and decreases after it has reached its maximum. Slow messengers form the homeostatic state together with certain levels of body conditions. The agent possesses body mechanisms that ensure the system's functionality. Body condition levels are an indicator for these mechanisms. Condition levels display the state of the stamina system, the nutrition system, the energy resource, the body integrity and the health system. They represent the basic set of body condition levels that are influenced by one another. For example, every action takes a certain amount of energy, fast movements reduce the stamina, while consumed nutrition types influence the energy level as well as the body integrity and health system. These internal systems form the homeostasis and must stay in balance.

The environmental sensor system is equipped with a visual, a tactile, and a gustatory modality. Every sensor possesses a specific sensor range. Fig. 4-1 shows the realization in the prototype implementation where the sensors range is divided into three areas. The visual sensor detects objects in every sensor range. Tactile and gustatory modalities depend on interactions with the object in the nearest area. An object is defined by a composition of various sensor characteristics. In case the *object* stays in the most distant area (*Area 3*), the agent receives sensor data only from the vision sensor. For the example in Fig. 4-1, detected characteristics correspond to those of an *obstacle* or an *energy source*. When the agent approaches, it receives additional sensor characteristics and identifies the object as energy source. In order to add additional complexity to the scenario, additional variation of the vision sensor granularity is introduced. The sensory representation becomes more detailed in dependence to the distance between the agent and the detected object. This varies from detecting only rudimental characteristics in the form of *shape* and *color* up to the detection of individual gestures. The sensor detail level's approximate the natural characteristics of vision and induces an additional complexity in the decision making process. Anyway, various acts and action plans can be sorted out in case the distance between the agent and the object of interest decreases.

Bodily sensations are initialized by signals from organic sensors and by changes in the actuators' position and state. In ARSi10 the agent possesses a stomach that converts consumed food to energy and thereby provides divers forms of nutrition to the body. The stomach interfaces a *nutrition sensor*, an *energy consumption sensor*, and a *tension sensor*. The tension sensor informs the decision units about the current stomach fill level. The energy consumption sensor submits the stomach's energy requirements to the overall energy level. The nutrition sensor influences the energy level in dependence to the nutrition components that are placed in the food. Regarding ARSi10 the bodily sensations are formed by the stomach sensors and the actuator states. The interaction between the internal system and the homeostatic

Examined Solution

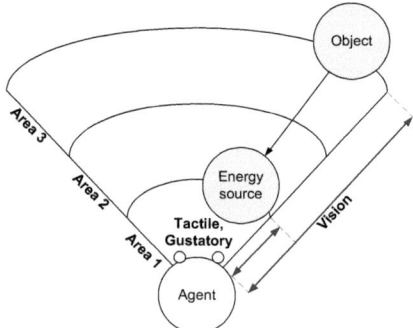

Fig. 4-1: External sensor system

The detail level of visual information decreases with the distance between the agent and a detected object. In this case, an object cannot be clearly identified as an energy source till the agent moves closer and it is located within area 1 of the field of vision. The agent additionally receives tactile and gustatory sensor information.

levels form a complex control loop that must be balanced by certain agent activities which are triggered by the decision making process.

The decision unit's output is used to drive actuators. The realized actuators enable the actions *move forward, turn left, turn right, eat, and seek*. These five actions form the agent's basic set of abilities and are processed by *action executors*.

In Section 3.3.2 the neuro-symbolic interface between the body and the decision unit is discussed. ARSi10 does not implement the neuro-symbolic layer and therefore passes through all the perceived sensor information to the decision unit. This procedure is adequate as the sensor information is read-out from detected Java objects and provides all required attributes like information about shape, color, and taste. Hence, the sensor information that is delivered by the *brain socket* (see Fig. 4-3) already has a level of detail that matches sub-unimodal and unimodal neuro-symbols. In case the neuro-symbolic layer is integrated to the BWsim, received object data must be de-symbolized. This step is disclaimed in ARSi10. The specification of sub-unimodal, unimodal and multimodal neuro-symbols provided by Velik et al. [VLBD08] determines that the information which is received by the sensor arrays already correspond to neuro-symbolic information. There, this work ties up. The implementation of the neuro-symbolic layer is not the topic of this work and is decided to be neglected for the evaluation of the proposed information representation system. This decision not only affects the *sensor-decision unit* interface but also the *decision unit-actuator* interface as the output is not de-symbolized as well. Action commands are mapped one to one to actuator control commands. The term actuator summarizes extremities and parts that provide facial expressions which are introduced to identify agents in the near distance.

Even though the ARS system takes the human being as archetype, it does not mean that the agent must be a human look alike. Only principles of the selected neurosciences (see Section 2.2) are assumed and transferred to computer science. As a first step the decision unit is not applied to the area of building automation systems, where the ARS project originates, but is realized in a software agent and tested in a multi-agent simulation toolkit. The agent implies principles of a life form, although these principles are strongly simplified. The reasons for these variations are the following:

- The ARS project does not have the aim to copy the human being.
- The controller must operate in an automation system that does not have much in common with the human being. However, the principles that let biological systems succeed in their daily life are promising for improving current and future automation systems.
- Issues regarding the ethical questions are limited[38].

In the following sections, the implementation is sketched by Unified Modeling Language (UML) class and sequence diagrams. UML is a standardized modeling language that is used in the area of software engineering. It is standardized by the International Organization for Standardization and International Electrotechnical Comission under the ISO/IEC 19501 standard [ISO05]. The notation style used is taken from the corresponding standards [uml09a] [uml09b]. Appendix A summarizes the graphical UML notations that are required for this work. Fig. 4-2 shows the class diagram for the ARSi10 agent. Every agent contains one complex body (*clsComplexBody*) and one decision unit (*clsDecisionUnit*). Only the agent that is controlled by the ARS decision unit (*clsARSi10*) has a complex body. Additionally, types of agents that represent food sources and enemies are introduced for the use case configuration. In contrast to the ARSi10 agent, they require only a restricted mass and variety of input data. Their decision unit does not possess the same functionalities and is based on simple if-then clauses instead. All decision units that are based on the class *clsDecisionUnit* are exchangeable as they are functionally decoupled from the agent body.

---

[38] Ethical questions always come up with the engineering use of biological mechanisms, especially when dealing with principles that are inspired by the human being. Even though a detailed discussion would exceed this work, though the influence of ethics to this work is given in Chapter 6.

Examined Solution

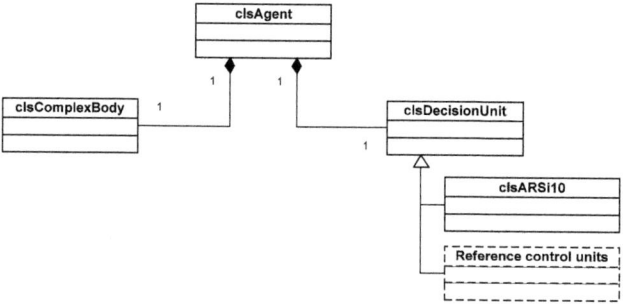

Fig. 4-2: ARSi10 agent structure

Every agent contains exactly one decision unit that either represents the ARSi10 decision unit or a reference controller which is used for the purpose of comparison.

Fig. 4-3 shows the UML class diagram of the complex body (*clsComplexBody*). The composed body systems that are represented by objects of the type *clsExternalIO* and *clsInternalIO* and introduce functionalities for internal and external interaction. The external component is divided to the external sensor array (*clsExternalSensor*) and an action processor (*clsActionProc*). The external sensor array detects the environmental state and bodily sensations and contains a set of sensors that introduces visual, gustatory and tactile abilities to ARSi10. In addition to the external and internal IO, the complex body contains a set of functionalities that is realized by internal systems (*clsInternalSystem*), intra-body systems (*clsIntraBodySystem*) and body-world systems (*clsBodyWorldSystem*). The internal systems implement slow messenger systems, fast messenger systems, and systems controlling body conditions like health-, stamina-, and stomach systems. The intra body and body-world systems enable the interaction between the internal systems. All three together are responsible

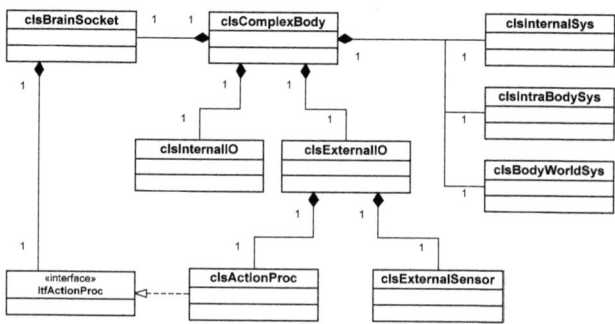

Fig. 4-3: Class structure of the complex body

110

for the bodily state. As this work does not focus on them, they are not discussed in more detail.

The class *clsBrainSocket* provides the interface between the body and the decision unit. This enables a decoupling of the decision unit from the body and its exchange by arbitrarily revisions and decision unit types. Hence, it is possible to compare the performance of different decision unit implementations for the same agent body and in identical environments. The socket receives sensor information from the body and forwards it to the decision unit. The other way round, it receives action commands from the decision unit and sends it to the action processor. The action processor controls the body's actuators. Therefore, it contains the interface *itfActionProc*. ARSi10 comes with the above defined basic set of actions. The brain socket forwards perceived data to the modules *E1*, *E10*, and *E12* (see Fig. 3-19) which represent the homeostatic-, the environmental- and the bodily sensor arrays. The modules *E2*, *E11*, *E13* are responsible for the neuro-symbolization of the incoming data. As discussed above, this layer is bypassed and the sensor data is directly forwarded to *E3* and *E14*.

The ARSi10 agent itself is represented as an instance of *clsEntity* that is the base class for any physical object which is placed within the simulation environment. Hence, obstacles, energy sources, and agents are entities as well. In Section 2.1 the requirements for embodiment are discussed, while they are listed in Section 2.4 with respect to an embodied software agent. The foundational prerequisite for embodiment is the physical interaction that

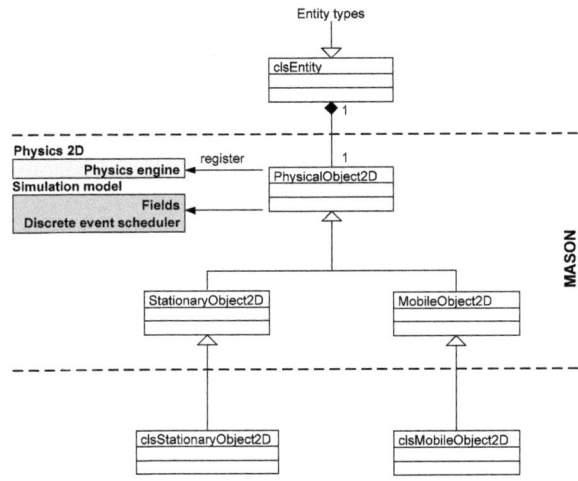

Fig. 4-4: UML class diagram of clsEntity

Examined Solution

leads to controversial discussions in the area regarding the claim that a software agent is embodied.

In the BWsim, physical dependencies are introduced by the MASON physics engine (Physics2D), which is optimized to provide physical rules for a two dimensional world. Any entity in the BW is a physical object and is registered at the *Physics2D*. As shown in Fig. 4-4, MASON provides a generalization of the class *PhysicalObject2D* to stationary (*StationaryObject2D*) and mobile objects (*MobileObject2D*). While the stationary object is immobile in the physics engine, the mobile object is moveable. Both classes are extended in the

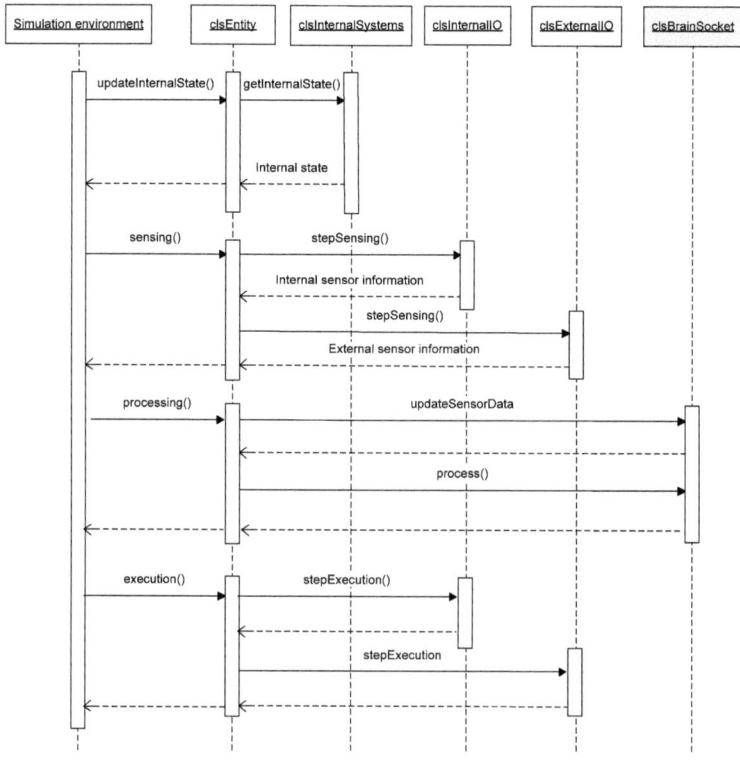

Fig. 4-5: Four phases of one simulation step in MASON

BWsim by *clsStationaryObject2D* and *clsMobileObject2D*. This has been done as the introduction of code changes to MASON are tend to be avoided.

As shown in Fig. 4-4 every entity must be registered at the *discrete event scheduler* that triggers an update of the object state with every simulation step. The localization within the simulation is done by a separation of the environment into *fields* of specific size. Every field registers its detected objects [LCRPS04]. This enables the discrete event scheduler to update their positions with every simulation step. The discrete event scheduler sequentially calls every entity for every simulation step. The step method is divided to four phases:

- Phase 1 – *Update the internal state*
- Phase 2 – *Sensing*
- Phase 3 – *Processing*
- Phase 4 – *Execution*

The UML sequence diagrams in Fig. 4-5 and Fig. 4-6 give an overview of the method calls. In *phase 1*, the states of the internal systems (*clsInternalSystems*) are updated. The term *internal system* summarizes internal system, intra-body system and the body-world system. The state changes result from interactions between these systems that are executed during the previous simulation step. When the update phase is completed, the sensing phase – *phase 2* – is initialized. The entity polls the internal and external IO interfaces in order to request data from the external and homeostatic sensor arrays. The perceived data is processed in

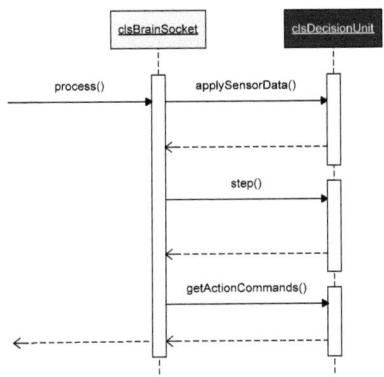

Fig. 4-6: Method calls during the process phase

phase 3. During the process phase, methods in *clsBrainSocket*, which represents the interface between the body and the decision unit, are invoked. First, the method *updateSensorData()* is invoked that forwards the perceived data to the decision unit. This input data is processed by the decision unit and results in action commands.

Fig. 4-6 shows the method calls during this phase in detail. First the method *applySensorData()* is invoked. It forwards data that is retrieved from the brain socket to the decision unit. Afterwards every decision unit module (see Fig. 3-19) is triggered by a *step()* method call. Finally, the generated action plan is transformed to action commands and retrieved by the brain socket. Afterwards *phase 4* is initialized that is started by the execution function call (see Fig. 4-5). It is responsible for the distribution of action commands to internal and external systems. First, the actuators are invoked and influence the environmental state. Second, physical forces are added to the BWsim entities and triggered by the physics engine after the step routines are finalized. Then the circle starts again at *phase 1*.

Summarized, the ARSi10 agent possesses a basic set of external- and internal systems as well as certain actuator abilities. These sensor and actuator systems belong to a physical body that is able to interact with the environment. The agent's decision unit is interfaced by the brain socket that manages the handover of data between the decision unit and the body (see Fig. 4-3). The received information is interpreted as sub-unimodal, unimodal and multimodal neuro-symbols and converted to *TPs*, *TPMs* and *drive demands*. The implementation of primary and secondary data structures is the subject of Section 4.2.

4.2 Realization of Primary and Secondary Data Structures

Section 3.2 discusses concept and model for a technical realization of psychoanalytically inspired data structures. Below their implementation into embodied software agents is discussed. It is differentiated between the methodology of describing the data structures in ontologies, storing them in a database (see Fig. 3-20), and their representation in a Java class structure. Data structures are realized as instances of classes that contain certain attributes and data-manipulation methods. Below the class structure as well as the manipulation processes are discussed.

While Section 3.2 explains the proposed data structure concept, Section 2.3.1 gives an overview of feasible techniques for a realization of knowledge bases. The differences between the groups of *neats* and *scruffies* as well as areas where their ideologies overlap are discussed. Even though the ARS approach is claimed to be closer to the scruffy approach, the proposed model is based on the technical expertise of both groups. The choice for a specific realization method is directed by data structure characteristics. The used tools must implement the following support:

1. Associative networks with the use of primary data structures as nodes
2. The declaration of node attributes
3. Search algorithms that are applied to a weighted network
4. The modeling of logic relations

The first three items aim at the use of associative networks and the frame approach, while the fourth item prefers the realization of a semantic net. Item 3 is not required for this work as the attribute association weights are static and set to the same level. However, it is a requirement for future implementations and therefore already considered for the realization in ARSi10. As discussed in Section 2.3.1 the knowledge frame and the semantic net approaches share various similarities regarding their creation of relational nets. Both areas will benefit from the continuous developments and achievements in the area of semantic web. Knowledge frames additionally support the assignment of properties to nodes. This fact contains an advantage regarding the definition of knowledge in the form of the proposed data structures. Regarding primary data structures, TPs, DMs, HMs, TPMs and TIs represent the nodes. Their edges are formed with associations. They are represented as frames themselves that include certain properties like associated data structures and an association weight. Regarding secondary data structures, WPs and acts form nodes that are linked to primary data structures by word presentation association objects. Secondary data structures string them together by *logic, action* and *temporal* relations. In ARSi10 WPs are represented by the object ID that is given by the ontology editor (see below). These IDs are set into relation by a basic set of *logic relations* (<, >, *to, or, and*). An extension of this set must be part of future work. The representation of WPs by *visual image for script* and *print, sound image*, and a *kinesthetic image* as it is proposed in Fig. 3-1, is not realized.

There exist a number of tools that support the design of ontologies which are based on frames and semantic nets. For ARSi10 it is decided to follow the frame approach and the use of the tool Protégé. This decision reasons in the similarities between the frame concept and object-oriented design. Protégé [InetProt] is a widely used ontology editor and knowledge base framework that is developed at the Stanford University School of Medicine by the Center for Biomedical Informatics Research. It is released under the Mozilla Public License version 1.1[39] and available for free. Its knowledge model is compatible with the Open

---

[39] Open source software license defined by the Mozilla foundation [InetMPL]

Examined Solution

Knowledge-Base Connectivity [CFF+98] protocol that defines an interface for accessing ontology repositories. Hence, Protégé allows the data exchange between different ontology repositories and increases the level of reusability. The application supports various storage formats like RDF and XML as well as a graphical user interface that eases the definition of knowledge. Beneath the ontology description in frame format, the editor supports OWL and provides a library that enables to integrate the ontology to a Java application. Protégé is released in two stable versions: versions 4.0.2 and 3.4.4. While version 4.0.2 brings only a partial support for OWL 2.0, version 3.4.4 is used for this work as it provides support for frames, OWL 1.0, and the general purpose language RDF (Resource Description Framework). It is possible to import project files defined with version 3.4.4 into Protégé 4.0.2.

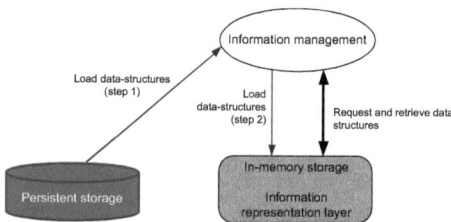

Fig. 4-7: Loading of knowledge from persistent storage to the information representation layer

A Protégé frame ontology is structured by *classes*, *slots*, and *facets* [NFM01] ontology is stored in a Protégé project file that is loaded at the simulation start to the *information representation layer*. It is also possible to export the ontology to an OWL or XML structure and load it from there. Fig. 4-7 sketches the loading process. The ontology that is stored in a Protégé project file is loaded by the ARSi10 *information management* unit at startup in two steps. In a first step stored data is retrieved from the persistent storage (step 1). Stored nodes and edges are mapped to Java objects and loaded to the main memory from where they are retrieved during runtime. Nodes and links are instantiated from their classes and accessed by the *information management*. In a second step the formed Java objects are sent to the in-memory storage. Even though the database is designed to cover the manipulation of stored data, the ARSi10 implementation does not realize this feedback to the database system. Hence, ontology changes during runtime are restricted in ARSi10. This step is justified due to the requirement for specific learning mechanisms that are not the focus of this thesis.

Fig. 4-8 shows the class structure that is proposed for the proposed information representation. The names of abstract classes are represented in italic font. The class *clsDataStructurePA* is the base class from which all data structures are inherited. "*PA*" stands for Psychoanalysis. The prefix "*cls*" is a notation to mark classes within the source code. Every Java object of the type *clsDataStructurePA* has attributes that specify a data structure identification, its value type and its content. The class *clsDataStructurePA* is directly extended by the abstract classes *clsPrimaryDS* and *clsSecondaryDS*. "*DS*" stands for data structure. They are differentiated by the interfaces that they realize.

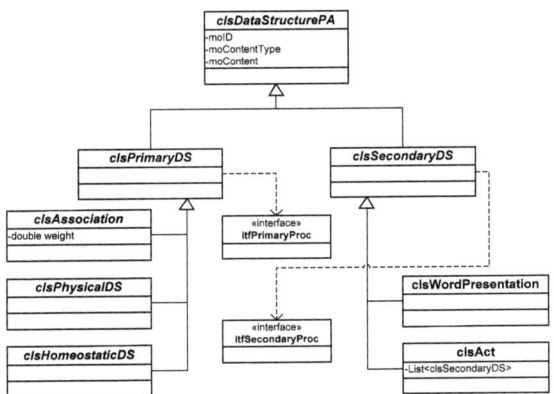

Fig. 4-8: Class diagram for the realization of the proposed information representation

Interfaces and modules, which are listed in Section 3.3, are either capable of handling primary data structures or secondary data structures. The category depends on the assignment of their functionality to the group of primary or secondary processes. The class *clsPrimaryDS* realizes *itfPrimaryProc* that marks the data structure as one that can be handled by primary processes only. Objects of type *clsSecondaryDS* are processed by decision unit modules that are based on the principle of secondary processes. Hence, this type of data structure realizes *itfSecondaryProc*. Both interfaces are introduced and described in [Lan10, p.94] in detail. Three abstract classes are extended from *clsPrimaryDS* that are categorized by the type of perceived information. Class *clsHomeostaticDS* forms the base class for all types of homeostatic data structures like DMs or affects. Class *clsPhysicalDS* defines the physical representation of entities and holds information perceived by the internal and external sensor system (*clsInternalIO* and *clsExternalIO* in Fig. 4-5). Class *clsAssociation* is the base class for *clsTemporalAssociation*, *clsAttributeAssociation*, *clsWordAssociation*, and *clsDriveMeshAssociation*. Fig. 4-13 and Fig. 4-14 give an overview of their specific realization.

Examined Solution

On the other hand, class *clsSecondaryDS* is extended by *clsWordPresentation* and *clsAct*. The class *clsWordPresentation* realizes the WP data structure. The content is defined by the *name* of the primary data structure with which the WP is associated. The class *clsAct* is defined by a list of secondary data structures. They define the act content by a combination of their content. Acts are used to select and evaluate upcoming system actions. As this thesis aims at showing the possibility of realizing psychoanalytic inspired data structures for an agent's control system basic planning abilities are implemented. In short, the act in ARSi10 includes a list of secondary data structures that define preconditions, an action (*action relation*), and consequences. Fig. 4-9 shows the structure of an act (see Section 3.2.2, p. 61) in a screenshot of the Protégé instance editor.

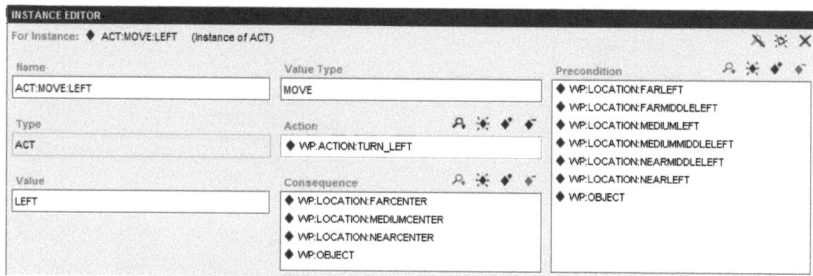

Fig. 4-9: Protégé instance editor view of act *MOVE:LEFT* (screenshot)

The example shows the act instance *ACT:MOVE:LEFT* that defines *precondition*, *action* and *consequence* which makes the agent to turn left (default value is set to 10 degree). Regarding the *precondition*, the entity (*WP:Object*) that should be reached must be on the left hand side of the field of vision. There exist six differentiations of the concept *LEFT* varying with the distance and the angle of the object in the field of vision. The *consequence* of the act is formed by its aim, which is in this case to have the object in the center of its view. This is reached by the *action TURN_LEFT*. The Protégé instance is mapped to a Java object by adding the different WPs to a list. *Precondition*, *action* and *consequence* are encoded to

```
ACT
||PRECONDITION||ENTITY|LOCATION:FARLEFT|LOCATION:FARMIDDLELEFT ...
||ACTION|ACTION:TURN_LEFT
||CONSEQUENCE|ENTITY|LOCATION:FARCENTER|LOCATION:MEDIUMCENTER ...
```

Fig. 4-10: String representation of an act

the act content in the form of a string object. The string representation for the instance in Fig. 4-9 is shown in Fig. 4-10.

During the simulation, micro-acts (see Section 3.2.2, p. 61) are combined to acts by the backward chaining[40] method. First, a micro-act is searched that holds the current goal as *consequence*. In case the retrieved micro-act does not define the current state as *precondition*, it is searched for an additional micro-act that completes the retrieved one. Therefore, the *consequence* of the latest retrieved micro-act is compared with the *preconditions* of other micro-act. Matching micro-acts are stringed together until the precondition of the whole act represents the agent's current state. This new act can be accomplished by the agent. A number of acts are introduced for ARSi10 in order to perform abilities that are required for the use cases that are discussed in Chapter 5. For ARSi10, the agent's abilities as well as the variety of logic, action, and temporal relations that an act possesses are limited. Temporal relations are introduced by a simple ordering of acts. The definition of durations upon the foundation of a time base is not part of ARSi10.

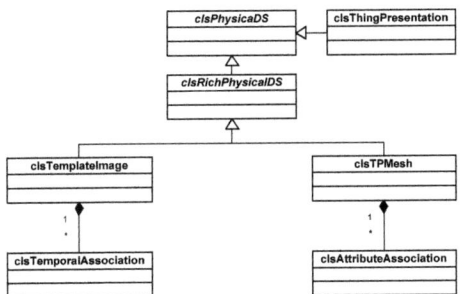

Fig. 4-11: Class diagram of *clsPhysicalDS*

Fig. 4-11 and Fig. 4-12 show the further division of *clsPhysicalDS* and *clsHomeostaticDS*. Class *clsPhysicalDS* forms an abstract base class for *clsThingPresentation* that introduces the atomic data structure TP to the model. The abstract class *clsPhysicalDS* is additionally extended by *clsBundeledPhysicalDS* that introduces data structure meshes as *clsTemplateImage* and *clsTPMesh*. Both own a list of associations as attribute. While *clsTemplateImage* is filled with associations from the type *clsTemporalAssociation*, the list in *clsTPMesh* is filled with associations of the type *clsAttributeAssociation*.

Pointed out in Fig. 4-14, the system's homeostatic representation is represented by *clsAffect*, *clsDriveMesh*, *clsHomeostaticMesh*, and *clsDriveDemand* that extend the class *clsHomeostaticRep*. In addition, every object of type *clsDriveMesh* or *clsHomeostaticMesh* owns ex-

---

[40] Inference algorithms that search backward from specified goals to facts by chaining through rules [RN03, p. 287].

Examined Solution

actly one instance of type *clsAffect* or *clsDriveDemand*. Their content is formed by a double value that defines the intensity of the particular homeostatic demand. Class *clsDriveMesh* additionally includes an array of double values that defines the categorizations of homeostatic demands that are proposed in [Lan10, p. 59].

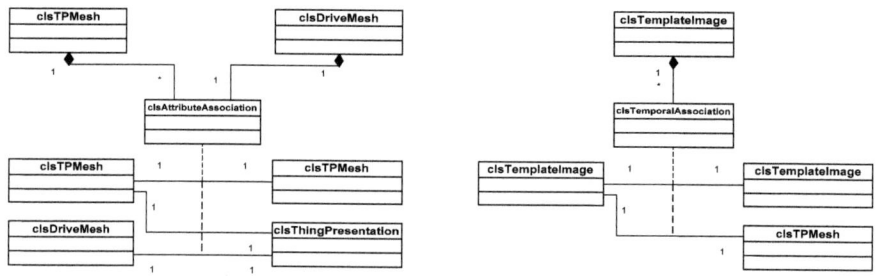

Fig. 4-13: Class diagrams of *clsAttributeAssociation* (left) and *clsTemporalAssociation* (right)

ARSi09 implies a simplified form of association that is not claimed to be psychoanalytically inspired [Lan10, p. 95]. In ARSi10, four types of associations are realized, which differ regarding the type of linked elements. Their theoretical background is defined in Section 3.2 and realized by association classes as shown in Fig. 4-13 and Fig. 4-14. Every association type includes exactly two objects that are linked with each other. As shown in Fig. 4-8, *clsAssociation* contains a weight that is predefined for ARSi10 as a learning mechanism is not realized.

As shown in Fig. 4-13, an attribute association connects TPs and TPMs to TPMs. They form bi-directional one to one links and are stored by *clsTPMesh*. In addition, objects of type *clsDriveMesh* are linked by an attribute association to a TP that represents the drive content. Hence, a DM owns exactly one attribute association.

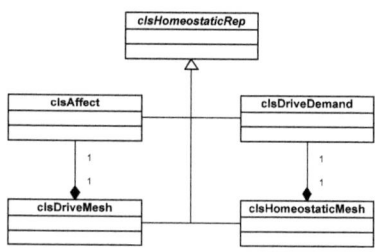

Fig. 4-12: Class diagram of *clsHomeostaticRep*

120

Temporal associations hold objects of the type *clsTemplateImage* and *clsTPMesh*. As stated in Section 3.2, TPMs and TIs are connected to a TI by a temporal association. The corresponding association class is shown in Fig. 4-13. TPMs that occur simultaneously are linked to the same TI (*clsTemplateImage*). It is possible to associate two objects of the type *clsTemplateImages* together in order to combine TIs together. While TPMs represent single physical objects, TIs represent the image of the current situation. An explicit time dependent association to TPs is restricted in ARSi10 as attribute associations implicitly include it. TPs

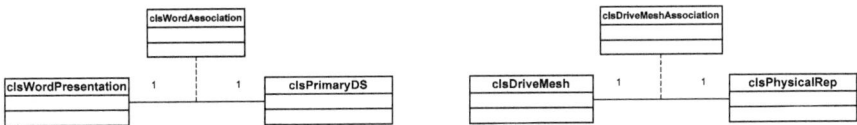

Fig. 4-14 Class diagrams of *clsWordAssociation* (left) and *clsDriveMeshAssociation* (right)

that are assigned to a TPM define an object and hence occur in parallel. An exceptional represents the occurrence of a single TP that does not belong to an object. In this case the TP is converted to a TPM with only one entry. However, the level of granularity regarding the temporal connection of sensor modalities is claimed to be sufficient at the level of TPMs for ARSi10. As is true of other association types, temporal associations are required for the activation process in order to trigger associated data structures.

Drive mesh associations (*clsDriveMeshAssociation*) are used to evaluate data structures that hold the physical representation of an object (TPMs, TIs and TPs). They are instances of *clsPhysicalRep*. Word presentation associations form the connection between primary data structures and secondary data structures. In theory it is possible to link one instance of *clsPhysicalRep* and *clsDriveSource* to a finite number of WPs and the other way round. Regarding language, an object may have different notations and one word may represent several types of objects. For ARSi10 this possibility is reduced to a bijective connection. Both types of associations are not part of another data structure as it is the case with attribute and temporal associations.

This section discusses the realization of the *information representation* concept that is proposed in Section 3.2. Any information that is processed by the agent is based on atomic information components that are formed by sensor data (TP, affect), their combinations (association), actuator commands (TP) or a predefined set of signs (WP). It must be differentiated between the way they are stored in persistent storage and the way they are presented during runtime. For ARSi10 the agent's knowledge base is defined on the base of knowledge frames by the use of the ontology editor Protégé. At startup, the ontology components are mapped to Java class objects. They are accessed by the *information management* module, which implements algorithms for the search and retrieval of data structures. The triggered results are manipulated by the ARS decision unit. ARSi10 extends ARSi09 by a bionically inspired *information representation* concept, a unified *information management system*, and required changes in the decision unit's interfaces. While this section focuses on the realization of the proposed *information representation* concept, Section 4.3 discusses the *information management* module's functionalities and the decision unit's interface structure.

4.3 ARSi10 Implementation

Fig. 3-19 shows the identified ARS decision unit functionalities. Every module has at least two interfaces that hold the input and output data. The modules are realized in terms of Java instances. As shown in Fig. 4-6, the decision unit is called once in every simulation step. Every module contains methods that execute the *receive*, *process* and *send* functionalities. When the decision unit processor (*clsProcessor*) is invoked, the *step()* method of all decision unit modules is called. This process starts at *E1* (see Fig. 3-19) and follows a predefined sequence up to *E32*.

The sequence diagram in Fig. 4-15 sketches this process. After triggering the *step()* method, the *process()*, *send()* and *receive_I1_1()* methods are called. The method *process()* manipulates the input data that is held by the module's interfaces following the functional task which is assigned to the decision unit module. The output data is forwarded to the output interfaces during the execution of the *send()* method. In Fig. 4-15, the *receive_I1_1()* method of module *E2* is called that concurrently follows *E1* in the step sequence. This triggers the reception of *E1*'s output by *E2*. Regarding the nomenclature of the *receive_I1_1()* method, "1_1" stands for the interface number. Every interface in Fig. 3-19 is realized by a *Java interface* that is implemented by the connected decision unit modules. Every ARS decision unit module extends the class *clsModuleBase* and is held by the container module (*clsModuleContainer*). The class *clsModuleBase* contains the methods *receive()*, *process()* and *send()*. The *module container* assigns decision unit modules regarding their affiliation to *function containers* that represent the different layers of the topological design (see Fig. 3-11). This approach is discussed by Lang in detail [Lan10, pp. 65-75].

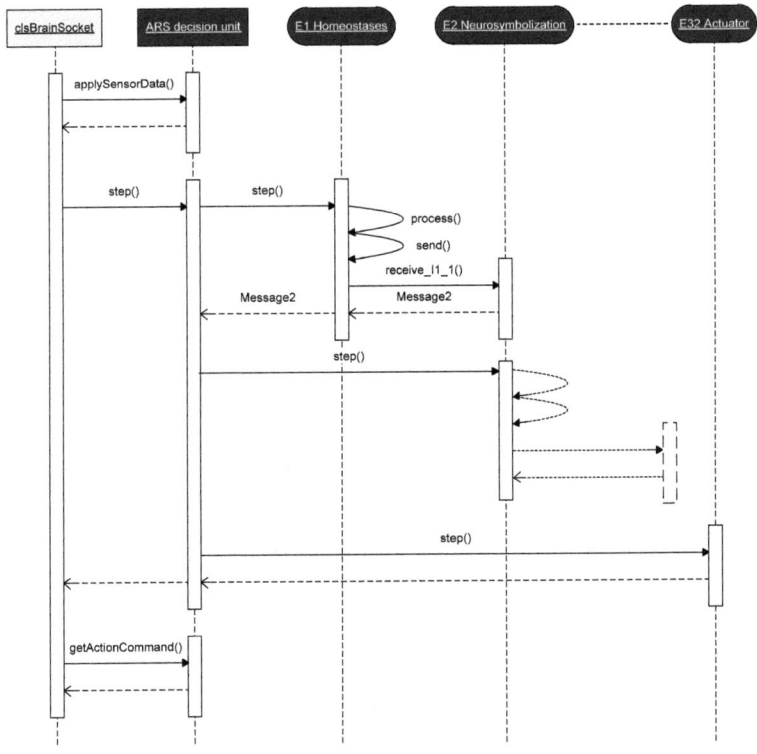

Fig. 4-15: Decision unit module calls during one simulation step

Besides the interfaces between the decision unit modules, the interfaces between the decision unit and the information representation layer must be discussed. In Section 3.4, concept and model are discussed. Fig. 3-22 lists the interfaces between the decision unit modules and the ARSi10 *information management* modules. ARSi10 differs from the proposed concept, as there is one common interface applied to the *information management* unit instead which is used by all decision unit modules.

Fig. 4-16 shows the class diagram of the information management's integration to ARSi10. The module container owns an instance of *clsInformationMgmt* that forms the interface to the underlying *information management system*. The class *clsInformationMgmt* serves as facade to the ARSi10 *information management module* and therefore decouples the *decision layer* from the *information system*. Hence, the decision unit modules need not to take care

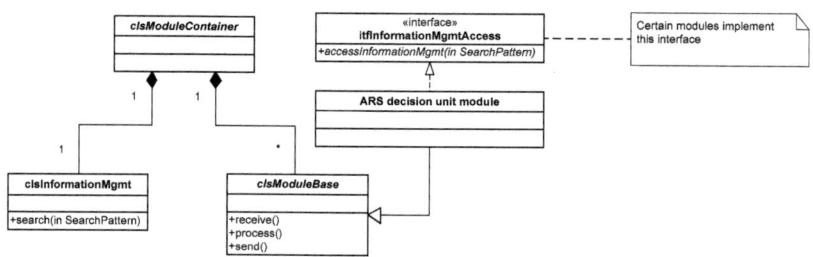

Fig. 4-16: *Information management system* class diagram

for the mechanisms in the *information management system*. This enables more flexibility for further developments. Revisions of the ARSi10 *information management system* can be developed independent from developments in the decision unit.

Every agent possesses one single *information management* instance. Decision unit modules that implement the interface *itfInformationMgmtAccess* are able to initiate a search space request by invoking the method *accessInformationMgmt(searchpattern)*. Section 3.4.1 lists these decision unit modules. Search patterns are defined by two components. First, unknown data structures are added whose correspondents are searched in the search space. Second, data structure types can be specified that additionally activate certain data structures which are associated to the search result.

Fig. 4-17 shows the sequence diagram of this process. A decision unit module invokes the *accessInformationMgmt(searchpattern)* method that initializes the search by calling *initMemorySearch (searchpattern)* in an instance of *clsInformationMgmt*. This retrieval process is executed by every module that implements the interface to the *information manage-*

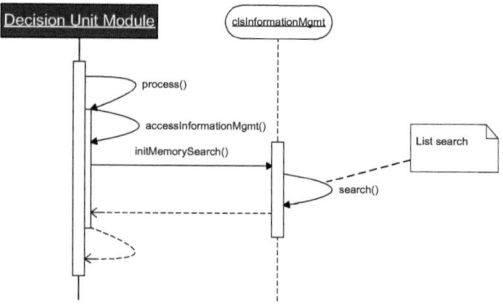

Fig. 4-17: *Information management* module method calls

ment system (see Fig. 3-22).

Fig. 4-18 defines the class structure of *clsInformationMgmtHandler* that is the super class of the ARSi10 *information management module* (*clsInformationMgmt*) which is designed to connect independent and fully decoupled knowledge systems to the ARS decision unit. For ARSi10, the *information management module* contains one instance of *clsSearchModuleContainer* and *clsSearchSpaceHandler*. Class *clsSearchModuleContainer* holds functionalities that implement different search algorithms with respect to processed data structure types. The search space handler owns a search space object that is extended from *clsSearchSpaceBase*. As it applies to the information management handler, the coupling is independent from the search space source either it is loaded from a database or a defined OWL file. In case of ARSi10 the Protégé ontology is loaded to a hash map where the data structures are ordered by their *type* and *value type*. While the search space is managed by the introduced handler, the search itself is accomplished within the modules that are extended from the *information management* module container.

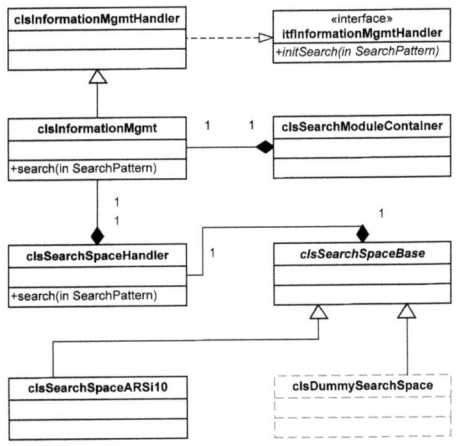

Fig. 4-18: Structural environment of the information management handler

The module container (*clsSearchModuleContainer*) is split into sub-modules according to the handled data structure types. This top-down design approach is adopted from the decision unit structure. As discussed in Section 3.4, the information representation management module is divided into the *secondary data structure management*, the *homeostatic perception management*, and the *external perception management* modules. Fig. 4-19 shows the corresponding class structure.

Examined Solution

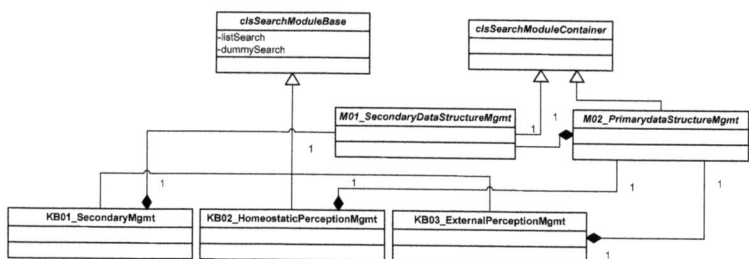

Fig. 4-19: Class diagram for the information management's search module

The module container is extended by *M01_SecondarydataStructureMgmt* and *M02_Primary-DataStructureMgmt*. M01 implements M02 and *KB01_SecondaryMgmt* that is inherited from the module base class *clsKBModuleBase*. The base class introduces the abstract search methods. They are realized by the deduced classes *KB01_SecondaryMgmt*, *KB02_InternalPerceptionMgmt* and *KB03_ExternalPerceptionMgmt*. *M01 contains KB01* that handles secondary data structures. In contrast, *M02* contains *KB02* and *KB03* which process primary data structures. In particular *KB02* manages homeostatic representations while *KB03* deals with externally perceived data structures. All modules integrate search mechanisms on their own that allow the adaptation to the particular data structure characteristics. For ARSi10 a list search algorithm is implemented that compares the search pattern with a list of stored data structures. In order to limit the list size, the objects of comparison are filtered by their data structure- and value types that are both member variables of *clsDataStructurePA*.

The search space is loaded at simulation startup from the specified Protégé ontology project file. Fig. 4-20 shows a screenshot from the Protégé's graphical user interface that sketches the defined class structure. Every class extends from the Protégé system class *:THING*. The introduced data structure types *TP*, *TPM*, *TI*, *WP*, *DM*, *ASSOCIATION*, *ACT* and *AFFECT* are inherited from it. The marked trunk shows the categorization of class *TPM* into its sub classes. As example, subclass *ENTITY* is highlighted that holds TPM as *value type* and is further divided into five entity types (bubble, can, wall, stone, cake).

In Fig. 4-21 the tree is expanded by instances of the node *BUBBLE* that is the name of the agent which holds the ARS control unit. Three different agents are identified. Fig. 4-22 shows the instance editor window of the agent with the *name TPM:ENTITY:BUBBLE:BUBBLE01*. The instance's *value type* as *ENTITY* and the value itself as *BUBBLE* are defined. In addition the frame slots *class association* and *instance association* are introduced. As discussed in Section 3.2.1, class associations bind data structures that are owned by the object type.

Examined Solution

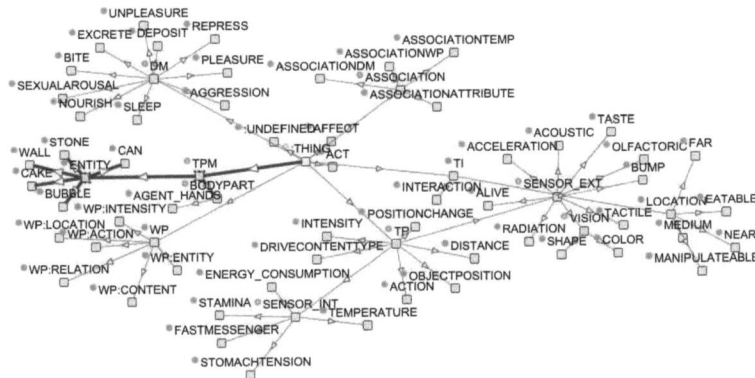

Fig. 4-20: ARSi10 Protégé ontology (screenshot)

For the example in Fig. 4-22 every bubble is defined by a shape in the form of a circle (*VISION:SHAPE:CIRCLE*), its antennas (*BODYPARTS:AGENT_ANTENNA:BASIC*) and hands (*BODYPARTS:AGENT_HANDS_BASIC*). Instance associations hold data structures that are individually different for every instance. In this case *BUBBLE01* includes an association to the TP that defines the color red (*COLOR_RED*).

Summarized, the tree in Fig. 4-20 can be split into the four atomic data structures TP, affect, WP and association. At startup, it is loaded by reading out the nodes by their data structure type and afterwards recursively initializing the tree leaves. Every data structure is loaded only once up to the search space. This means that a search space lookup is started before a data structure is created as there is a chance that it already exists due to the initialization of

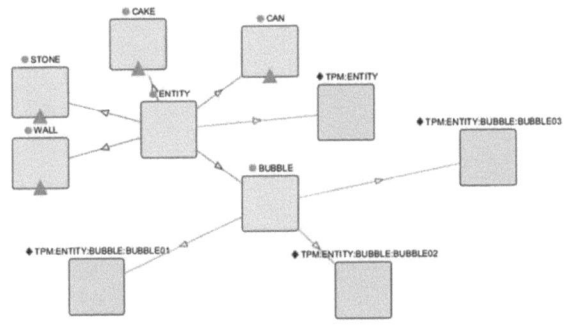

Fig. 4-21: ENTITY ontology structure (screenshot)

127

Examined Solution

another data structure mesh. The loaded objects are stored in a composition of hash maps. There, entries are ordered by *data structure type* and *value type*. This categorization allows selecting groups of data structures by the characteristics of the search patterns and therefore helps to limit the list size through which it searches.

In ARSi10 a *linear search* is used to accomplish the comparison process. It is a simple algorithm, but feasible for a prototype implementation. In case the search space increases, the arising costs exceeds the advantage of simplicity. The worst-case cost for using linear search on an unsorted list is $O(n)$ [41]. The variable n stands for the size of the input data set. The given Bachman-Landau notation indicates that the worst-case cost grows linearly and in direct proportion to n. Hence, the search space must be pre-filtered before the comparison process is started. In a first step, only data structures are added to the list which realize the same *data structure type* as the search pattern. In case the *value type* is known, the list can be additionally limited in its size while an identification number avoids the comparison process. A correspondence between data structure attributes result in an increasing *match factor*. Class associations are higher valuated than instance associations. The search result is retrieved to the decision unit in a list that is ordered by the match factor.

An alternative to the implementation of a search algorithm into *KB01_SecondaryMgmt* would be the use of the reasoning mechanism that is provided by the knowledge framework Protégé. It is useful in networks of logic relations where a search context must be provided and a simple data structure comparison brings unsatisfactory results. However, this works only for semantic net based ontologies that are not used in ARSi10. The integration into the

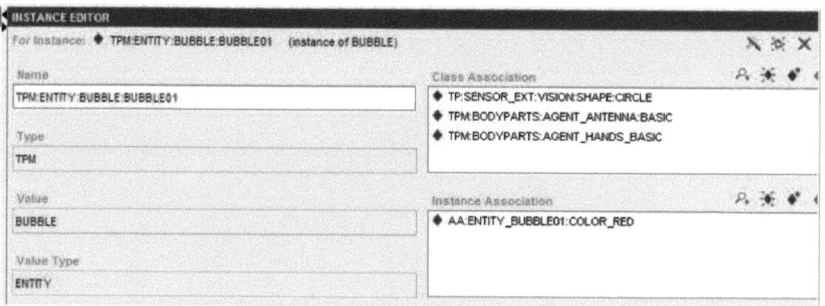

Fig. 4-22: Instance editor of BUBBLE01 (screenshot)

---

[41] The Bachman-Landau notation, or O-notation, is used to specify an upper bound on a function and applied to measure the worst-case running time of algorithms [CLRS03, pp. 44-45].

ARS project can be useful for an extension of action plans. At the current states, standard search algorithms are sufficient.

For ARSi10, association weights are introduced but remain static during runtime. Proper mechanisms for adapting data structures as well as the learning of new ones depend on the data structure types – primary or secondary. For ARSi10, loaded data structures are not changed within the search space during runtime though they are adapted and merged in the decision unit.

Above, the realization of the bionically inspired *information representation system* is given. Any information that is processed by the agent is based on at least one of the atomic data structures. They, in turn, are derived from sensor data and actuator commands. The model is implemented to an embodied software agent that is situated[42] in a game of artificial life. The simulator BWsim is based on the multi-agent toolkit MASON and is implemented in Java. The proposed implementation is labeled as ARSi10 and extends ARSi09 by a well-defined *information representation concept*, the *information management system* and interface adaptations in the decision layer.

In Chapter 5, use cases are introduced to verify ARSi10. Three critical points are thus identified which have great influence on the feasibility of the proposed model.

First, the definition of the data structures in the ontology and their handling by the information management modules affect the overall system performance; not in terms of speed, which is an incidental characteristic here, but in retrieving correct data structure matches. The introduction of a match factor helps to order the search results and helps to filter the required data structures. The differentiation between class associations and instance associations adds an additional differentiation to the process.

Second, it must be proven that the proposed data structure model provides the right data structures to close the gap between perceived raw sensor data and action plans with the ARS decision unit in between. The mapping of sensor data to primary data structures as well as the same process between primary data structures and secondary data structures are of specific interest as they represent the ties between data structures of different abstraction levels. This is also true for the transition from secondary data structures back to actuator commands.

Third, not only the generation of action plans out of sensory input is important but also the influence of predefined knowledge to the plan selection process. System engineers must

---

[42] Situated in this context means that the agent is embedded into its environment.

Examined Solution

define rules to avoid safety-critical system states. The integrity of these rules within the ARS decision unit is important for real world applications. The specification of WPs and acts intends to allow the inhibition or activation of specific input data.

These three points are part of the model examination in Chapter 5, where use cases are specified and their simulation results analyzed.

5. Simulation and Results

Chapter 3 provides the technical specification of a psychoanalytic model on *information processing* and *information representation* by going along with Premise 1 and therefore proves Hypothesis 1, both listed in Section 1.3. As it is stated in Chapter 1, the evaluation of the proposed *information management system* cannot be decoupled from the decision unit layer as the functionality of the overall system must be discussed in order to make a feasibility statement. First, it must be shown that the gap between sensory input and action plans can be closed by the proposed *information representation* concept. Every secondary data structure is derived from atomic primary data structures. Second, it must be proved that ARSi10 is not only equal to ARSi09 but leads to an explicit improve in functionality and flexibility. Here, the specific challenge is to store information in one single search space and structure it the way that required information is retrieved from it. In Chapters 3 and 4, these questions are handled in theory. Below, the developed model is tested in practice in a simulation of artificial life. Following Hypothesis 3 in Section 1.3, this is done by the integration into an embodied software agent and investigating the system's behavior with therefor specified use cases (Hypothesis 4).

5.1 Evaluation Toolkit

As discussed in Section 4.1, the BWsim simulation framework is based on a toolkit for multi-agent simulations called MASON. The world setup is inspired by M. Toda's *Fungus Eater* thought experiment. An agent is placed within an environment that assigns specific tasks to it and drives it to conflictive situations. The agent possesses certain actuator and sensor characteristics that can be used to solve these tasks. Sensors and actuators are available by a body that is grounded with a physics engine to physical laws. Even though a physics engine cannot replace realistic conditions, the provided physical dependencies are sufficient in a first step. It is not the aim of the simulation to prove the agent's abilities in a physical environment but its functionality and behavior in certain situations. Therefore a world-body interaction is required that in turn requires physical laws in a simple specificity. A simple

Simulation and Results

world setup is shown in Fig. 5-1. It consists out of an agent and an energy source. The agent is surrounded by circles that represent the sensor ranges, which differ in respect to the sensor type. The agent contains the ARS decision unit as controller. A simulated world is designed and configured in a way that confronts an embodied software agent with certain tasks. Within this artificial world the functionality of the ARSi10 *information representation system* is verified.

First, use cases are introduced that trigger certain agent functionalities. In Chapter 4 three objectives are specified whose compliance must be fulfilled by the use cases.

1. It must be shown that the *information representation* concept closes the gap between raw sensor data and action plans.
2. The functionality of the *information management system* must be verified.
3. It must be verified if rules can be integrated into the *information representation system* and in which way they influence the decision process.

These use cases must not exceed a certain complexity as the agent's functionality must remain traceable by observing only its behavior. Hence, the use case setup is limited to a minimum number of objects and agents.

Second, even though behavior must be traceable it is a tightrope walk to deduce between functionality and behavior. Hence, to prove the correct processing of sensed information a debugging tool in the form of inspectors is introduced. They are used for global measurement analysis as well as for the representation of information that circulates within the decision unit. Every module input and module output is provided with an inspector. A set of inspectors is provided that differ in the type of data that are visualized. They are categorized into three groups. The first summarizes certain data to tables and visualizes their static and textual content with Hypertext Markup Language. The second group uses charts to visualize their input values. They are applied in case dependencies between certain dimensions must be shown, as it is true for the internal sensor system. They are displayed by the use of the open source library JFreeChart that is available under the GNU/LGP license. The third group of inspectors visualizes dependencies in the form of tree structures. This kind of inspector is applied to the proposed ARSi10 data structures. The open source graph visualization tool JGraphX, also available under the GNU/LGP license, is used for this task. JGraphX is provided by its Java archive file[43] and is available by Version 6. Beneath displaying decision unit data, the inspectors are used to represent a global state like the per-

---

[43] Java archive files (jar) are used to distribute Java libraries and class libraries.

centage of consumed energy sources or the number of accomplished tasks. Especially the last value is used to evaluate the agent's performance.

ARSi09 [Lan10] has provided the first implementation of a psychoanalytic inspired decision unit for autonomous software agent. Hence, the possibility to merge neuropsychoanalytic concepts in a technical concept is approved and applied to a system controller. ARSi10 goes one step forward and unifies the data storage and *information representation* concept. Control units that are inspired by the multi-store model (see Section 2.3), differ by the type of information content and define a separate data storage for every type. In contrast, the ARSi10 *information representation* concept is realized in a single ontology without paying attention to the information content but only to the way it is represented. This leads to an *information representation system* that interconnects low-level sensor data with high-level[44] symbol sets. This concept is tested by the use cases, defined below.

5.2 Definition of Use Cases

Section 5.1 lists three objectives that must be fulfilled by the defined use cases. Regarding Objective 1, every use case presented in this work implicitly tests the functionality of the knowledge base and the interaction with the decision unit. There must not be introduced an extra use case. Objective 2 is handled in Use case 1. Basic agent functionalities as well as the reaction of the ARS decision unit to environmental changes and their influence on the agent's action plans are shown. Use case 2 satisfies Objective 3 and shows the influence of

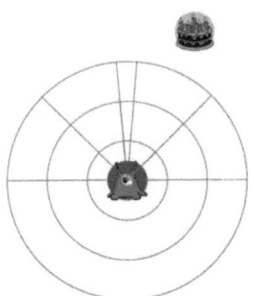

Fig. 5-1: Simulation setup for Use case 1

---

[44] The terms low and high are not mapped to different hierarchies but to the different types of processes that operate on data on different abstraction levels. Low-level data is processed by primary processes while secondary processes operate on high-level data.

rules (micro-acts) to the selection of action plans. The use cases do not introduce high-level social interactions between agents like communication or any kind of cooperation. They require a *system-environment* and a *body-decision unit* interaction instead which is based on the basic set of *sensors*, *actuators*, and *abilities*. At this stage of the simulator development, the basic functionalities must be verified in order to form the foundation for more AI focused objectives like navigation and learning. The feature that the detail-level of sensor information changes with varying sensor range, which is proposed in Section 4.1, is deactivated for the use cases as it is not required to fulfill Objectives 1 to 3.

5.2.1 Use Case 1

For satisfying Objective 1, the hierarchical way of information processing (sensor data to actuator commands) must be verified. This is done based on Use case 1 that is shown in Fig. 5-1. Its setup includes two objects, an ARS decision unit driven agent, and an energy source. The agent is visualized in the middle of the figure together with its sensor ranges, while the energy source can be seen in the upper right corner marked by a bitmap showing a cake. Any of the agent's actions require a certain amount of energy. Hence, it periodically runs low on energy and is driven by the demand to consume energy sources. The primary use case task is to deal with this requirement. The agent therefor requires a basic set of actions that is limited to the moves *MOVE_FORWARD*, *TURN_LEFT*, *TURN_RIGHT*, *SEEK*, and the object manipulating action *EAT*. In case no energy source is detected, the seeking action is triggered, which is a randomized call of the actions *MOVE_FORWARD* and

Fig. 5-2: Internal and external state (screenshot)

The current simulation setup is shown on the left while the outcome is shown on the right by the external data. The combination of slow messengers and fast messengers affects the demand to refill the energy sources. In this case the stomach tension and blood sugar level are already rather high (0.7, 0.55) and therefore represent a high demand for consuming an energy source.

Simulation and Results

TURN_RIGHT. The agent roams its environment in order to find an object that it can use for satisfying its internal requirements. Fig. 5-2 shows the energy source within the agent's field of vision on the left. The seeking procedure is rejected and the agent searches for a sequence of acts that enables it to reach the goal that is consuming the detected energy source. On the right currently received external and internal data is shown. An object is detected in the distance *FAR* to the agent towards the direction *MIDDLERIGHT*. This corresponds to the current position of the energy source within the sensor segments.

The internal sensor data gives an overview of the agent's homeostatic state that is defined by its health status, blood sugar, adrenalin, stomach tension and energy consumption. As it is discussed in Section 4.1 it is differentiated between slow messengers and fast messengers. All together form the homeostatic input to the decision unit. The slow messengers *blood sugar*, *adrenalin* and fast messenger *stomach tension* evaluate the agent's demand to refill its energy sources and are mapped to DMs as it is shown in Fig. 5-3. In short, both DMs represent the need to consume an energy source. The internal state of *energy consumption* implicitly triggers this demand while the *health system* affects different ways to satisfy it. The agent is initialized without any injury (100% health system) and a minimal energy consumption level (0.02 per simulation step). In case of increasing interaction with the environment, the chance to be harmed as well as the energy consumption increases. The current system requirements are defined and passed on to the subsequent modules. The internal data as shown in Fig. 5-2 on the right, are mapped to DMs labeled as NOURISH and BITE. Each contains a TPM that defines the *drive content* and an affect that marks the *intensity* of the demand. This process is discussed in detail by Lang et al. [Lan10] [LKZD10, pp. 715-721].

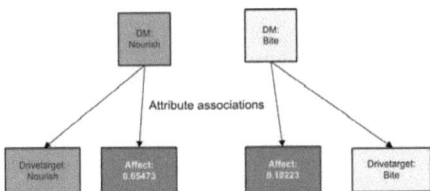

Fig. 5-3: Perceived homeostatic information (screenshot)

The external sensor data is converted to TPs and TPMs the way it is shown in Fig. 5-4. Up to this processing step the identity of the perceived object is not known. Its identity number is set to "*-1*" that characterizes data structures that are not compared to stored ones and therefore have not been identified yet. The perceived physical attributes are converted to TPs and TPMs whose *value type* and *value* are derived from the attribute characteristics. For the sit-

Simulation and Results

uation sketched in Fig. 5-2 the agent perceives an object of type *ENTITY* with the visual characteristics *SHAPETYPE* circle, a RGB[45] value for *COLOR*, and an *ALIVE* status false. This information is forwarded to the decision unit module E16 (see Fig. 3-19).

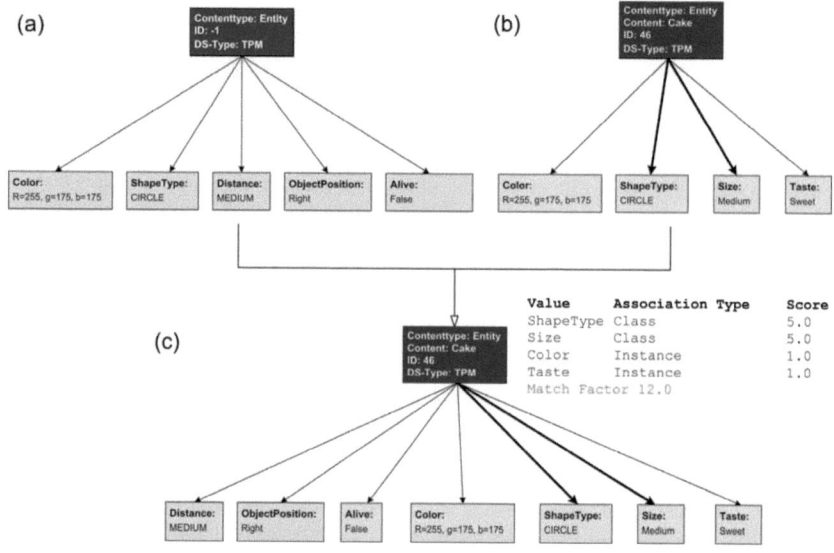

Fig. 5-4: Data structure manipulation in E16

Data structures in (a) and (b) are compared. There correspondence is evaluated by calculating a *match factor* that depends on the weights of the different associations. For ARSi10 it is differentiated between class and instance associations. A correspondence with class associations is higher weighted (5.0) than a correspondence with instance associations (1.0).

In Fig. 5-4 the knowledge representation of energy source (object cake) is compared with its sensory representation (see (a) and (b)). It is obvious that the sensory representation adds additional information like a *location* or an *alive* status information to the object. The different dash weight in (b) and (c) mark the differentiation regarding instance associations and class associations (thick dashes). This kind of information depends on the environmental situation, which is dynamic and cannot be stored to every object in the *information representation layer*. Hence, stored object information holds static characteristics that compose the object. Dynamic information like locational data is stored independent to an object in the form of TPs. As shown in Fig. 5-4(c), *E16* merges the input information and forwards it to the output.

---

[45] RGB represents the fraction of red, green and blue in a specific color.

1. The input object is compared with the stored data structures. The *information management system* retrieves a list of possible matches that are ordered by their match factor.

2. Additional information like locational data is send to the *information management* module in order to retrieve corresponding data structures. In case the search result list is not empty, its content is merged with the previously retrieved data. Otherwise, perceived sensor data is not known and therefore ignored.

3. In addition to dynamic sensory data, the perceived information is completed by stored homeostatic evaluations of objects in the form of associated DMs.

4. Any information that is forwarded to the subsequent modules has an identification number that is assigned by the *information management system*. This speeds up further data structure comparisons as not the whole attribute tree must be searched through but only those parts that are generated by the decision unit and therefore do not possess any identification number.

Before the conversion from primary to secondary data structures takes place, the current snapshot of perceived information is compared with stored images. These images merge information that coincidentally occurs and define similar content. For Use case 1 the similarity between distance and direction values defines a TI that represents an object location. A TI of the current situation is composed of multiple predefined TI. As a side effect, the number of perceived data structures is reduced. The formed image is forwarded to the modules E8 and E21 via I1.6 and I2.10 (see Fig. 3-19) where they are converted to secondary data structures. A request for the secondary data structure pendants of primary data structures is sent to the *information management system*. As the data structure identification numbers are already known, they do not must be identified and their associated WPs are directly read out of the search space. In Section 3.2.1 it is specified that for ARSi10 only a one to one association between primary data structures and WPs is realized. Hence, the returned list contains exactly one match for every search pattern. This data is forwarded to the subsequent modules.

There they are ordered by their affect intensities and the current homeostatic state. The decision for the current goal is influenced by theses evaluations. The goal deliberation process is broadly discussed by Lang [Lan10, pp. 107-111]. Summarized, the goal represents a homeostatic need that is elected by the decision making process to get satisfied. For Use case 1, this corresponds to the requirement to refill the agent's energy resource. Beneath the goal, also the current possibilities to accomplish this task are defined. An object is used to satisfy

Simulation and Results

an internal requirement. In case there does not exist an object that meets the current requirements, the seeking procedure is invoked and the agent roams its environment by randomly triggered moves (see Fig. 5-1). When an adequate object is detected, as it is the energy source in Fig. 5-2, the goal is combined with the object's status to a new WP and forwarded to the decision unit module *E28* (see Fig. 3-19). For the sketched situation, the new WP's content is a string object in a form that is shown in Fig. 5-5. For the string representation, ":", "|", and "||" are introduced as delimiters. The char ":" delimits *value type* and *value* of a data structure, "|" differentiates between associated data structures and "||" marks specific information groups, goal and current state in case of Fig. 5-5. In case more than one corresponding object is detected, a list of WPs is generated that includes the adapted WP content.

```
WP:GOAL|NOURISH||ENTITY:CAKE|LOCATION:FARRIGHT|NOURISH:HIGH
```

Fig. 5-5: Representation of the current goal

Delimiter: ":" *separates content and value type of a data structure;* "|" *separates data structures;* "||" *separates goal and object that is used for achieving the goal*

In the next step, the information management searches for acts whose consequence match with the *goal state*. This means that in a first step stored micro-acts and acts, whose actions lead to a satisfaction of the nourish drive, are retrieved. For Use case 1, a micro-act is activated that reaches the goal state by eating the detected object and therefore contains the action *EAT*. In order to accomplish an act, its precondition, which lists required objects or specific object positions, must be fulfilled.

Fig. 5-6 shows the micro-act that leads to the goal state in Use case 1. As precondition, the object of interest must be within the eatable area. In this configuration, the eatable area is within the gustatory sensor range (see Fig. 4-1). For BWsim, this distance is the lowest pos-

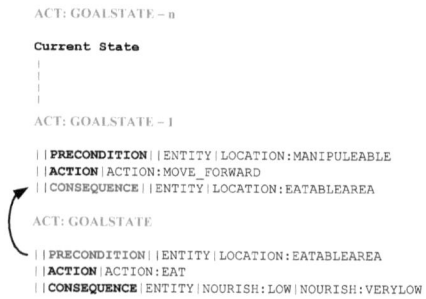

Fig. 5-6: Act generation process

Delimiter: ":"*separates content type and value type of a data structure;* "|" *separates associated data structures;* "||" *separates parts of the act*

sible one. In the next step, an act is searched whose consequence corresponds to the localization of the object within the eatable area. The corresponding micro-act is shown in Fig. 5-6 and labeled as ACT:GOALSTATE-1. The procedure is repeated n-times until the precondition of an act corresponds to the current state. In ARSi10 an exit condition is integrated that stops this process in order to avoid an endless loop. In case a result cannot be found, the seeking process is invoked again after a defined number of iterations. Only if every precondition is fulfilled an action is triggered. As mentioned in Section 4.3, act entries of the same type (e.g. LOCATION in ACT:GOALSTATE-1) are linked by a disjunction. The same object cannot be at two locations at the same time. Entries of the same condition type are linked by a conjunction. This makes perfect sense for the described use cases. However, it must be verified in future work if this implicit definition of logical relations is sufficient or if they must be explicitly introduced by additional WPs. Fig. 5-6 shows the generalized definition of acts. They possess a generic format that allows applying them to more than one object or more than one situation. For example, acts that define a locational change are decoupled from any restriction to a special entity type. Only the entity's position is important. Hence, no specific categorization of the required *ENTITY* is defined in the act in Fig. 5-6. On the other hand, some actions can only be accomplished by the use of specific entity types. Though, the generic *ENTITY* tag in the act entries must be replaced by the particular entity type.

The generated act-sequence is submitted to E27. In case more than one sequence leads to the goal state, they are evaluated in terms of the micro-act number that is directly mapped to the duration of the act. For ARSi10 the act with the shortest length is taken which is reasonable for Use case 1 but may turn up with challenges in case of more complex scenarios. The selected action sequence is converted to action commands, which are send to the actuator control and correspond to the content of the act's action entry. The same action commands are triggered as long as the next act's precondition is fulfilled. Table 5-1 summarizes the main processing steps by the ARS control unit within one single simulation step. The BWsim set-up corresponds to the situation shown in Fig. 5-2, Fig. 5-7(a) and Fig. 5-8(a).

Step	Layer	Module	Description
1	Decision Layer (PP: Primary Process)	E3, E14	1. External sensor data (see Fig. 5-2) is received in the form of neuro-symbols. 2. Conversion to psychoanalytic inspired data structures (affects and TPs). 3. The identification number is set to *minus 1*.
2	Decision Layer (PP)	E4-E5	The homeostatic input (TPs and affects) is merged to the DMs of type *nourish* and *bite*.
3	Decision Layer (PP)	E15	So-called *repressed content* in the form of DMs is added to the perceived input.

Simulation and Results

4	Decision Layer (PP)	E16	External information is forwarded to the *information management system*. In addition to search pattern matches, associated DMs are requested.
5	Information Management System	EPM	1. Search patterns are compared with stored information; the calculated match factor depends on the weights of class and instance associations 2. The search results are ordered by their match factor and retrieved to E16.
6	Decision Layer (PP)	E16	1. Best search result match replaces the corresponding input parameter (in this case the detected object is identified as *cake*). 2. Additional information that is familiar to the system but not part of the replaced data structures (e.g. *location*), are associated to the result (see Fig. 5-4). 3. The new formed TPMs have an identification number higher than zero.
7	Decision Layer (PP)	E17, E18	1. Identified TPMs are merged with repressed content (DMs) and homeostatic impact information about the particular TPM (retrieved from the information representation layer in Step 5) 2. This results in the homeostatic evaluation of externally perceived input.
8	Decision Layer (PP)	E6, E19	1. Perceived information is transformed to WPs. 2. Information is filtered with respect to their homeostatic evaluation. Homeostatic demands must exceed a threshold in order to pass the defense mechanisms. *For Use case 1 the detected energy source is associated with high effect on satisfying nourish and bite demands.*
9	Decision Layer (SP: Secondary Process)	E8, E21	1. Received data structures are merged to TIs with respect to their value type (e.g. location information like distance and angle). 2. Resulting TIs are assigned to the search pattern. 3. The search pattern additionally defines the requested data structure type that is associated to the search matches (WPs in this case).
10	Information Management System	EPM	1. The knowledge base is searched by the EPM for TIs that match the received search pattern; instance associations and class associations do not have an effect as temporal associations are not categorized into these groups. 2. Found matches and associated WPs are returned.
11	Decision Layer (SP)	E8, E21	E8 and E21 select the best matching search results and forward their associated WPs to E22, E23, E26, and E29.
12	Decision Layer (SP)	E23	Homeostatic and external perception is synchronized and ordered by priority (VERY LOW to VERY HIGH). *For Use case 1, the detected energy source takes the first position in this list*
13	Decision Layer (SP)	E26	1. The current goal is selected in dependence to the homeostatic input and prioritized external input. 2. For Fig. 5-1, a new formed WP includes the goal only. 3. For Fig. 5-2, the WP that is shown in Fig. 5-5 is generated and includes the goal and the current state *For Use case 1 the current goal is NOURISH while the Super-Ego rules are ignored*
14	Decision Layer (SP)	E28	Micro-acts are retrieved from the *information representation layer* for establishing an act

Simulation and Results

			(search pattern = goal state).
15	Information Management System	SDSM	Micro-acts are searched whose *consequence* corresponds to the *goal state*. The returned list is ordered by the match factor. The final filtering process is done by E28.
16	Decision Layer (SP)	E28	1. Retrieved micro-acts are compared with the current state. 2. An act is formed in an iterative process (see Fig. 5-6). 3. The resulting act is shown in Fig. 5-7 (left).
17	Decision Layer (SP)	E27	Actions are extracted from the act.
18	Decision Layer (SP)	E30	Actions (WPs) are converted to action commands (neuro-symbols) and sent to the actuator interface.

Table 5-1: Main steps for accomplishing Use case 1

Fig. 5-7 defines the steps that must be set to accomplish Use case 1. The complete act is shown on the left hand side as well as the corresponding simulator screenshots are shown on the right hand side. The act starts with the *initial situation* (a) and ends with the *goal state* (e). The rectangles represent the different states while the arrows in between define the actions that must be triggered. The action is repeated as long as the next state has been

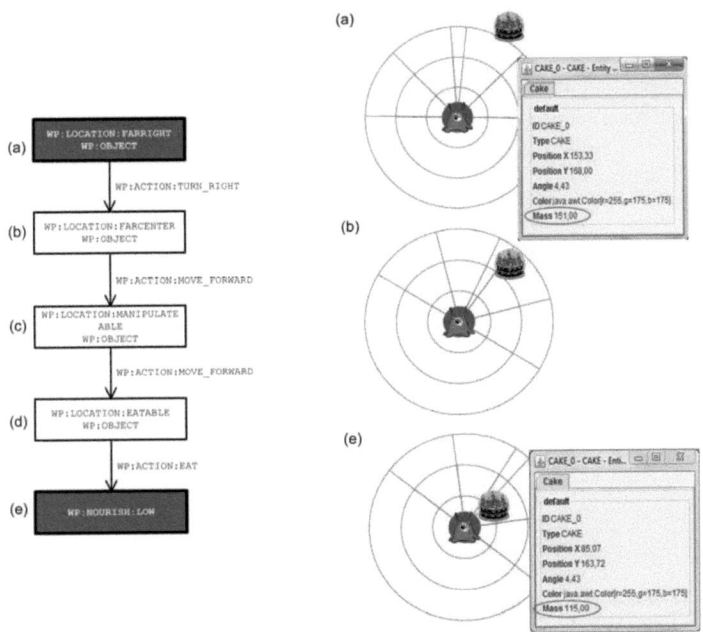

Fig. 5-7: Use case 1 (screenshot) – Action plan (left) and simulator screenshots (right)

141

reached. The agent starts at state (a) and decides to turn right in order to reach state (b). Afterwards the required object is in the center of its field of vision. In order to reach the detected entity, first the agent moves forward to the manipulable area and then goes on to the eatable area (see (c) and (d) on the left hand side). Now the precondition for ACT:GOALSTATE in Fig. 5-6 is reached as the energy source is located within the eatable area. Now, the action command EAT can be executed on it. In Fig. 5-7 (a) and (e) the energy source characteristics are additionally presented. It is shown that the energy source's mass is reduced in (e) after the invocation of the action *eat*.

The invoked actions influence the homeostatic state as it is represented in Fig. 5-8 that shows the gradient of the homeostatic requirements *nourish* and *bite* on the left. On the right, the corresponding action selection is represented. The x-axis marks the number of simulation steps while the y-axis lists the actions *SEEK, TURN_LEFT, TURN_RIGHT, MOVE_FORWARD* and *EAT* and defines their current activation level (0 for deactivated and 1 for activated). Only one action can be executed during a simulation step. Labels (a) to (e) in Fig. 5-8 correspond to the act-states marked in Fig. 5-7. In the beginning the nourish demand is on a medium level while the bite demand is rather low. In the course of the simulation both values increase and reach a maximum at state (d). Than the agent starts to eat the energy source (see Fig. 5-7 (e), Fig. 5-8 simulation step 162) which results in a sharp decline of the homeostatic demands between (d) to (e). The action state diagram in Fig. 5-8 shows this sequence in dependence to the simulation steps. After the energy source is detected, the

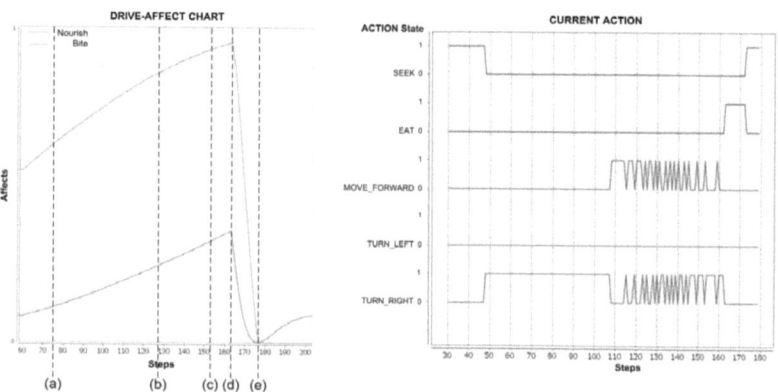

Fig. 5-8: Correlation between homeostatic demands and executed actions – Gradient for the homeostatic demands *nourish* and *bite* (screenshot) on the left, the current action state on the right

Simulation and Results

agent stops seeking and starts to turn right (around simulation step 50). At around simulation step 110 the energy source is located in front of the agent. From there on, the agent moves forward and alternately turns right in order to keep the object in the center of its field of view. After 160 simulation steps, the *EAT* action is activated and lasts for 15 steps. When the system's demands are satisfied, the seeking action restarts again. Fig. 5-7 and Fig. 5-8 show the correlation between the agent's internal demands, the environmental state, and the selection of goals and acts.

Use case 1 shows the feasibility of realizing the proposed *information representation* concept in combination with the ARS decision unit. External as well as internal sensor data are converted to primary data structures. After their comparison with stored data structures, they are associated with high-level information in the form of WPs and used to define and evaluate acts. This complies with the conditions to accomplish Objective 1 in Section 5.1. The agent is able to accomplish the given task by interacting with the environment, based on its set of abilities. ARSi10, hence, is the first implementation that provides a fully functional controller for autonomous agents that is inspired by neuropsychoanalytic information processing and *information representation* concepts. This applies to Objective 2 of this chapter.

5.2.2 Use Case 2

While Use case 1 verifies the basic control functionalities of ARSi10, Use case 2 goes one step further targeting directly at Objective 3 in Section 5.1. In addition to the knowledge that is required to form simple action plans, rules in terms of micro-acts are introduced which inhibit and enforce actions. Regarding Use case 2, rules are specified that are handled by the module E22 (see Fig. 3-19). This is important for the Super-Ego module's task that is to manage rules which specify boundary conditions for the system operation. Hence, this

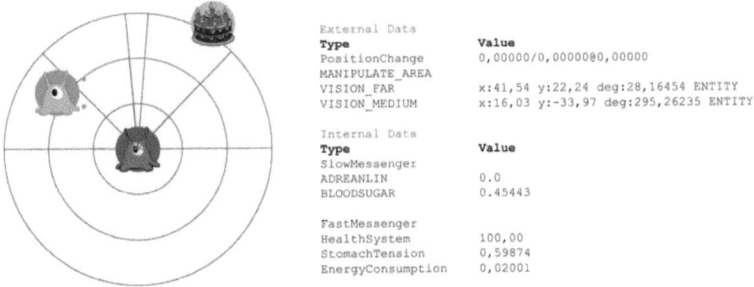

Fig. 5-9: Simulation setup for Use case 2 and internal/external sensor data(screenshot)

143

Simulation and Results

section verifies the rule structure and shows its activation as well as influence on the control unit.

Fig. 5-9 shows the setup for Use case 2. Use case 1 is extended by one *remote agent* that is placed left to the agent. A remote agent does not possess a decision unit and is controlled by a human being. However, the ARSi10 agent identifies it as one of its kind as both have the same body. While the agent's environment has changed in comparison to Use case 1, the basic task does not. It is still the aim of the agent to stay alive by refilling its energy resources in time. In contrast to Use case 1, two types of energy sources are available to fulfill the given task. Fig. 5-10 shows the perceived *environmental* and *bodily state* in terms of secondary data structures at the scenario startup. The presented WPs are sent by *E21* and *E8* to the Super-Ego module *E22* (see Fig. 3-19).

```
WP||BUBBLE:ARSINO|LOCATION:MEDIUMLEFT|NOURISH:HIGH
WP||ENTITY:CAKE|LOCATION:FARRIGHT|NOURISH:HIGH
WP||NOURISH:MEDIUM
WP||BITE:MEDIUM
```

Fig. 5-10: Input of Super-Ego module E22
Delimiter: ":" *separates content type and value type of a data structure;* "|" *separates associated data structures;* "||" *separates data structure type from content*

Simulation and Results

The agent in the middle of Fig. 5-9 detects a *cake* at the far right and an additional agent on the left hand side within medium distance. The agent is labeled *ARSINO*. Both detected entities have high effect on the energy level. In *E26* (see Fig. 3-19) the current goal is selected

```
ACT:
||PRECONDITION|ENTITY:BUBBLE|LOCATION:EATABLEAREA
||ACTION|ACTION:EAT
||CONSEQUENCE|ENTITY:BUBBLE|PLEASURE:VERYLOW|NOURISH:LOW
```

Fig. 5-12: Super-Ego rule (micro-act)

Delimiter: ":" *separates content type and value type of a data structure;* "|" *separates associated data structures;* "||" *separates different parts of the act*

based on the state that is presented in Fig. 5-10. The goal selection leads to a verification of possible action plans that invokes actuator commands. As this process is already discussed for Use case 1, it is not shown here. The accomplished actions are summarized in Fig. 5-11. The decision for an energy source aims at the most effective way, which is in this case the fastest way, to satisfy the energy requirement. As the ARSi10 driven agent is closer to the remote agent than to the cake, the shortest action plan leads to the consumption of the remote agent and is selected therefore. Hence, the agent turns left (Fig. 5-11 (a)), moves forward and eats the remote agent (Fig. 5-11 (b)).

For the second simulation run, which is shown in Fig. 5-14, a rule is introduced whose task is the limitation of the number of potential energy sources to one. This is guaranteed by the micro-act that is shown in Fig. 5-12. The micro-act in Fig. 5-12 specifies a Super-Ego rule that avoids considering the remote agent as an energy source. Rules are specified by micro-acts and therefore contain preconditions, action and consequences. Super-Ego rules in particular evaluate the level of *pleasure* that results out of a specific act represents the main difference to micro-acts that are used to form an action plan. The Super-Ego rule in Fig. 5-12 additional-

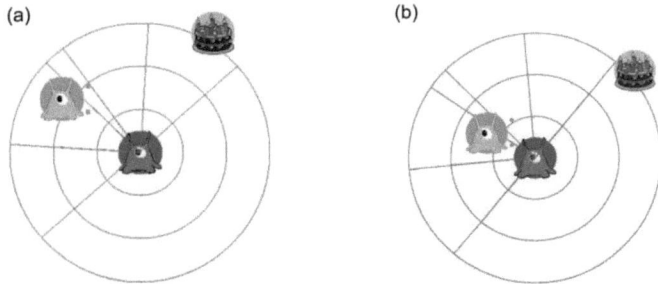

Fig. 5-11: Use case 2 without Super-Ego rule (screenshot)

Simulation and Results

ly introduces limitations regarding the type of entity. In this case, the rule applies to entities

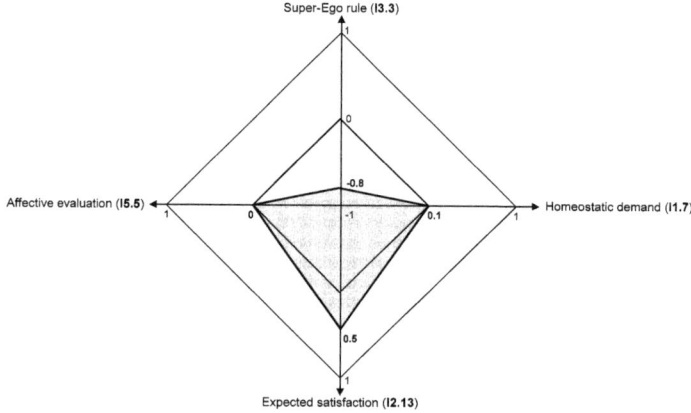

Fig. 5-13: Aggregation of individual input data of *E26*

of the type *BUBBLE*. As the remote agent belongs to this group, the rule is applied to it.

The defined rule is retrieved from the *information management system* and evaluates the consumption of an agent for satisfying the *NOURISH* demand with very high unpleasure (*PLEASURE:VERYLOW*). The information is processed by the Super-Ego module *E22* that maps its input, shown in Fig. 5-10, to the retrieved rules. For this particular scenario, information about the perceived agent is compared with the *precondition* in Fig. 5-12. As both match, the rule is activated and forwarded to the decision making module (*E26* in Fig. 3-19).

E26 selects a goal with respect to *environmental information*, *bodily information*, *affective evaluation of the situation* and *Super-Ego rules*. Fig. 5-13 shows the correlation of these four input parameters. The discreet values *very low, low, medium, high, very high* are mapped to the intervals

[-1, -0.75[, [-0.75, -0.25[, [-0.25, 0.25[, [0.25, 0.75[, [0.75, 1.0].

The exact value is randomly assigned. For the startup conditions in Use case 2, the expected satisfaction (see Fig. 5-10) is assigned to 0.5 (*high*), the impact of the Super-Ego rule (see Fig. 5-12) is assigned to -0.8 (*very high*) while the other parameters have a *medium* impact factor and are assigned to 0.0 and 0.1 (see Fig. 5-13). These factors (α) are used to calculate the weight $g_k(\omega)$ (see Equation 5-2) for the goals that are received by I2.13. Equation 5-1 shows the normalization of the factors α with respect to the number of input parameters (n). Index k labels the goal while index i labels the specific input parameter.

$$\varpi_{k_i} = \frac{\alpha_{k_i}}{n} \quad \forall \alpha_{k_i} \in [-1,1] \wedge n \in \mathbb{N} \tag{5-1}$$

$$g_k(\varpi) = \sum_{i=1}^{n} \varpi_{k_i} \quad \forall \varpi_{k_i} \in [-1,1] \wedge n, i \in \mathbb{N} \,\Big|\, \Big|\sum_{i=1}^{n} \varpi_{k_i}\Big| \leq 1 \tag{5-2}$$

$$g_k(\varpi) \geq g_{th}(\varpi) \wedge g_{th}(\varpi) \geq 0 \tag{5-3}$$

This concept is inspired by Lang [Lan10, p. 109] and Engel [Eng10, p. 48] but has had to be adapted to the ARSi10 concept of rules. In case the above-mentioned values are applied to the equations 5-1 and 5-2, the goal of discharging the requirement *nourish* by consuming the remote agent is evaluated with *minus 0.05*. As these calculations result in a *negative* value, the information that ARSINO can be used to satisfy the *nourish requirement* is discarded as the threshold value $g_{th}(\omega)$ for considering goals is set to zero (see Equation 5.3). Hence, the remote agent is not considered for the generation of action plans. The entity *cake* is the last remaining object that is able to refill the agent's energy resources. Fig. 5-14 shows the impact on Use case 2. In Fig. 5-14(a), the agent ignores the remote agent. Even though it is closer to the agent it turns right towards the cake. Afterwards it moves on to the cake and consumes it (Fig. 5-14(b)).

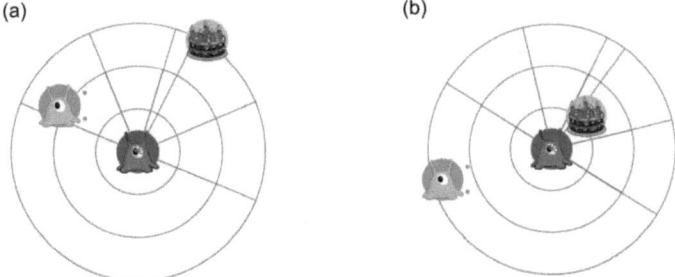

Fig. 5-14: Use case 2 with activated Super-Ego rule

The weight of a Super-Ego rule is defined by the level of *pleasure* that is specified as *consequence*. Hence, the possibility that a Super-Ego rule is considered varies with the simulation setup. In case the cake is not placed within the sensor range and the agent is *very low* on energy, the requirement to satisfy the homeostatic state gets very high. As a consequence, the expected level of unpleasure is lower than the current requirement. Hence, the remote agent is not ignored but incorporated to the definition of action plans. This particular scenario leads to a consumption of the *remote agent*, even though the Super-Ego rule is still active. Hence, it is possible to define rules with a different level of priority and allow a system en-

Simulation and Results

gineer to differentiate between non safety-critical (bids) and safety-critical (bans) rules. Table 5-2 summarizes the influence of Super-Ego rules to the decision making process.

Step	Layer	Module	Description
1	Decision Layer (SP: *Secondary Process*)	E22	1. Internal and external information is matched regarding their associated DMs. 2. External information in the form of TIs is defined as search pattern and micro-acts are requested from the *information management system*. For Use case 2 the homeostatic requirement nourish is matched with the detected energy source.
2	Information Management System	SDSM	Received TIs are compared with stored micro-acts (*preconditions* and *consequence states*)
3	Decision Layer (SP)	E22	1. Returned micro-acts are investigated. 2. Micro-acts whose consequence tags contain *PLEASURE* tags are extracted. 3. The current homeostatic state (WP) is compared with the *consequence* states of extracted rules. 4. Externally perceived information is compared with the *preconditions* of extracted rules. 5. Corresponding matches from 3. and 4. are loaded to a list and forwarded to E26.
4	Decision Layer (SP)	E26	1. Homeostatic input is compared with prioritized external input. 2. Received Super-Ego rules are incorporated; level of *UNPLEASURE* and *PLEASURE* is compared with homeostatic demands and the capability of externally perceived objects to satisfy them. 3. In case the level of expected unpleasure is higher than the expected satisfaction of the corresponding homeostatic demand, one possible way to reach the goal is blocked. As a consequence the possibility to satisfy the nourish demand by consuming the detected agent is blocked (see Fig. 5-14).

Table 5-2: Influence of Super-Ego rules on the decision making process

The realization of the proposed bionically inspired *information representation system* leads to the ARSi10 controller for autonomous software agents. Two use cases are defined that aim at the objectives which are listed in Section 5.1. Both use cases verify the information representation layer functionalities and therefore handle Objective 2. It is shown that the differentiation between *instance associations* and *class associations* allow a steady identification of detected objects regarding the current knowledge base dimensions. The selection of the requested data structure type can be individually adapted.

Even though both use cases adhere to Objective 1, it is discussed based on Use case 1 in detail by dividing one specific action sequence to five snapshots (see Fig. 5-7) and combining it with the analyzes of one single simulation step (see Table 5-1). It is shown that the pro-

Simulation and Results

posed *information representation* provides data structures that enable to convert homeostatic and external sensor data to semantic symbols, merge them to images in order to reduce the amount of input data, and transfer them to secondary data structures. Especially the conversion between primary and secondary data structures poses a challenge as the corresponding processes are based on completely different principles. Obtained secondary data structures are used to reason about goals and plans and result in action commands. Hence, it is shown that Objective 1 is accomplished.

Table 5-3 lists all defined interfaces between the *decision layer* and the *information representation layer*. The *requirement level* defines the interfaces that are required for a minimal reasonable functionality and therefore to accomplish Use case 1. The decision unit modules *E8*, *E16*, *E21*, and *E28* (see Fig. 3-19) hold a minimum required interface and implement at least the basic information processing functionality (implementation state) as well. Otherwise retrieved data structures would not be feasibly manipulated which inhibits the decision making process. Fig. 5-15 shows the outcome in case any of the mandatory information representation layer accesses are deactivated. *E22* is not required for accomplishing Use case 1 and therefore introduces additional functionality by means of Super-Ego rules.

Module	Implementation status	Requirement level	Impact
E8	Active	Mandatory	Executes the conversion of primary data structures to secondary data structures. In case IR-I 1.9 and IR-I 1.10 are deactivated the conversion is inhibited. Externally perceived data could not be evaluated and prioritized by homeostatic information. The decision making process could not define a goal, therefore an action plan cannot be defined. Hence, the agent accomplishes the seeking action (see Fig. 5-15).
E16	Active	Mandatory	In case IR-I 1.5 and IR-I 1.6 are disabled, externally perceived information cannot be compared with stored knowledge and therefore remains unidentified and cannot be interpreted. External information gets lost and a decision making is impossible.
E21	Active	Mandatory	As E8 it converts primary to secondary data structures. In this case externally perceived data is converted. By disabling IR-I 1.11 and IR-I 1.12, WPs cannot be retrieved and not all subsequent modules possess information about the environment. The decision making process does not result in a goal. The seeking action is activated (see Fig. 5-15).
E28	Active	Mandatory	By deactivating IR-I 2.8 and IR-I 2.7, action plans cannot be defined as micro-acts cannot be retrieved from the data storage. As for the other mandatory interfaces, a deactivation leads to a behavior as shown in Fig. 5-15.
E22	Active	Additional	Super-Ego rules are used by the decision making process but are not mandatory for the basic model functionality. They enable additional evaluation mechanisms as it is described for Use case 2. The action state diagram is similar to the one that is shown in Fig. 5-8. However for

Simulation and Results

				a larger and more crowded environment the phases between eat actions become longer on average as the possibility to find an adequate energy source is reduced.
E7, E9, E25, E34	Inactive		Additional	See below

Table 5-3: Active and inactive information representation layer access

The impact of Super-Ego rules to the decision making process is shown in Use case 2. Rules are modeled in the form of micro-acts and are stored in the same search space as any other type of acts. The *consequence* state in Super-Ego rules contains a specific attribute that holds the expected pleasure level. Apart from that attribute, rules (facts) are not differentiated from experiences as it is done for the multi-store approach. In ARSi10 both types of information are stored in acts. The feasibility of defining rules by the use of the proposed *information representation* concept is shown as well as their usage is proved. Hence, Objective 3 is considered as accomplished.

As it is listed in Table 5-3, the access to the information representation layer of the decision unit modules *E7*, *E9*, *E25* and *E34* (see Fig. 3-19) is not mandatory. In addition, they are not realized in ARSi10. Their impact to the overall system is discussed below in order to elaborate a focus for future implementations.

Super-Ego (primary proc.) – E7

E7 deals with restrictions that arise due to social interactions that do not exist in the current BWsim. While these restrictions are factored into the ARSi10 *information representation* design the current use cases do not support them as the first step is to verify basic functionalities. Any type of social interaction introduces additional complexity to the implementation and the verification process. Without these interactions, *E7* lacks on any influence to the decision making process and is deactivated therefore.

Knowledge about reality (primary proc.) – E9

E9 is deactivated in ARSi10 as it deals with the handling of system demands in case of failing system abilities. However, for ARSi10 an operative system is expected and *E9* is currently not required. It must be verified if the decision unit can get along without *E9* for further revisions of the ARS decision unit in a simulated world. An activation would require the definition of an additional failure model that does not have an additional value except for the realization in a real world application. Therefore, its functionality depends on hardware malfunctions and the activation of E9 could be an advantage. The required knowledge must be implemented by the system engineer in advance.

Simulation and Results

Knowledge about reality 1 and 2 – E25, E34

The modules *E25* and *E34* depend on the development level of *E24* and *E33*. For ARSi10 both reality check modules are deactivated and map input to output data without manipulating it. Apart from that the *information representation system* supports this kind of rules as they do not differ from the Super-Ego rules which are processed by *E22*. As for *E7* rules, the basic use cases do not require knowledge about reality rules.

From the author's point of view currently deactivated modules and *information management* interfaces are not required for accomplishing basic functionalities. However, the ARS project aims at interactions between systems as well. Hence, it makes sense to consider them in future realizations and use case definitions. Those may base on an own language or on the use of acts like attacking or fleeing. Currently deactivated modules and interfaces must be activated for that.

Summarized, the proposed *information representation system* is implemented into an embodied software agent. It enables the ARSi10 agent to operate in observance of the environmental, homeostatic and bodily state as well as stored knowledge. This satisfies hypotheses 3 and 4 in Section 1.3. Functionalities are based on the same data structure principle. These principles are deduced from the same theories as the ARS decision unit. In Section

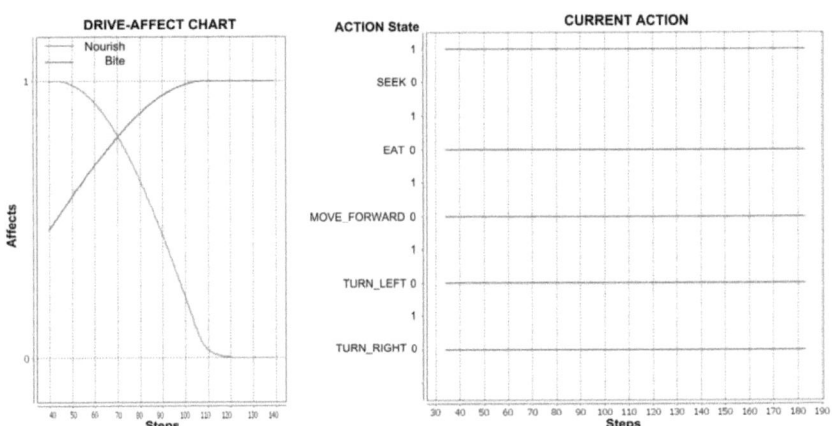

Fig. 5-15: Drive-affect chart and current action state

In case one or more minimum required interfaces between the decision layer and the *information representation layer* (see Table 5-3) are deactivated, the agent is not able to fulfil its task. As long as it does not run out of energy, the nourish and bite demands evolve towards a static level (see on the left, step 110). As it is impossible to identify or derive stored acts, the agent activates the *default* act (*SEEK*) and executes it for the whole simulation run (see on the right).

151

Simulation and Results

1.3 the *decision layer* is decoupled from the *information representation layer*. This is not common for bionically inspired control units in autonomous agents.

Memory based control structures as SOAR and ACT-R, which are discussed in Section 2.3.2, mix functional and informational structures. They focus on the definition of knowledge and define a set of operators for manipulating this data. Contrarily, the ARS model is designed with a balance between stored knowledge and functional modules in mind. There is a clear differentiation between the functional description and stored data that is compared to input data. The underlying theories, which also support this distinction, are thus observed.

The aspects of data structures are discussed theoretically first and hence allow a conceptual technical design. Only then is the incorporation of information and mechanisms specified. Information and functional model share the same underlying theory. The technical model is completely based upon bionics. Lastly, the feasibility of this concept is shown by the use cases above.

ARSi10 covers the conversion and filtering of sensor data up to the definition and selection of action plans, as well as the introduction of environmental and social rules. The proposed model introduces adaptable data structures that merge low-level sensor signals from three different sources with stored knowledge and convert them to actuator commands. In order to reduce the amount of data, TPs are bound to TPMs and TIs with respect to their associative context. The conversion to secondary data structures introduces temporal and logical relations that lead to the generation of action plans by combining predefined acts. In ARSi10 the shortest plan is carried out. This simple assumption is feasible for the discussed use cases, even though it must be rethought in case the planning mechanisms are extended to allow higher complexity in the selection process. The differentiation between primary and secondary data structures allows an optimization of their composition regarding the specific functional definitions. This is done by categorization into homeostatic, physical, and secondary representation that leaves space open for further optimizations due to different types of incorporated associative data structures. In fact, the introduction of primary and secondary data structures allows the use of different concepts regarding the definition of knowledge (semantic nets vs. frame structure) and search mechanisms.

ARSi10 represents the first implementation that realizes principles of human-like information representation and information processing in one technical model. This fusion of psychoanalytically inspired data structures and the ARS decision unit's functions is shown in the use cases above. The underlying findings are transferred to a technical specification in extensive interdisciplinary work. This allows extension of the model by future neuroscientific findings, an advantage that would be lost were the theories interpreted by engineers only.

The discussed use cases are configured to prove the functionality of the identified concept. Implementation details like search or planning algorithms must be evaluated in comparison to alternative AI technologies. They leave space for the improvement of system performance in their current state, but this has no effects on the fundamental concept of the model. While Chapter 5 proves the feasibility of the proposed model, Chapter 6 gives a conclusion and prospects for further research and refinement.

"Trust me, everything's gonna be fine."

[Edward Norton as narrator – Fight Club]

6. Conclusion and Outlook

The term information has a central role in the area of AI. The way information is represented within a system has been the subject of much research and is covered in many theories. They range from purely mathematical approaches to biological inspired ones. Representatives of the respective areas of science are discussed in Section 2.3. They lack a description of the data structure or do not possess a common basis for different types of information. Another issue is the integration of developed memory systems into their host systems, as there is no distinction between control functions and information flow. One reason for this is the lack of coherent biological models that unify a functional description of the mind's processes and a structural description of the processed information. Even though research disciplines in neurosciences may not require this separation, computer scientists cannot rely on such. ARSi10 deals with these issues and introduces the *information representation system* to the ARS control unit which has neuropsychoanalytic concepts as its basis.

6.1 Achieved Solution

Dealing with the transfer of concepts between different scientific disciplines is a challenge that engineers must face in interdisciplinary work. The interpretation of theories and neuroscientific concepts is part of common research work in the area of AI. This interdisciplinary work offers great possibilities, but it is also fraught with traps. The benefits lie in obtaining another point of view on the examined problem, learning from other sciences and using their theories to find new solutions. However, the greatest trap is using the knowledge gained thereby in the wrong way. When transferring knowledge from one scientific discipline to another, this knowledge must be interpreted and described appropriately. One example is the engineering use of neuroscientific findings, which is discussed in this work. Problems occur when the interpretation of a model and its technical specification is done by the engineer only. The engineer generally does not have the expertise to achieve a correct interpretation. Hence, the result is a technical model whose original theoretical basis is insufficiently implemented.

This challenge is faced in the ARS project by cooperation with scientists from neurology, neuropsychoanalysis and psychoanalysis. This helps to avoid misinterpretations and inconsistencies with the original theory. The model definition is clearly separated from the implementation in order to avoid mixing up both disciplines. In a first step a model is defined in scientific interdisciplinary work. Later, this model is implemented with the use of common computer scientific methods. The proposed ARSi10 is developed in line with this methodology.

ARSi10 extends ARSi09 and adds bionically inspired data structures that are processed by the decision unit. While ARSi09 focuses on the decision unit's functional description, ARSi10 additionally introduces a dedicated structure of processed information and the interface to the *information representation layer* (see Fig. 1-1). Thus, the technical specification of the decision unit and the *information representation* both have neuropsychoanalytic concepts as basis. The proposed interface is formed due to the separation between processing and storing of data. It is labeled as *information management* and controls the access to the search space. The *information representation layer* defines the way this data is stored in the search space.

The proposed *information representation* is based on four atomic data structures labeled TP, affect, association and word presentation. Their description corresponds to the psychoanalytic definition and is translated to a technical specification in cooperation with neuropsychoanalysts and psychoanalysts. It turns out that these terms can be used to describe any type of information processed in the decision unit or stored in the *information representation layer*. This is also the reason why they are identified as atomic data structures. Together with the restrictions defined in 3.2, the resulting search space defines a network where nodes correspond to TPs, affects and word presentations, while associations form the edges in between. In order to simplify this description, additional data structures are introduced. They define meshes of atomic data structures with certain characteristics. The type of association that is used to bundle them differentiates them in particular. Hence, the data structures TPM, TI, DM and acts are introduced. Questions that remain open in the theory of psychoanalysis are solved by the use of findings from the related research discipline neuropsychoanalysis. For the definition of acts and TIs preliminary work in [R07] and [DZ08, p. 16-17] is analyzed and adapted. DMs and TPM are novel and introduced with ARSi10.

While Section 3.2 introduces psychoanalytically inspired data structures, Chapters 4 and 5 discuss their technical realization in autonomous software agents. Proof is shown that the proposed *information representation* model is technically realizable and allows mapping of perceived sensor data to atomic data structures. Even though additional data structures are introduced they are traced back to the atomic ones. In contrast to other realizations in AI, in ARSi10 the functional description of the decision unit as well as the definition of the data structures are based upon the same theory. This creates the drawback that the proposed model is only realizable in combination with the ARS decision unit. Similarly, the decision unit requires the proposed data structures in order to exercise its functionalities.

The proposed data structures are categorized into primary and secondary data structures. They are mapped one to one to primary and secondary processes that define the functional principles applied to the decision unit. The work at hand provides the required data structures for both process types and closes the gap between perceived data and secondary data structures. Every decision on upcoming actions bases upon secondary data structures that introduce logic and temporal relations. This results in the settlement of *Hypothesis 1* and *Hypothesis 2* stated in Section 1.3.

Common implementations of bionically inspired memory systems in autonomous agents categorize information with regard to its content. As discussed in 2.3, the multi-store model that introduces different memory systems for specific information content has a lot of influence in this area. However, this model does not possess a structural description of the processed information nor does it offer a shared basis for the different types of data structures. As the structural information is important for a technical specification, its definition must be generated by engineers. Hence, the outcome is a memory system whose outlines are inspired by a bionic approach, but engineers produce the definitions that are required for the technical realization on their own. This is different for the model specified in this thesis. Information is not categorized according to its content, but instead is described in three different ways. First, it is mapped to its physical representation by external and internal perception. Second, the impact on the agent is defined by drives and affects. Third, it is set into a logical context by secondary data structures. The proposed model is a technical description of an already existing model, which is devised in interdisciplinary work, and not a concept introduced by engineers.

Psychoanalytic concepts provide a functional description of the human mind and a structural description of the processed information. This distinction between information and control flow is upheld in this work by the differentiation between the *information representation* and *information processing*. In addition, the data storage is decoupled from any functional description. It is located parallel to the decision layer that holds the ARS decision unit (see Fig. 1-1). The decision layer holds the functional description of operations that lead from input parameters to a decision and the resulting output. The *information representation layer* contains knowledge that helps to deal with the environmental and internal state. It must not be mistaken for information that influences the transfer function of decision unit operations. These are static operations. Further research may go towards a dynamic functional change. The *information management* forms the interface between the decision layer and the *information representation layer*. Information management as well as the *information representation layer* are not the subject of any theoretical conditions. They must be defined in order to realize the introduced model. Hence, they are an engineering solution without any background in psychoanalysis or neuropsychoanalysis.

For ARSi10 knowledge is defined in an ontology by use of the knowledge framework Protégé. Due to its correspondence to the object-oriented approach, the frame structure approach was chosen for the definition of this ontology. The data structures specified in the ontology can be easily mapped to Java objects at the simulation startup.

It must be pointed out that implementation details like the selection of search algorithms or the definition of the ontology structure are not based upon performance requirements. The implementation of ARSi10 is purely a feasibility study of transferring neuropsychoanalytic concepts of *information representation* to a technical specification and implementing it in autonomous software agents. In a next step, optimization criteria and performance tests can be applied to the implementation. Hence, Chapter 5 does not define performance tests for the ARSi10 operations but use cases that verify specific functions of the proposed *information representation system*. This acknowledges *Hypothesis 3* and *Hypothesis 4* claimed in Section 1.3.

Unlike ARSi09, ARSi10 introduces a single ontology that holds the required knowledge to handle upcoming situations. In [Lan10] the specification of several data stores is pointed out as a possible issue that is solved with ARSi10. All static knowledge is stored in one search space. The term static points out a minor limitation that is discussed in Section 6.2.

In summary, psychoanalytic theory provides a model of the human mind whose principles can be consigned to a technical specification. All four hypotheses that are stated in Section 1.3 are approved in this work. Together with the neuropsychoanalytic approach and neuroscientific theory a control unit for autonomous agents can be defined. Psychoanalytic theory not only provides a model for information processing but also a definition for the structure of processed information. The discussed artificial life simulation BWsim defines a first test bed for the ARS model and the proposed ARSi10. In the future, it is destined for an implementation in real world applications as discussed in Section 6.3.

6.2 Future Research Hot Spots

The aim of this thesis, to create a technical specification of bionically inspired information representation in the context of the ARS decision unit in cooperation with psychoanalytic advisors, is completed with this work. However, ARSi10 leaves several questions unanswered which are common in prototype implementations but represent possible starting points for future research work. These open questions are summarized below.

Feedback Loops

Up to now the modules of the ARS model are accessed in a one-way process. With the exception of one loop around the module E15 (see Fig. 3-19) no recursions are implemented in the model. This is not because recursions are not intended. It is planned to define a recursion between the decision unit output and input in order to enable filtering of perceived data depending on to the current action plan. This means that secondary process operations influence primary processes. Further recursions also must be discussed in the lower layers where neuro-symbolization operations are carried out. For example, a reactive loop between decision unit and perceptive processes can integrate a focusing mechanism that is able to filter relevant data. This would result in a performance gain for systems where a great amount of data is expected. Recursions can also assist learning mechanisms that are required within the decision unit and the neuro-symbolization layers. However, recursions may also introduce stability issues that must be avoided within a system. The influence of every newly introduced reactive loop must be analyzed in detail. This is an extensive procedure within a complex system like the ARS system and must be done step by step. It is a costly topic that raises additional issues and highlights drawbacks of the ARS model, but it is also a prerequisite for further steps.

Search Algorithm

The *information management module* introduces the *list search* algorithm. Certain parameters like data structure and value type define the search space structure and therefore limit the list size. However, the cost for a list search as well as its limited scalability demands the integration of alternative search methods. In case the search space grows larger by the integration of knowledge for further use cases, the list search algorithm's drawbacks become obvious. This is pointed out in Section 4.3. In order to improve the performance, the search algorithm should be adapted to the respective data structures. Hence, there is not a single solution for all data structures. Primary data structures give different boundary conditions to the search method than secondary data structures do. However, the *information management system* design in ARSi10 allows the implementation of various search algorithms.

Temporal Information Storage

Section 6.1 mentions a possible extension of the *information representation layer* to dynamic knowledge. In ARSi10, knowledge that is required to handle common situations is stored. The defined search space is not adapted during the simulation run in the current implementation. However, some of the modules require certain information like knowledge of the present location of the system or the actions currently being triggered. This information should not change for every simulation step and must be provided for upcoming simulation steps. As they are parameters that change dynamically during the simulation run, this information cannot be predefined in the proposed *information representation layer*. Hence, a temporal storage must be introduced that provides a buffer for this information beyond the current simulation step. In ARSi10, knowledge about the current context as well as so-called repressed content is affected by this drawback. For this implementation the solution from ARSi09, which predefines this kind of information, was adopted. This works for use cases that test individual capacities but must be adapted for unbounded simulation runs. The temporal storage must not be confused with the term *working memory*. The latter is defined in psychology and holds the information that the human being is dealing with in a given situation. The required solution contains a lot more information.

Ontology Restructuring

The ARSi10 ontology is not optimized regarding a specific search algorithm or towards the advantages or disadvantages that are introduced by the frame approach. It must be evaluated whether an adaptation towards the stored information structure leads to better system performance. A possible improvement may be a stronger structuring of the ontology. For example, the categorization of TPMs to specific entity types can be extended to a greater number of groups. This higher granularity can become an advantage for search algorithms.

Frame vs. Semantic Net Representation

As stated above, the frame approach was chosen to define the agent's knowledge due to the advantages frames offer when dealing with object-oriented design and programming. However, future extensions to ARSi10 should investigate the advantages of a semantic net approach by introducing it to the ARS model. Even though the frame approach seems to fit better with an object-oriented design, semantic net technologies like OWL are standardized and broadly used. In addition, knowledge frameworks like Protégé include reasoning concepts for OWL that may support the ARS model in retrieving certain information from the search space. A semantic net description can be an alternative especially to the ARSi10 implementation of secondary data structures and the logical relations between them. Another possibility may be to combine the advantages of both approaches and remain with the frame method for the primary data structures but use the semantic net approach for secondary data structures.

Introduction of Learning Algorithms

As mentioned above, retrieved data structures are adapted by the ARS decision unit during runtime, but these changes are not stored to the search space or established in the ontology. Machine learning is required therefor, which is not included in ARSi10. Possible implementations are discussed elsewhere [LZD+08, pp. 639-644]. A discussion thereof requires the specification of information structures that is done in this work. Future work can thus deal with this topic based upon ARSi10. It must be stressed again that the data structure type on which the learning algorithm is to be used is an important factor. An adaptation of association weights of primary data structures requires different learning strategies than the definition of relations between word presentations. In addition, a differentiation must be made between a learning mechanism that adapts already existing data structures and one that introduces new ones. For the latter case a value must be defined to mark the threshold between recognizing a data structure as new and matching it to an existing one.

Logic and Temporal Dependencies

For ARSi10, conjunctions and disjunctions are implicitly integrated into secondary data structures. When word presentations with the same value type are merged into one act they are said to be linked by a conjunction, while word presentations with diverse content are linked by a disjunction. This assumption is sufficient for ARSi10. However, the flexibility in designing acts increases in case these relations are explicitly introduced by word presentations. In addition, negations or temporal dependencies expand the possibilities of defining goals and acts for the agent. For ARSi10 temporal dependencies are limited to an order on the timeline. Neither the duration of actions nor a common time base is defined. Future work on this topic should be done in combination with the restructuring of the frame ontology or the integration of a semantic net approach.

Perception, Symbolization of Sensor Data

As for ARSi09, the neuro-symbolization between the sensor array and the decision unit remains an open issue in ARSi10. Even though it is theoretically described by Velik et al.

[Vel08], no implementation exists thus far due to various open questions. Their solution is part of current research in the ARS project. For ARSi10 a shortcut for bundling sensor data is introduced. This is possible for the software simulation, as the required data can be transferred from the detected object to the sensor arrays. However, neuro-symbolization must be introduced in case the ARS model is integrated into a real world application. Even though this part of the ARS model is not within the scope of this work, the proposed concept and model are based upon the outcome of the neuro-symbolization. Following the theoretical description [Vel08], assumptions for the input parameters to the decision unit are made. In order to guarantee the functionality of the ARS model, these assumptions must be taken into account for the neuro-symbolic realization.

Real World Application

ARSi10 is realized in a simulated environment. This enables testing the model's functionality in a predefined environment without unexpected influences. However, the ARS model is developed to be applied to real world applications. Besides the issue of neuro-symbolization, additional challenges will emerge on the path to this goal due to real world conditions. The inaccuracy of sensor data or highly dynamic environmental changes represents only two of possible challenges that influence the ARS model's functionality as well as the definition of predefined knowledge. Before the decision is ported from the ARS model to a real world application, a detailed investigation on upcoming issues must be undertaken.

In summary, ARSi10 is an enclosed implementation and therefore the aim of this work is accomplished. This merely forms the basis for further research towards different ways. Their priority must change with the type of application in which the ARS model is integrated. Section 6.3 discusses a number of possible areas of application.

6.3 Ethical Questions and Upcoming Challenges

The ARS project originates from building automation. Although its development is conducted in a simulated environment, it is obvious that the long-term goal is to return to this area. In doing so, ethical questions must be addressed regarding the human-system interaction. Some of them must be discussed in the near future, others become relevant further on and are to be kept in mind, but are not considered to be of immediate concern in the initial development phases.

Thoughts about the influence of machines on human beings belong to the first group. In order to assist human beings in their daily routines, machines must be able to interact with their environment. A balance must be found, however, between helpfully impacting people's lives and invading their privacy. Automated systems are perceived differently depending on the application area. For example, video surveillance systems are more accepted when used in public space (e.g. an airport) than in private areas (e.g. a nursing home). This distinction must be considered for any building automation system. The area of ambient assistant living is often highlighted regarding the use of smart systems as the demography for the European Union shows a rising average age over the next decades. The old age dependency ratio, which defines the percentage of persons who are older than 65 years among the overall population, is estimated by Eurostat to rise from 25.4% today to 38% in 2030 [Gia10, p. 6]. Hence, the increasing number of elderly people as well as limited expenses in this area requires new ways of assisting health care staff. Since this is nearly impossible to achieve without machine support, two basic use cases emerge. While the assistance of nursing staff by surveillance systems is a short-term goal, applying active care is a long-term goal and requires systems capable of coping with their environments. In the second, long-term category of issues, not only the ethical usage of machines with respect to human privacy but also the ethical behavior of machines towards people must be discussed as part of the area of machine ethics [AA07].

The replacement of nursing staff with machines is more fiction than reality, and rumors about such concepts most likely originate from people's fears (like the fear of unchecked engineering omnipotence) and journalistic interpretation, rather than from the actual chance of them being realized in the near future. From the author's point of view the primary goal of AI is not to design a 'human being clone' but to improve systems. Among other concepts, this can be achieved by the use of biological mechanisms that are designed to be more effective than any known algorithm. The human being, of course, is based on numerous such principles and is therefore used as archetype in the ARS project. Discussion of the ethical consequences of creating smart systems should be accompanied by a certain sense of reality, although the author does not think that issues such as robot rights regarding their use for military combat – except for the obvious ethical questions about military combat itself – or the consequences of shutting down a personal computer possessing human-like intelligence, become relevant soon.

Computer scientists have always searched for a way to integrate the principles of human decision making into a technical system. However, they have lacked a theoretical model that covers wide areas of human perception up to decision making. This is why the author is confident that the ARS approach leads to new ways and chances for AI and the area of building automation in particular. The way internal and external sensor data is processed by the use of bionic findings enables to deal with future challenges of integrating complex systems and processing huge amount of sensor data. This legitimates the introduction of psychoanalysis and neuropsychoanalysis to the area of engineering. While psychoanalysis provides a functional description of the human mind, neuropsychoanalysis combines psychoanalytic and neuroscientific concepts of the connection between higher brain functions and the sensor system. The ARS model is the first technical description of these principles and ARSi10 extends its current implementations by data structures designed upon a novel approach and a consistent memory system. This work however represents neither the first nor the last step on the way to a complete control system that is based upon new principles. ARSi10 must be taken to reach final goal and provides a basis for upcoming research work.

The idea of the airport that detects security issues and supports the staff in handling them, as it is proposed in the course of the SENSE project [BVZ08, pp. 1092-1096], is only one of the possible scenarios where the ARS model can be applied. Ambient assistant living is one of the crucial factors in future health care. Ethical components as discussed above must be taken into account and the system must be adapted towards them. A building automation system within a nursing home has limited use of video surveillance while an airport will not do without it.

Besides the integration into a building automation system different application areas are possible. The implementation in autonomous robots is the real life application that comes to mind. It would be the first contact of the ARS model with the real world and could provide additional clarity on the usability of the ARS model in the real world. First investigations are undertaken that go in this direction.

The use of an artificial life simulation as an intermediate step before current reality opens doors to the growing areas of intelligent avatars and game logic. Both areas face increasing interest but cannot actually cope with the set of requirements. They depend on rule-based decision making that does not allow any deviations from a predefined concept and hence is not sufficient for game intelligence. It must be investigated if the ARS approach can improve on these concepts. Another possible area of application is the use in avatars for e-learning systems or any kind of product support. In these areas, extensive system-user interaction is required, which predestines them for the use of the ARS approach.

There is still a lot of research work to be done. Even though psychoanalysis and neuropsychoanalysis provide the most consistent model of the human mind, they leave questions unanswered. For the technical realization in ARSi10, some of these questions have been elaborated in cooperation with scientists from the aforementioned areas. Others are handled by a shortcut. Future work aims at closing these gaps, thus providing knowledge flow not only towards the engineering side. The author is convinced that the scientific areas of neuropsychoanalysis and psychoanalysis can benefit from engineering findings and developments. Computer science can introduce simulation frameworks for testing neuropsychoanalytic models and therefore provide tools to verify them. This requires open minds, a lot of convincing and research work on both sides.

This work extends the ARS decision unit by a bionically inspired *information representation* concept. Both have the same theoretical foundation and complete one another to a unit. This results in the first model that introduces neuropsychoanalytic inspired functional and information processing principles to engineering and additionally covers a huge area with which a system controller must deal. In effect, the computational framework ARSi10 is described in a consistent model of human-like information representation and processing. Therefore, the author is confident that the concept proposed in this work takes advantage of knowledge from neuropsychoanalysis in an effective way and helps the ARS project on its way towards a new generation of AI and the design of systems that are able to cope with future requirements. Maybe the project brings computer science one step closer to the aim that was announced by scientists at the Dartmouth conference in 1956 and whose attainment has been delayed so often: the design of a machine with human-like intelligence.

References

[AA07] Michael Anderson and Susan Leigh Anderson. Machine ethics: Creating an ethical intelligent agent. *AI Magazine*, 28 No. 4:4–15, 2007.

[AL98] John R. Anderson and Christian Lebiere. *The Atomic Components of Thought*. Lawrence Erlbaum Associates, 1998.

[Ari64] Silvano Arieti. The rise of creativity: From primary to tertiary process. *Contemporary Psychoanalysis*, 1:51–68, 1964.

[AS68] Richard C. Atkinson and Richard M. Shiffrin. *The psychology of learning and motivation*, volume 2, chapter Human memory: A proposed system and its control processes, pages 89–195. New York: Academic Press, 1968.

[Bad97] Alan Baddeley. *Human Memory: Theory and Practice*. Psychology Press, 1997.

[BDK+04] Elisabeth Brainin, Dietmar Dietrich, Wolfgang Kastner, Peter Palensky, and Charlotte Rösener. Neuro-bionic architecture of automation systems : Obstacles and challenges. *Proceedings of 2004 IEEE AFRICON, 7th Africon conference in Africa, Technology Innovation*, 2:1219–1222, 2004.

[Ber08] Matthew J. Berryman. Review of software platforms for agent based models. Technical report, Defence Science and Technology Organisation, 2008.

[BL04] Ronald J. Brachman and Hector J. Levesque. *Knowledge Representation and Reasoning*. Elsevier, 2004.

[BLPV07] Wolfgang Burgstaller, Roland Lang, Patricia Pörscht, and Rosemarie Velik. Technical model for basic and complex emotions. *Proceedings of 2007 IEEE International Conference of Industrial Informatics*, pages 1033–1038, 2007.

[Bov06] Simon Bovet. Emergence of insect navigation strategies from homogeneous sensorimotor coupling. In *In proceedings of the 9th International Conference on Intelligent Autonomous Systems*, pages 525–533, 2006.

[BP05a] Simon Bovet and Rolf Pfeifer. Emergence of coherent behaviors from homogenous sensorimotor coupling. In *12th International Conference on Advanced Robotics*, pages 324–330, 2005.

[BP05b] Simon Bovet and Rolf Pfeifer. Emergence of delayed reward learning from sensorimotor coordination. *IEEE/RSJ International Conference on Intelligent Robots and Systems*, pages 2272–2277, 2005.

References

[Bra84] Valentino Braitenberg. *Vehicles: Experiments in Synthetic Psychology*. MIT Press, Cambridge, 1984.

[Bre02] Cynthia Breazeal. *Designing Sociable Robots*. MIT Press, Cambridge, MA, USA, 2002.

[Bre03a] Cynthia Breazeal. Emotive qualities in lip-synchronized robot speech. *Advanced Robotics*, 17, No. 2:97–113, 2003.

[Bre03b] Cynthia Breazeal. Toward sociable robots. *IEEE Journal of Robotics and Autonomous Systems*, 42(3-4):167–175, 2003.

[Bro86a] Rodney A. Brooks. A robust layered control system for a mobile robot. *Robotics and Automation, IEEE Journal of [legacy, pre - 1988]*, 2(1):14–23, Mar. 1986.

[Bro86b] Rodney A. Brooks. A robust layered control system for a mobile robot. *IEEE J. Robotics and Automation*, pages 14–23, 1986.

[Bro91a] Rodney A. Brooks. Intelligence without reason. In John Myopoulos and Ray Reiter, editors, *Proceedings of the 12th International Joint Conference on Artificial Intelligence (IJCAI-91)*, pages 569–595, Sydney, Australia, 1991. Morgan Kaufmann publishers Inc.: San Mateo, CA, USA.

[Bro91b] Rodney A. Brooks. New approaches to robotics. *Science*, 253(5025):1227–1232, 1991.

[Bru07] Dietmar Bruckner. *Probabilistic Models in Building Automation: Recognizing Scenarios with Statistical Methods*. PhD thesis, Vienna University of Technology, Institute of Computer Technology, 2007.

[BTW01] Harold Boley, Said Tabet, and Gerd Wagner. Design rationale of ruleml: A markup language for semantic web rules. In *SWWS'01*, 2001.

[Buc00] Wilma Bucci. The need for a "psychoanalytic psychology" in the cognitive science field. *Psychoanalytic Psychology*, 17(2):203–224, 2000.

[Bul02] Andrzej Buller. Volitron: On a psychodynamic robot and its four realities. *Proceedings Second International Workshop on Epigenetic Robotics: Modeling Cognitive Development in Robotic Systems*, 94:17–20, 2002.

[Bul05] Andrzej Buller. Building brains for robots: A psychodynamic approach. *Invited talk on the First International Conference on Pattern Recognition and Machine Intelligence, PReMIT'05*, pages 17–20, 2005.

[BVZ08] Dietmar Bruckner, Rosemarie Velik, and Gerhard Zucker. Network of cooperating smart sensors for global-view generation in surveillance applications. In *Proceedings of the 6th Conference on Industrial Informatics*, pages 1092–1096, 2008.

[Cañ97] Dolores Cañamero. Modeling motivations and emotions as a basis for intelligent behavior. In *AGENTS '97: Proceedings of the first international confer-

	ence on Autonomous agents, pages 148–155, Marina del Rey, California, United States, 1997. New York, NY, USA. ISBN: 0-89791-877-0.
[Cañ05]	Lola Cañamero. Emotion understanding from the perspective of autonomous robots research. *Neural Networks*, 18:445–455, 2005.
[CFF+98]	Vinay K. Chaudhri, Adam Farquhar, Richard Fikes, Peter D. Karp, and James P. Rice. Open knowledge base connectivity 2.0.3. Technical report, Artificial Intelligence Center of SRI International and Knowledge Systems Laboratory of Stanford University, 1998.
[CLRS03]	Thomas H. Cormen, Charles E. Leiserson, Ronald L. Rivest, and Clifford Stein. *Introduction to algorithms*, volume 4. MIT Press, 2003.
[Dam94]	Antonio Damasio. *Descartes' Error: Emotion, Reason, and the Human Brain*. Penguin, 1994. Published in Penguin Books 2005.
[Dam98]	Antonio Damasio. Emotion in the perspective of an integrated nervous system. *Brain Research Reviews*, 26(2-3):83–86, 1998.
[Dam00]	Antonio Damasio. *The Feeling of What Happens: Body, Emotion and the Making of Consciousness*. Vintage, new edition, October 2000.
[Dam03]	Antonio Damasio. *Looking for Spinoza: Joy, Sorrow, and the Feeling Brain*. Harvest Books, 2003.
[DC96]	Kerstin Dautenhahn and Thomas Christaller. Remembering, rehearsal and empathy - towards a social and embodied cognitive psychology for artifacts. In Sean O'Nuallain Paul Mc Kevitt, editor, *Two sciences of the mind. Readings in cognitive science and consciousness*, pages 257–282. North America Inc, 1996.
[Den87]	Daniel C. Dennett. *The Intentional Stance*. The MIT Press, Cambridge, MA, 1987.
[DFKU09]	Dietmar Dietrich, Georg Fodor, Wolfgang Kastner, and Mihaela Ulieru. Considering a technical realization of a neuropsychoanalytical model of the mind – a theoretical framework. In Dietmar Dietrich, Georg Fodor, Gerhard Zucker, and Dietmar Bruckner, editors, *Simulating the Mind – A Technical Neuropsychoanalytical Approach*, pages 99 – 115. Springer, Wien, 1st edition, 2009. invited contribution for the 1st ENF - Emulating the Mind, 2007, Vienna.
[DFZB09]	Dietmar Dietrich, Georg Fodor, Gerhard Zucker, and Dietmar Bruckner. *Simulating the Mind - A Technical Neuropsychoanalytical Approach*. Springer, Wien, 2009.
[DGLV08]	Tobias Deutsch, Andreas Gruber, Roland Lang, and Rosemarie Velik. Episodic memory for autonomous agents. In *Proc. Conference on Human System Interactions*, pages 621–626, 25–27 May 2008.
[Die00]	Dietmar Dietrich. Evolution potentials for fieldbus systems. volume 1, pages 145–146, 2000. Invited Talk.

References

[Dor06] Martin Dornes. *Die frühe Kindheit - Entwicklungspsychologie der ersten Lebensjahre*, volume 8. Fischer Taschenbuch, 2006.

[DS00] Dietmar Dietrich and Thilo Sauter. Evolution potentials for fieldbus systems. In *Proceedings of 4th IEEE Int. Workshop on Factory Communication Systems*, pages 343–350, 2000.

[DZ08] Dietmar Dietrich and Gerhard Zucker. New approach for controlling complex processes. an introduction to the 5th generation of AI. *Human System Interactions, 2008 Conference on*, pages 12–17, 2008. invited keynote speech.

[DZL07] Tobias Deutsch, Heimo Zeilinger, and Roland Lang. Simulation results for the ARS-PA model. In *Proc. 5th IEEE International Conference on Industrial Informatics*, volume 2, pages 995–1000, 23–27 June 2007.

[DZLZ08] Tobias Deutsch, Tehseen Zia, Roland Lang, and Heimo Zeilinger. A simulation platform for cognitive agents. In *Proc. 6th IEEE International Conference on Industrial Informatics INDIN 2008*, pages 1086–1091, 13–16 July 2008.

[Eng10] Robert Engel. Goal deliberation in a bionically inspired autonomous agent. Master's thesis, Vienna University of Technology, Institute of Computer Technology, 2010.

[ET01] Fergus Craik Endel Tulving. *The Oxford Handbook of Memory*. Oxford Handbook Series. Oxford University Press, 2001.

[FAD+04] Miriam Fend, Roland Abt, Marco Diefenbacher, Simon Bovet, and Martin Krafft. Morphology and learning - a case study on whiskers. In *in Proc. 8 th Int. Conf. on the Simulation of Adaptive Behavior*, pages 114–122, 2004.

[Fog95] David. B. Fogel. Review of computational intelligence: Imitating life. In *Proc. of the IEEE*, volume 83(11), pages 1588–1592, 1995.

[Fre91] Sigmund Freud. *Zur Auffassung der Aphasien*. Fischer Taschenbuch, 1891.

[Fre00] Sigmund Freud. The interpretation of dreams. *The Standard Edition of the Complete Psychological Works of Sigmund Freud*, Volume IV (1900): The Interpretation of Dreams (First Part):ix–627, 1900.

[Fre15a] Sigmund Freud. Instincts and their vicissitudes. *The Standard Edition of the Complete Psychological Works of Sigmund Freud*, XIV (1914-1916): On the History of the Psycho-Analytic Movement, Papers on Metapsychology and Other Works:109–140, 1915.

[Fre15b] Sigmund Freud. Repression. *The Standard Edition of the Complete Psychological Works of Sigmund Freud*, 14:146–158, 1915.

[Fre15c] Sigmund Freud. *The Unconscious*, volume XIV (1914-1916) of *On the History of the Psycho-Analytic Movement, Papers on Metapsychology and Other Works*. 1915.

[Fre20]   Sigmund Freud. *The Standard Edition of the Complete Psychological Works of Sigmund Freud*, volume 19, chapter Beyond the Pleasure Principle, pages 7–64. London: Hogarth Press, 1920.

[Fre23]   Sigmund Freud. The ego and the id. *The Standard Edition of the Complete Psychological Works of Sigmund Freud*, XIX (1923-1925):1–66, 1923.

[Fre72]   Sigmund Freud. Trieblehre. *Gesammelte Werke chronologisch geordnet*, XVII:70–73, 1972.

[Fre98a]   Sigmund Freud. *Gesammelte Werke: I*, chapter Studien über die Hysterie. 1998.

[Fre98b]   Sigmund Freud. *Gesammelte Werke: XI*, chapter VORLESUNG: DIE ANGST, pages 407–426. 1998.

[Fre08]   Sigmund Freud. Zur Psychologie der Traumvorgänge. *Gesammelte Werke chronologisch geordnet: II/III*, pages 513–626, 2008.

[Fue03]   Clara Tamarit Fuertes. *Automation System Perception - First Step towards Perceptive Awareness*. PhD thesis, Faculty of Electrical Engineering and Information Technology, Vienna University of Technology, 2003.

[Gia10]   Konstantinos Giannakouris. Regional population projections europop2008: Most EU regions face older population profile in 2030. Technical report, Eurostat - statistics in focus, 2010.

[GL88]   Robert M. Galatzer-Levy. On working through: A model from artificial intelligence. *Journal of the American Psychoanalytic Association*, 36:125–151, 1988.

[GL09]   Robert M. Galatzer-Levy. A primer of psychoanalysis for Alan Turing. In Dietmar Dietrich, Georg Fodor, Gerhard Zucker, and Dietmar Bruckner, editors, *Simulating the Mind – A Technical Neuropsychoanalytical Approach*, pages 367 – 381. Springer, Wien, 1st edition, 2009.

[Har05]   Stevan Harnard. *Handbook of Categorization in Cognitive Science*, chapter To Cognize is to Categorize: Cognition is Categorization, pages 20–45. Elsevier, 2005.

[HDN03]   Wan Ching Ho, Kerstin Dautenhahn, and Chrystopher L. Nehaniv. Comparing different control architectures for autobiographic agents in static virtual environments. *Intelligent Agents, 4th International Workshop, IVA 2003, Kloster Irsee, Germany, September 15-17, 2003, Proceedings*, pages 182–191, 2003.

[HDN05]   Wan Ching Ho, Kerstin Dautenhahn, and Chrystopher L. Nehaniv. Autobiographic agents in dynamic virtual environments - performance comparison for different memory control architectures. *Proceedings of IEEE Congress on Evolutionary Computation IEEE*, pages 573–580, 2005.

[HDN06]   Wan Ching Ho, Kerstin Dautenhahn, and Chrystopher. L. Nehaniv. A study of episodic memory-based learning and narrative structure for autobiographic agents. In *Adaptation in Artificial and Biological Systems AISB 2006 Confer-*

References

[HDN08] *ence*, volume 3, pages 26–29, 2006.

Wan Ching Ho, Kerstin Dautenhahn, and Chrystopher L. Nehaniv. Computational memory architectures for autobiographic agents interacting in a complex virtual environment: a working model. *Connection Science*, 20(1):21–65, 2008.

[HDNB04] Wan Ching Ho, Kerstin Dautenhahn, Chrystopher L. Nehaniv, and Rene Te Boekhorst. Sharing memories: An experimental investigation with multiple autonomous autobiographic agents. *IAS-8, 8th Conference on Intelligent Autonomous Systems*, pages 361–370, 2004.

[HMK+08] Bernd Hanke, Günter Meyer, Thomas Kohlhoff, Marius Hartel, Volker Pregizer, and Frank Schubert. Airport tests bacnet devices - competition at high stage. *BACnet Europe*, 8:41–43, 2008.

[IN87] Asghar Iran-Nejad. The schema: A long-term memory structure or a transient functional pattern. In R. J. Tierney, P.L Anders, and J.N. Mitchell, editors, *Understanding Readers' Understanding: Theory and Practice*, pages 109–128. Hillsdale, Lawrence Erlbaum Associates, 1987.

[ISO05] ISO/IEC. Iso/iec 19501:2005 information technology — open distributed processing — Unified Modeling Language (UML) version 1.4.2, 2005.

[Kan99] Eric R. Kandel. Biology and the future of psychoanalysis: A new intellectual framework for psychiatry revisited. pages 505–524. McGraw-Hill, 1999.

[Köh98] Lotte Köhler. *Erinnerung von Wirklichkeiten: Psychoanalyse und Neurowissenschaften im Dialog, Vol. 1: Bestandsaufnahme*, chapter Einführung in die Entstehung des Gedächtnisses, pages 131–222. Stuttgart: Cotta / Verlag Internat. Psychoanalyse (VIP), 1998.

[KL98] Martha Koukkou and Dietrich Lehmann. *Erinnerung von Wirklichkeiten: Psychoanalyse und Neurowissenschaften im Dialog, Vol. 1: Bestandsaufnahme*, chapter Ein systemtheoretisch orientiertes Modell der Funktionen des menschlichen Gehirns, und die Ontogenese des Verhaltens: eine Synthese von Theorien und Daten, pages 287–415. Stuttgart: Cotta / Verlag Internat. Psychoanalyse (VIP), 1998.

[Knu97] Donald E. Knuth. *The Art of Computer Programming - Fundamental Algorithms*, volume 1. Massachusetts: Addison-Wesley, 3rd edition, 1997.

[Lan10] Roland Lang. *A Decision Unit for Autonomous Agents Based on the Theory of Psychoanalysis*. PhD thesis, Vienna University of Technology, 2010.

[Lap73] Jean Laplanche. *Das Vokabular der Psychoanalyse*. Suhrkamp Taschenbuch Wissenschaft, Frankfurt am Main, 1973.

[LBP02] Marianne Leuzinger-Bohleber and Rolf Pfeifer. Remembering a depressive primary object: Memory in the dialogue between psychoanalysis and cognitive science. *International Journal of Psychoanalysis*, 83:3–33, 2002.

[LCRPS04] Sean Luke, Claudio Cioffi-Revilla, Liviu Panait, and Keith Sullivan. Mason: A new multi-agent simulation toolkit. In *Proceedings of the 2004 Swarmfest Workshop*, 2004.

[LKZD10] Roland Lang, Stefan Kohlhauser, Gerhard Zucker, and Tobias Deutsch. Integrating internal performance measures into the decision making process of autonomous agents. In *Proceedings of 3rd International Conference on Human System Interaction (HSI'10), Rzeszow*, 2010.

[LMP08] Vladimir Lifschitz, Leora Morgenstern, and David Plaisted. *Handbook of Knowledge Representation*, chapter Knowledge Representation and Classical Logic, pages 3–88. Elsevier Science & Technology, 2008.

[LNR87] John E. Laird, Allen Newell, and P. S. Rosenbloom. Soar: An architecture for general intelligence. *Artificial Intelligence*, 33:1–64, 1987.

[LP73] Jean Laplanche and Jean-Bertrand Pontalis. *The Language of Psycho-Analysis: Translated by Donald Nicholson-Smith*. The Hogarth Press and the Institute of Psycho-Analysis, 1973.

[LZD$^+$08] Roland Lang, Heimo Zeilinger, Tobias Deutsch, Rosemarie Velik, and Brit Muller. Perceptive learning - a psychoanalytical learning framework for autonomous agents. In *Proc. Conference on Human System Interactions*, pages 639–644, 25–27 May 2008.

[MBLA96] Nelson Minar, Roger Burkhart, Chris Langton, and Manor Askenazi. The swarm simulation system: A toolkit for building multi-agent simulations - report no.: 96-06-042. Technical report, Santa Fe (NM): Santa Fe Institute, 1996.

[Mer98] Wolfgang Mertens. *Erinnerung von Wirklichkeiten: Psychoanalyse und Neurowissenschaften im Dialog, Vol. 1: Bestandsaufnahme*, chapter Einige Aspekte der psychoanalytischen Gedächtnistheorie, pages 48–130. Stuttgart: Cotta / Verlag Internat. Psychoanalyse (VIP), 1998.

[Min75] Marvin Minsky. *The Psychology of Computer Vision*, chapter A framework for representing knowledge, pages 211–277. McGraw-Hill, 1975.

[Min06] Marvin Minsky. *The Emotion Machine: Commonsense Thinking, Artificial Intelligence, and the Future of the Human Mind*. Simon & Schuster Paperbacks, 2006.

[MMRS55] John McCarthy, Marvin L. Minsky, Nathaniel Rochester, and Claude E. Shannon. A proposal for the dartmouth summer research project on artificial intelligence. Technical report, 1955.

[MN05] Charles. M. Macal and Michael J. North. Tutorial on agent-based modeling and simulation. In *Proceedings of the 37th conference on Winter simulation*, pages 2–15, 2005.

[Núñ99] Rafael Núñez. Could the future taste purple? reclaiming mind, body, and cognition. *Consciousness Studies*, 6:41–60, 1999.

References

[Nac02] Werner Nachtigall. *Bionik*. Springer, Berlin, 2nd edition, 2002.

[New94] Allen Newell. *Unified Theories of Cognition*. Harvard Univ Press, 1994.

[NFM01] Natalya F. Noy, Ray W. Fergerson, and Mark A. Musen. The knowledge model of protege-2000: combining interoperability and flexibility. pages 17–32. Springer, 2001.

[Ode02] James J. Odell. Objects and agents compared. *Journal of Object Technology*, 1:41–53, 2002.

[Pal08] Brigitte Palensky. *From Neuro-Psychoanalysis to Cognitive and Affective Automation Systems*. PhD thesis, Faculty of Electrical Engineering and Information Technology, Vienna University of Technology, 2008.

[Pan05] Jaak Panksepp. On the embodied neural nature of core emotional affects. *Consciousness Studies*, 12(8-10):158–184, 2005.

[Par04] Domenico Parisi. Internal robotics. *Connection Science*, 16:325–338, 2004.

[PB07] Rolf Pfeifer and Josh Bongard. *How the body shapes the way we think*. MIT Press, 2007.

[PB09] Adrian Paschke and Harold Boley. Rules capturing events and reactivity. *Handbook of Research on Emerging Rule-Based Languages and Technologies: Open Solutions and Approaches*, page Section I, 2009.

[PBTD08] Peter Palensky, Dietmar Bruckner, Anna Tmej, and Tobias Deutsch. Paradox in AI – AI 2.0: the way to machine consciousness. *Proceedings of IT Revolutions 2008, Venice*, 2008.

[Pea98] Judy Pearsall, editor. *The New Oxford Dictionary of English*. Oxford University Press Inc. New York, 1998. ISBN 0-19-861263-X.

[PI03] Rolf Pfeifer and Fumiya Iida. Embodied artificial intelligence: Trends and challenges. *Embodied Artificial Intelligence*, pages 1–26, 2003.

[PIB05] Rolf Pfeifer, Fumiya Iida, and Josh Bongard. New robotics: Design principles for intelligent systems. *Artificial Life*, 11(1-2):99–120, 2005.

[Pic99] Rosalind Picard. Response to sloman's review of affective computing. *AI Magazine*, 20(1):134–137, 1999.

[PIG06] Rolf Pfeifer, Fumiya Iida, and Gabriel Gómez. Designing intelligent robots – on the implications of embodiment. *Journal of Robotics Society of Japan*, 24(7):783–790, 2006.

[PLD05] Gerhard Pratl, Brigitte Lorenz, and Dietmar Dietrich. The artificial recognition system (ARS): New concepts for building automation. *Fieldbus Systems and their Applications*, 6(1), 2005.

[PLOS08] Rolf Pfeifer, Max Lungarella, and Yasuo Kuniyoshi Olaf Sporns. *On the information-theoretic implications of embodiment – principles and methods*, volume 4850, pages 76–86. 2008.

[PP05]	Gerhard Pratl and Peter Palensky. Project ARS – the next step towards an intelligent environment. *Proceedings of the IEE International Workshop on Intelligent Environments*, pages 55–62, 2005.
[PPC09]	Peter Palensky, Brigitte Palensky, and Andrea Clarici. Cognitive and affective automation: Machines using the psychoanalytic model of the human mind. In Dietmar Dietrich, Georg Fodor, Gerhard Zucker, and Dietmar Bruckner, editors, *Simulating the Mind – A Technical Neuropsychoanalytical Approach*, pages 178 – 227. Springer, Wien, 1st edition, 2009. invited contribution for the 1st ENF - Emulating the Mind, 2007, Vienna.
[Pra06]	Gerhard Pratl. *Processing and Symbolization of Ambient Sensor Data*. PhD thesis, Faculty of Electrical Engineering and Information Technology, Vienna University of Technology, 2006.
[PS99]	Rolf Pfeifer and Christian Scheier. *Understanding Intelligence*. MIT Press, 1999.
[R07]	Charlotte Rösener. *Adaptive Behavior Arbitration for Mobile Service Robots in Building Automation*. PhD thesis, Vienna University of Technology, Institute of Computer Technology, 2007.
[RLJ06]	Steven F. Railsback, Steven L. Lytinen, and Stephen K. Jackson. Agent-based simulation platforms: Review and development recommendations. *SIMULATION*, 82 No. 9:609–623, 2006.
[RN03]	Stuart J. Russell and Peter Norvig. *Artificial Intelligence: A Modern Approach*. Pearson Education, 2003.
[Ros58]	Frank Rosenblatt. The perception: A probabilistic model for information storage and organi-zation in the brain. *Psychological review*, 65(6):386–408., 1958.
[Rot92]	Gerhard Roth. Das konstruktive Gehirn: Neurobiologische Grundlagen von Wahrnehmung und Erkenntnis. In Siegfried J. Schmidt, editor, *Kognition und Gesellschaft*. Suhrkamp Verlag, 1992.
[RR96]	Juan Rodado and Marion Rendon. Can artificial intelligence be of help to psychoanalysis ... or ... vice versa? *The American Journal of Psychoanalysis*, 56(4):395–412, 1996.
[Rus03]	Gerhard Russ. *Situation-dependent Behavior in Building Automation*. PhD thesis, Vienna University of Technology, Institute of Computer Technology, 2003.
[Sim65]	Herbert A. Simon. The new science of management decisions. In *The Shape of Automation for Men and Management*. Harper and Row, 1965.
[Slo04]	Aaron Sloman. What are emotion theories about? In *Symposium Technical Report*, pages 128–134. AAAI Spring, 2004.
[Sol09]	Mark Solms. What is the 'mind'? a neuro-psychoanalytical approach. In Dietmar Dietrich, Georg Fodor, Gerhard Zucker, and Dietmar Bruckner, editors,

References

	Simulating the Mind – A Technical Neuropsychoanalytical Approach, pages 115 – 123. Springer, Wien, 1st edition, 2009. invited contribution for the 1st ENF - Emulating the Mind, 2007, Vienna.
[SRF00]	Stefan Soucek, Gerhard Russ, and Clara Tamarit Fuertes. The smart kitchen project - an application on fieldbus technology to domotics. *Proceedings of the 2nd International Workshop on Networked Appliances (IWNA2000)*, page 1, 2000.
[ST02]	Mark Solms and Oliver Turnbull. *The Brain and the Inner World: An Introduction to the Neuroscience of Subjective Experience*. Karnac/Other Press, Cathy Miller Foreign Rights Agency, London, England, 2002.
[Ste00]	Robert J. Sternberg, editor. *Handbook of Intelligence*. Cambridge University Press, 2000.
[Ste03]	Luc Steels. Intelligence with representation. *Philosophical Transactions: Mathematical, Physical and Engineering Sciences*, 362(1811):2381–2395, 2003.
[TH04]	Robert Tobias and Carole Hofmann. Evaluation of free java-libraries for social-scientific agent based simulation. *Journal of Artificial Societies and Social Simulation*, 7(1), 2004.
[Tod82]	Masanao Toda. *Man, Robot and Society*. Martinus Nijhoff Publishing, 1982.
[Tul72]	Endel Tulving. *Organization of memory*, chapter Episodic and semantic memory, pages 381–403. New York: Academic Press, 1972.
[Tul83]	Endel Tulving. *Elements of Episodic Memory*. Oxford: Clarendon Press, 1983.
[Tur89]	Sherry Turkle. Artificial intelligence and psychoanalysis: A new alliance. In S. R. Graubard, editor, *The Artificial Intelligence Debate: False Starts, Real Foundations*, pages 241–268. MIT Press, Cambridge, MA, 1989.
[uml09a]	OMG Unified Modeling Language (OMG UML), infrastructure; version 2.2, 02 2009.
[uml09b]	OMG Unified Modeling Language (OMG UML), superstructure; version 2.2, 2 2009.
[Vel08]	Rosemarie Velik. *A Bionic Model for Human-like Machine Perception*. PhD thesis, Vienna University of Technology, Institute of Computer Technology, 2008.
[VLBD08]	Rosemarie Velik, Roland Lang, Dietmar Bruckner, and Tobias Deutsch. Emulating the perceptual system of the brain for the purpose of sensor fusion. In *Proc. Conference on Human System Interactions*, pages 657–662, 25–27 May 2008.
[Weh01]	Thomas Wehrle. The grounding problem of modeling emotions in adaptive artifacts. *Cybernetics and Systems*, 32(5):561–580, 2001.

[WR10] Alfred North Whitehead and Bertrand Russell. *Principia mathematica*. Cambridge: University Press, 1910.

[ZDML08] Heimo Zeilinger, Tobias Deutsch, Brit Müller, and Roland Lang. Bionic inspired decision making unit model for autonomous agents. In *Proc. IEEE International Conference on Computational Cybernetics ICCC 2008*, pages 259–264, 27–29 Nov. 2008.

[Zie03] Tom Ziemke. What's that thing called embodiment. In *25th Annual Meeting of the Cognitive Science Society*, pages 1305–1310. Lawrence Erlbaum, 2003.

[ZL09] Tom Ziemke and Robert Lowe. On the role of emotion in embodied cognitive architectures: From organisms to robots. *Cognitive Computation*, 1:104–117, 2009.

[ZLM09] Heimo Zeilinger, Roland Lang, and Brit Müller. Bionic inspired information representation for autonomous agents. In *Proceedings of 2nd International Conference on Human System Interaction (HSI '09), Catania*, pages 24–30, 2009.

[ZPK10] Heimo Zeilinger, Andreas Perner, and Stefan Kohlhauser. Bionically inspired information representation module. In *Proceedings of 3rd International Conference on Human System Interaction (HSI '10), Rzeszow*, 2010.

Internet References

[InetACTR] ACT-R Research Group, "Homepage – ACT-R research group," Available: http://act-r.psy.cmu.edu/ [Accessed: February 15th, 2010].

[InetMPL] Mozilla foundation, "Mozilla Public License," Available: http://www.mozilla.org/MPL/ [Accessed:April 30th, 2010].

[InetOde] Tilmann Zäschke, "ode4j – A Java 3D Physics Engine & Library," Available: http://www.ode4j.org/ [Accessed: March 24th, 2010].

[InetOra] Oracle Technology Network, "Java Developer Center," Available: http://www.oracle.com/technology/tech/java/index.html [Accessed: March 24th, 2010].

[InetProt] Stanford Center for Biomedical Informatics Research, "Protégé" Available: http://protege.stanford.edu [Accessed: September 19th, 2010].

[InetRC] RoboCode sourceforge group, "Homepage – RoboCode Sourceforge," Available: http://robocode.sourceforge.net/ [Accessed: February 21st, 2010].

[InetRDF] RDF Working Group, "Resource Description Framework," Available: http://www.w3.org/RDF/, [Accessed: April 29th, 2010].

[InetOWL] Deborah. L. McGuinness, Frank van Harmelen, "OWL Web Ontology Language Overview," Available: http://www.w3.org/TR/owl-features/ [Accessed:April 28th, 2010].

[InetXML] XML Working Group, "Extensible Markup Language," Available: http://www.w3.org/XML/ [Accessed:April 28th, 2010].

A. Unified Modeling Language Notation

For the presentation of program code and timing dependencies the Unified Modeling Language version 2.2 infrastructure [uml09a] and superstructure specifications [uml09b] are used.

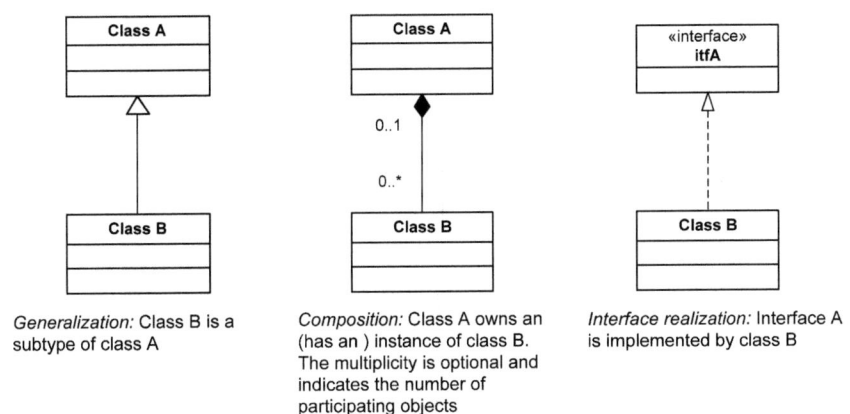

Fig. A-1: Path type notations for UML class structure diagrams [uml09b, pp. 140-142]

Fig. A-1 specifies the used path type notations *generalization*, *composition*, and *interface realization*. The composition can include an additional notation that is named *multiplicity* and is explained in Fig. A-3.

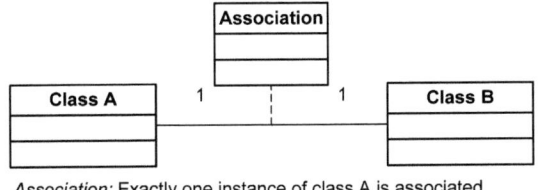

Association: Exactly one instance of class A is associated with exactly one instance of class B

Fig. A-2: Notation for the UML association path type [uml09b, pp. 140-142]

The definition of an association class is given in Fig. A-2. An association links an instance of class A with an instance of class B.

177

Appendix

Fig. A-3 defines the *multiplicity* notation. The multiplicity specifies the number of instances that participate in an association. One number defines an exact value while two numbers, for example 0..1 define an interval between a lower boundary (left number) and an upper boundary (right number).

Multiplicity:

0..1	0 to 1 instance
1	exactly 1 instance
0..*	0 or more instances
1..*	1 or more instances

Fig. A-3: Association multiplicity notations for UML class structure diagrams [uml09b, pp. 94-97]

Fig A-4 shows the UML sequence diagram notation. There are instances of class A and class B. The bars define class functions while the arrows define messages. There exist different types of messages. In this case the upper arrow defines a function call that invokes a method in a class B instance. The lower arrow defines the reply message of the invoked function.

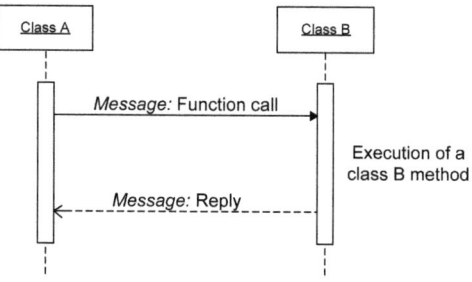

Fig. A-4: UML sequence diagram notation [uml09b, pp. 506-524]

178

B. Additional Acknowledgment

This work was conducted using the Protégé resource, which is supported by grant LM007885 from the United States National Library of Medicine.

Die VDM Verlagsservicegesellschaft sucht für wissenschaftliche Verlage abgeschlossene und herausragende

Dissertationen, Habilitationen, Diplomarbeiten, Master Theses, Magisterarbeiten usw.

für die kostenlose Publikation als Fachbuch.

Sie verfügen über eine Arbeit, die hohen inhaltlichen und formalen Ansprüchen genügt, und haben Interesse an einer honorarvergüteten Publikation?

Dann senden Sie bitte erste Informationen über sich und Ihre Arbeit per Email an *info@vdm-vsg.de*.

Sie erhalten kurzfristig unser Feedback!

VDM Verlagsservicegesellschaft mbH
Dudweiler Landstr. 99
D - 66123 Saarbrücken

Telefon +49 681 3720 174
Fax +49 681 3720 1749

www.vdm-vsg.de

Die VDM Verlagsservicegesellschaft mbH vertritt

Printed by Books on Demand GmbH, Norderstedt / Germany